Berlitz

SUT

30119 026 659 31 0

GREAT BRITAIN

D0808202

Contents

Top **25** attractions

1 **Shakespeare's Stratford** The home town of Britain's greatest playwright has lovely timbered houses and a famous theatre *(see pp.39 and 159)*

2 **Buckingham Palace** View the art collection, the State Rooms and the horse-drawn coaches at the Queen's London residence *(see p.65)*

3 **The Eden Project** Lush vegetation thrives in the tropical climate simulated within these futuristic greenhouses in Cornwall *(see p.130)*

4 **British Museum** One of the world's largest museums charts human culture back to prehistory *(see p.75)*

5 **Tate Modern** An art museum in a disused power station is one of London's most popular attractions *(see p.83)*

7 **London department stores** Harrods, Selfridges and the like are perfect for shopaholics *(see p.74)*

6 **The Royal Crescent** Bath's semi-circle of houses is a wonder of Georgian architecture *(see p.123)*

8 **Stonehenge** No one quite knows why this spectacular prehistoric monument was first built *(see p.119)*

9 **Royal Mile, Edinburgh** The historic thoroughfare linking the Castle with Holyrood Palace *(see p.223)*

10 **King's College Chapel, Cambridge** Hear one of the finest choirs in an exquisite building *(see p.137)*

11 **Changing the Guard** A chance to see a colourful display of military discipline and pomp *(see p.65)*

12 **Brighton Royal Pavilion** This exotic palace was created by the profligate George IV *(see p.111)*

13 **Portmeirion** A quaint village in Wales with buildings made from architectural salvage *(see p.182)*

14 **High tea at The Savoy** Treat yourself to tea, scones, strawberries and champagne at this top London hotel (see p.94)

15 **York Minster** Gothic splendour makes it one of the great medieval buildings (see p.209)

16 **Premier League football** Experience Britain's football fever at a live game (see p.56)

17 **Chatsworth House** See how the other half live at one of Britain's grandest stately homes (see p.165)

18 **Hiking in the Lake District** The hills and lakes of Cumbria provide rewarding terrain for walkers (see p.47)

19 **Legoland** This theme park near Windsor is great fun for the whole family and very popular with kids (see p.103)

20 **St Andrews Golf Club** Perhaps the most famous course in Scotland, the homeland of golf (see p.229)

21 **Hay-on-Wye** Bibliophiles flock to the bookshops and festival in the Welsh Borders *(see pp.39 and 176)*

22 **Buxton** A Derbyshire spa town, famous for Georgian architecture and its opera festival *(see p.165)*

23 **Fine dining at Bray** This pretty Thameside town has two Michelin-starred restaurants *(see p.115)*

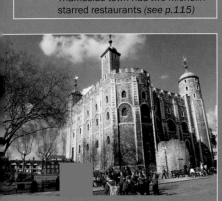

24 **Tower of London** Meet the Beefeaters and view the Crown Jewels at this Norman fortress *(see p.81)*

25 **Kelvingrove Art Gallery** Just one of the many outstanding art museums in Glasgow *(see p.54)*

Great Britain fact file

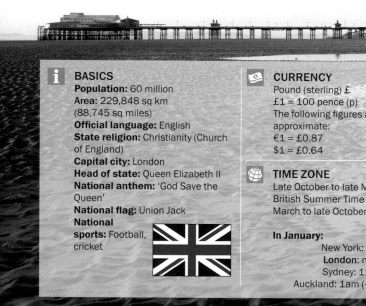

Great Britain is the largest European island, and one of Europe's most densely populated countries. While a quarter of its population lives in and around London, other regions – especially parts of Wales and the Scottish Highlands – are quite sparsely populated. The country therefore offers the unusual combination of great cities and unspoilt wilderness within relatively short distance of each other.

BASICS
Population: 60 million
Area: 229,848 sq km
(88,745 sq miles)
Official language: English
State religion: Christianity (Church of England)
Capital city: London
Head of state: Queen Elizabeth II
National anthem: 'God Save the Queen'
National flag: Union Jack
National sports: Football, cricket

CURRENCY
Pound (sterling) £
£1 = 100 pence (p)
The following figures are approximate:
€1 = £0.87
$1 = £0.64

TIME ZONE
Late October to late March is GMT
British Summer Time (BST), from late
March to late October, is GMT + 1

In January:
New York: 7am
London: noon
Sydney: 11pm
Auckland: 1am (+13 hours)

In July:

New York: 7am
London: noon
Sydney: 9pm
Auckland: 11pm

IMPORTANT TELEPHONE NUMBERS

Country code: +44
International calls: 00 + country code + number
Police: 999
Ambulance: 999
Fire: 999

AGE RESTRICTIONS

Driving: 17
Drinking: 18
Age of consent: 16

Smoking is banned in all enclosed public spaces, including bars and workplaces

ELECTRICITY

230 volts, 50 Hertz
Square 3-pin plug; nearly all visitors will need adaptors to use their own equipment

OPENING HOURS

Banks: usually Mon–Fri 9am–4pm
Shops: usually Mon–Sat 9am–5.30pm, Sun 11am–5pm
Many museums are closed on Mondays

Postal service: Royal Mail
Post office opening hours: Mon–Fri 9am–5.30pm, Sat 9am–noon
Post boxes: Red
Standard post: 46p (1st class)
Airmail: 68p to Europe, £1.10 to rest of the world

Trip planner

WHEN TO GO

Climate

Britain's climate is temperate and generally mild. It is unusual for any area in the country to have a dry spell for more than three weeks, even in the summer months, from June to September. It is advisable, therefore, to keep an umbrella handy at all times. It rains most frequently, though, in the mountainous areas of north and west Britain, where temperatures are also cooler than in the south.

In summer, the average maximum temperature in the south of England is around 70°F (23–25°C), although over 80°F (27°C) is not unusual. The temperatures in the large cities can soar, as the buildings and streets store heat, and the

Though beautiful, the Yorkshire Dales can be cold and wet

Public holidays

Compared to most of Europe, the UK has few public holidays:

1 January	New Year's Day
March/April	Good Friday, Easter Monday
First Monday of May	May Day
Last Monday of May	Spring Bank Holiday
Last Monday of August	Summer Bank Holiday
25 December	Christmas Day
26 December	Boxing Day

On public holidays, banks and offices are closed, though most shops are open (except on Christmas Day). Roads are often congested as people head for the coast or the countryside or to see relatives.

atmosphere can become stuffy (air conditioning is not universal). July and August are the worst months in this respect. In Scotland, temperatures tend to stay within the mid-60s°F (17–19°C) in summer.

During the winter (November to February), most of Britain, with the exception of mountainous regions in the north, tends to be cold and damp rather than snowy. Snow is unusual, and January temperatures have an average minimum of about 1°C (34°F) in England and Wales, and 0°C (32°F) in Scotland.

For weather information, visit www.metoffice.org, or http://news.

On the beach at Porthcurno, Cornwall, in summer

bbc.co.uk/weather for region- or city-specific forecasts.

High/low season
Holiday seasons in Britain generally coincide with school holidays. High season in the summer is July and August, while Easter and Christmas are also busy times, with hotels and airlines generally increasing rates.

In the more remote areas of the country – especially the Highlands of Scotland, rural Wales and the Lake District – many hotels and restaurants will close for part or all of the winter. Stately homes and some other visitor attractions also close from October to March.

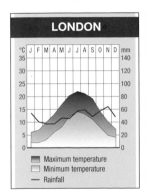

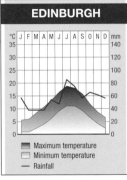

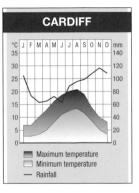

ESSENTIAL EVENTS

The crowd enjoying the show
at the Edinburgh Festival

January

Celtic Connections, late January, Glasgow. The city comes to life with a fortnight of concerts celebrating Celtic music and dance.

February–March

Rugby Six Nations Championship, February–mid-March, various venues. This annual international rugby union competition is conducted between six European sides: England, Scotland, Wales, Ireland,

France and Italy. Matches in Britain take place at Twickenham, Murrayfield and the Millennium Stadium in Cardiff.

May

Hay-on-Wye Festival of Literature and the Arts, late May–early June, Powys, Wales. A small town on the Welsh Borders enjoys the limelight for ten days of talks, book-signings and Q&As by big names in the world of literature.

June

Aldeburgh Festival of Arts & Music, mid-June, Snape, Suffolk. A two-week festival of classical music centres around the concert hall fashioned from an old maltings building by Benjamin Britten in the 1960s.

The Glastonbury Festival of Contemporary Performing Arts, late June, Somerset. This five-day festival of rock and pop is organised by a farmer on his land a few miles east of Glastonbury. Hundreds of acts play to crowds of over 100,000. Most of the profits go to charity.

Trooping the Colour, 14 June, Horse Guards Parade, London. The Queen's official birthday is marked with a military march. Thousands turn up to enjoy the spectacle, which is filled with plenty of pomp and revelry.

July

Buxton Festival, mid-July, Derbyshire. For three weeks every summer, the opera house in the Georgian spa town of Buxton hosts a major opera, theatre and music festival.

British Grand Prix, second weekend, Silverstone, Northamptonshire. Formula One comes to Britain for the biggest event in the British motor-racing calendar.

August

Edinburgh International Festival, mid-August, Scotland. The world's biggest arts festival attracts world-class theatre companies, musicians and comedy acts. During the same period, there is also the Festival Fringe and various other festivals – see www.edinburghfestivals.co.uk for a full list.

Notting Hill Carnival, Bank Holiday weekend, London. This event draws the crowds in London. The colourful West Indian carnival features floats, steel bands, an assortment of food stalls and various types of live music.

September

Royal Highland Gathering, early September, Braemar, Scotland. This traditional festival of Highland sports, music and dance is often attended by the Queen and other members of the royal family.

October

London Film Festival, second half of October, BFI Southbank. Britain's largest film event screens more than 300 features, documentaries and shorts from all over the world.

December

Hogmanay, 31 December, central Edinburgh. The New Year's Eve revels are best celebrated on the streets of Edinburgh – with fireworks, singing, street entertainment and a few drinks.

Notting Hill Carnival

ITINERARIES

It can be difficult to know where to start when visiting Britain for the first time – there is such a wealth of cultural heritage, such variety in landscape, and so many activities to engage with on this densely packed island. While the temptation may be there to pack in as much as possible, a certain ruthlessness when making your selection can yield a viable itinerary that enables you to see a good many highlights within a few days.

A weekend shopping in London

Day 1: **West London**. Harvey Nichols is a mecca for fashionistas, while Harrods in nearby Knightsbridge is the ultimate emporium. In the afternoon, head down to the King's Road, Chelsea, to browse the boutiques and high-street fashions. If you fancy a break from the high streets, head over to Portobello Road Market in Notting Hill (open Saturdays), with chic offerings for stylish shoppers.

Independent designers have stalls here, so browsing them (and the odd boutique) should unearth some unique creations.

Day 2: **East End to West End**. Start in the East End at Columbia Road's dazzlingly colourful Sunday morning flower market, before heading down to vibrant Spitalfields for a range of fashion and art treasures. Then head west to Bond Street – check out the latest fashion at Chanel or

Westminster Abbey's grand exterior

In costume at the Jane Austen Club, Bath

DKNY and window-shop at Bulgari. At its north end, Bond Street meets Oxford Street, and department store Selfridges offers homewares, more designer clothes, restaurants and bars. Over on Regent Street, peruse the Apple Store, or delight your kids at toy giant Hamleys.

Five days for history buffs

Day 1: London. Visit Westminster Abbey before taking the boat from outside Parliament to travel downriver to Greenwich and the National Maritime Museum.

Day 2: Oxford. This handsome university city is about an hour's train ride away. Be sure to make time for the particularly grand Christ Church.

Day 3: Stratford-upon-Avon. Shakespeare's home town is an easy drive north. The town's old timber-framed houses remain intact.

Day 4: Bath. The couple of hours' drive southwest to this Georgian spa town is well worth it to see the setting for so many scenes of Jane Austen's novels.

Day 5: Salisbury. Visit perhaps Britain's greatest cathedral, about an hour's journey to the southeast.

One week for the sights of Scotland

Days 1–2: Edinburgh. Starting at Edinburgh Castle, amble down the Royal Mile to Holyrood Palace and the new Scottish Parliament. On the next day, try shopping on Princes Street and a tour of the Royal Yacht *Britannia* in Leith Docks.

Days 3–4: Glasgow. Just 40 miles (65km) to the west, Glasgow has wonderful art museums, plenty of shops, and theatres, cinemas and concerts for the evenings.

Day 5: Loch Lomond. From Glasgow, it's an easy drive northwest to Balloch, from where you can explore the landscape around Loch Lomond.

Day 6: Fort William. It's a longer drive to Fort William, but well worth it for the views of Ben Nevis and your first taste of the Highlands.

Day 7: Inverness. The road from Fort William to Inverness is 68 miles (109km) long, skirting the banks of Loch Ness. Inverness, capital of the Highlands, is a historic city, with Culloden Battlefield, scene of Bonnie Prince Charlie's defeat, on its doorstep.

Trip planner

BEFORE YOU LEAVE

Visas and entry requirements

To enter the UK you need a valid passport (or any form of official identification if you are an EU citizen). Health certificates are not required unless you have arrived from Asia, Africa or South America.

Nationality	Visa Required
Australia	✗
Canada	✗
Ireland	✗
New Zealand	✗
South Africa	✗
US	✗

If you wish to stay for a protracted period or apply to work in Great Britain, contact the UK Border Agency. Look at the website: www.ind.home office.gov.uk or write to Croydon Public Enquiry Office (PEO), Lunar House, 40 Wellesley Road, Croydon, CR9 2BY, tel: 0870-606 7766.

Embassies and consulates

Australia: Australia House, Strand, London WC2 4LA, tel: 020-7379 4334; www.australia.org.uk
Canada: 1 Grosvenor Square, London W1K 4AB, tel: 020-7258 6600; www.dfait-maeci.gc.ca/canadaeuropa
India: India House, Aldwych, London WC2 4NA, tel: 020-7836 8484; www.hcilondon.org
New Zealand: 80 Haymarket, London SW1Y 4TQ, tel: 020-7930

8422; www.nzembassy.com
South Africa: South Africa House, Trafalgar Square, London WC2N 5DP, tel: 020-7451 7299; www.south africahouse.com
United States: 24 Grosvenor Square, London W1A 1AF, tel: 020-7499 9000; www.usembassy.org.uk

Booking in advance

Visitors should try to book in advance for major sporting events, big-name concerts and perhaps also for tickets to go inside Buckingham Palace (open from late July until early October).

Tourist information

Visit Britain (formerly The British Tourist Authority) has offices world-wide. See www.visitbritain.com or

The crowds outside Buckingham Palace

Stanfords bookstore

write to request information.

Australia: Level 16, Gateway, 1 Macquarie Place, Sydney, NSW 2000. Tel: 02-9377 4400

Canada: 5915 Airport Road, Suite 120 Mississauga, Ontario, L4V 1T1. Tel: 1888-VISITUK

New Zealand: 17th Floor, NZI House, 151 Queen Street, Auckland 1. Tel: 9-303 1446

Singapore: 01-00 GMG Building, 108 Robinson Road, Singapore 068900. Tel: 65-6227 5400

South Africa: PO Box 41896, Lancaster Gate Hyde Park Lane, Hyde Park, 2196. Tel: 11-325 0343

USA – New York: 7th Floor, 551 Fifth Avenue, NY 10176-0799. Tel: 1-800-GO 2 BRIT or 212-986 2266

Maps

Insight Guides' best-selling Flexi-Maps are laminated for durability and easy folding, with clear cartography and practical information. Titles include: London, Edinburgh and Great Britain.

In London, you should head for Stanfords (12–14 Long Acre, in the Covent Garden area; www.stanfords. co.uk); it's one of the world's best map and guidebook stores.

Websites

www.visitbritain.com The UK's tourism authority website.

www.nationalrail.co.uk Provides train times and fares.

www.theaa.com/route-planner/ index.jsp Provides routes, distances and estimated times for your car journey anywhere in the UK.

www.petrolprices.com Locates the cheapest petrol station nearby.

http://news.bbc.co.uk/weather Five-day weather forecasts for wherever you are in the country.

www.guardian.co.uk Free online content for this national newspaper.

www.rspb.org.uk The Royal Society for the Protection of Birds lists details of its nature reserves online.

www.nationaltrust.org.uk Heritage organisation that owns hundreds of stately homes and scenic spots.

www.bachtrack.com A quick way to find concerts, operas and ballet.

Books to get you in the mood

In England, **Don McCullin.** A compelling portrait in pictures of the British people.

Blimey! – From Bohemia to Britpop, **Matthew Collings.** Funny, readable, and copiously illustrated account of the London art world of the last few decades.

Waterlog: A Swimmer's Journey Through Britain, **Roger Deakin.** A travelogue, written with wit, style and humanity.

The Last Resort, **Martin Parr.** A Magnum photographer presents a poignant and at times edgy view of the British on holiday.

London Caffs, **Edwin Heathcote.** A tongue-in-cheek survey of a British culinary institution.

UNIQUE EXPERIENCES

The Royal Family

Access to the Royal Family has never been so easy. You can go inside Buckingham Palace, gawp at the Queen's bedroom on the old royal yacht, goggle at the Crown Jewels in the Tower of London and watch the Queen inspecting the Household Guards or enjoying the horse racing at Ascot.

The Royal Family form an important ingredient in Britain's self-identity, and in the image of Britain overseas. Nowhere else is there a monarchy as grand, with such a long and colourful history, and that is so conspicuous in the life of the country.

Recent opinion polls suggest that the vast majority of Britons support the idea of the monarchy – despite, of course, the fact that it's not easy to square it with the idea of democracy. Technically, the Queen has the power to refuse her assent to legislation proposed by parliament, and so prevent it passing into law, but this right has not been exercised since at least 1707. Indeed, were a king or queen to defy parliament's wishes today, it would probably spell the end of the institution of the monarchy itself.

The modern monarch's power is rather of a softer kind. For one thing, it provides unity and continuity. As the British Empire disintegrated in the 1950s and '60s, for example, the monarchy helped smooth the

The splendid interior of Buckingham Palace

transition in relations between Britain and former colonial nations by heading up the more symbolic Commonwealth. The monarch also provides a sense of unity precisely because he or she has been born into it, rather than having to elbow competitors out of the way, pay off cronies, or compromise their integrity – which is, of course, what politicians have to do in order to get to the top.

Moreover, some members of the Royal Family – notably Prince Charles and Princess Anne – have successfully carved out roles for themselves in promoting charitable causes and certain ethical and cultural values. Prince Charles, for example, initiated the building of Poundbury, a 'heritage' village in Dorset, and has championed eco-friendly countryside management through his own farms and estates. He has used his own charity, the Prince's Trust, to help thousands of young people.

Where does the Royal Family live?

The Royal Family's role in British life is also evident in its remarkable portfolio of castles and palaces, that stretches from the very tip of Scotland to the Isle of Wight, off the south coast of England. The Royal Family's official website – www. royal.gov.uk – lists about 10 residences for the Queen, and a further two dozen properties that were formerly occupied by British monarchs.

In addition, there are dozens of other grand houses occupied by

The ornate entrance gates at Buckingham Palace

The Royal Family

other members of the Royal Family. Each of the Queen's children has their own grand pile in the country. Prince Charles has **Highgrove**, a particularly beautiful Georgian mansion in Gloucestershire. The **gardens** are open to the public from April to mid-October (Doughton, near Tetbury; tel: 020-7766 7310; www. highgrovegardens.com; booking ahead is essential). By contrast, Prince William merely rents a farmhouse on the Isle of Anglesey, in order to be near the Air Force base where he flies a search-and-rescue helicopter.

Of the Queen's residences, **Buckingham Palace** (tel: 020-7766 7300; www.royalcollection.org.uk) in London is the most famous. Despite its enormous size, when Queen Victoria took possession of it in 1837, she complained that it had too few bedrooms, and had another wing built. Visitors today can see the State Rooms in August and September, while the **Changing the Guard** ceremony takes place outside on alternate days (see www.changing-the-guard.com for details).

Nearby is **St James's Palace**, a castellated brick building commissioned by Henry VIII in the 16th century. It was here that Charles I spent his last night before being executed in 1649. Today, however, it functions as the administrative headquarters of the monarchy, and is, unfortunately, not open to the public. Situated almost next door, **Clarence House** (tel: 020-7766

St James's Palace is now the royal family's administrative headquarters

7303; access is from The Mall), is the London residence of Prince Charles. His sons, William and Harry, also have apartments here. Guided tours of some of the rooms are offered daily during August and September.

During the late summer, when tourists are traipsing round her London home, the Queen goes to stay at **Balmoral Castle** (tel: 01339-742 534; www.balmoralcastle.com), on her 50,000-acre (20,234-hectare) Scottish estate. Visitors can see the gardens daily from April until late July, when the Queen arrives. Famously, this is where the Royal Family was staying when Princess Diana died. The Queen's decision not to come back to London immediately was portrayed by the media as a sign of aloofness. The episode was memorably dramatised in the film, *The Queen*, with Helen Mirren playing the role of Her Majesty.

Just before the Queen goes to Balmoral – in late June and early July – she stays at **Holyrood Palace** (tel: 0131-556 5100; www.royal collection.org.uk), her official Scottish residence in Edinburgh. Her stay here coincides with Holyrood Week, during which the Queen undertakes a number of official engagements, including the giving out of knighthoods and other honours in the palace's Great Gallery, and hosting a garden party for around 8,000 guests. The palace itself is otherwise open daily for tourist visits.

At Christmas the Queen boards a train at King's Cross in London and makes the journey up to her **Sandringham Estate** (tel: 01485-545

Holyrood Palace is the Queen's preferred residence in early summer

408; www.sandringhamestate.co.uk) in north Norfolk. The Queen's father, King George VI (who was portrayed in the recent film, *The King's Speech*) died at Sandringham in 1952. It is the Queen's custom to remain at the estate until the anniversary of her father's death in early February. Members of the public are able to visit the house from late April until the end of October.

The Queen's other major home is **Windsor Castle** (tel: 020-7766

The Royal Family

Top five royal castles and palaces of yesteryear

- **Hampton Court Palace**
  Located just upriver from London, this magnificent Tudor palace (tel: 0844-482 7777; www.hrp.org.uk/HamptonCourtPalace) was originally built for Cardinal Wolsey, a favourite of Henry VIII, until the latter's marriage problems led to the former's downfall. A highlight of any visit is the famous maze in the grounds, which was created in the 1690s for William III.

- **Brighton Royal Pavilion**
  This exuberant seaside palace (tel: 03000-290 900; www.royalpavilion.org.uk) was designed by John Nash for the Prince Regent (later George IV) with Indian-style cupolas on the outside, and exotic oriental decoration inside. Its extravagance reflects the lifestyle of its former owner, who racked up enormous debts, had numerous mistresses, and gorged himself until his waistline measured 50 inches (127cm).

- **Osborne House**
  Queen Victoria's summer residence on the Isle of Wight (tel: 01983-200 022; www.english-heritage.org.uk) exhibits a fascination with Indian style. The Durbar Room, designed when the Empire was at its height, satisfied the Queen's mania for all things Indian (she even had an Indian secretary who taught her Hindi).

- **Castle of Mey**
  The summer home of the late Queen Mother in the very north of Scotland remains just as she left it, with her coat and wellington boots left just inside the door (tel: 01847-851 473; www.castleofmey.org.uk).

- **Queen's House, Greenwich**
  Built between 1614 and 1617 by Inigo Jones for Anne of Denmark, the wife of James I, this sublime building introduced the Palladian style to Britain. It now houses the art collection of the National Maritime Museum (tel: 020-8858 4422; www.nmm.ac.uk).

Changing the Guard at Windsor Castle

Unique experiences

7304; www.royalcollection.org.uk), in Berkshire, to the south west of London. This is the Queen's weekend home. Parts of the castle were badly damaged by a fire in 1992 – the year which the Queen notoriously termed her 'annus horribilis' (it was also a year in which three of her children had announced marriage break-ups). A full restoration of the castle, if not the broken relationships, has since been completed, and the public can view the results daily, all year round.

Finally, **Kensington Palace** (tel: 0844-482 7777; www.hrp.org.uk/KensingtonPalace) also remains a royal residence, and is especially popular with visitors since it is where Princess Diana lived until her death in 1997. The palace still contains a number of apartments for minor members of the Royal Family – including the Dukes and Duchesses of Kent and Gloucester – who are often dubbed 'hangers on' by the media. The State Rooms, however, are open daily to members of the public.

Royal collections

Extravagant buildings are not the only treasures to have been left behind by centuries of monarchy. The royal collections include 7,000 paintings, 3,000 miniatures, 40,000 drawings and watercolours, 150,000 prints, 350,000 photographic images, 125,000 books and manuscripts, not to mention thousands of sculptures, items of furniture, ceramics, clocks, silver, jewellery, arms and armour, fans and textiles.

Many items from the collections are on loan to museums and galleries around the world, but most

The Royal Yacht *Britannia*

There have been 83 royal yachts since the restoration of King Charles II in 1660, and this was the very last. The present Queen launched *Britannia* in 1953, and witnessed her decommissioning in 1997. She has not been replaced owing to budgetary constraints. During her working life as the royal yacht, *Britannia* undertook almost 700 official foreign visits, hosted several US presidents, and took Prince Charles and Princess Diana on their honeymoon. Her last foreign trip was to Hong Kong, to convey the colony's last governor and Prince Charles away after handover to China on 1 July 1997.

Today, *Britannia* is moored at Ocean Terminal in Leith, near Edinburgh, and is open to the public daily (tel: 0131-555 5566; www.royalyachtbritannia.co.uk). As well as the Queen's bedroom – and Prince Philip's separate, and rather spartan bedroom – highlights include the State Dining Room and an old Rolls Royce in its own on-board garage. Visitors can now also enjoy refreshments in the recently opened Royal Deck. Another new attraction is the 1936 racing yacht, *Bloodhound*, which was owned by the Queen in the 1960s, and is now moored alongside *Britannia*. Both the Prince of Wales and Princess Royal learned to sail in her, and she is still used for yachting trips away at sea in July and August each year.

are held within the royal palaces. **The Queen's Gallery** (tel: 020-7766 7301; www.royalcollection.org.uk) at Buckingham Palace is open daily, and puts on exhibitions derived from the collections. Similarly, there is another gallery at Holyrood Palace in Edinburgh (tel: 0131-556 5100), and the Drawings Gallery at Windsor Castle (tel: 020-7766 7304). Masterpieces from the collections include paintings by Holbein, Rembrandt and Vermeer.

The Queen also owns one of the finest collections of postage stamps in the world, which is continually being added to. This is the personal property of the Queen, and is held in St James's Palace. Although it is not generally made accessible to the public, selections are loaned for major exhibitions from time to time.

Perhaps the most famous of royal

The Imperial State Crown is encrusted with thousands of gems

treasures, however, are the **Crown Jewels**. These are guarded by the famous 'Beefeaters' at the **Tower of London** (tel: 0844-482 7777; www.hrp.org.uk/toweroflondon). Among the priceless objects are the coronation regalia – sceptres, orbs, rings, swords, spurs, bracelets and robes which date back centuries. The Imperial State Crown is particularly impressive – encrusted with over 3,000 diamonds, rubies, sapphires and pearls. The First Star of Africa, mounted on top of the Sovereign's Sceptre, is the largest flawless cut diamond in the world, while the legendary Koh-i-Nur diamond, presented to Queen Victoria in 1850, is now set in the platinum crown made for the late Queen Mother for the 1937 coronation. This diamond, which originally belonged to the early Mughal emperors, is only worn by a queen or queen consort, since it brings bad luck to any man who wears it.

Another of the essential components of coronations is the Gold State Coach. This, together with a collection of horse-drawn carriages and motor cars can be seen next door to the Queen's Gallery at the **Royal Mews** (tel: 020-7766 7302; www.royalcollection.org.uk; daily Apr–Oct, Mon–Sat Nov–Dec). If you're lucky, you may also see the horses – the Cleveland Bays and Windsor Greys. By tradition, only the latter are used to draw the carriage in which the Queen is travelling.

Royal events

If you're not content with merely seeing the Royal Family's trappings,

Trooping the Colour is a highlight of the royal calendar

Examining a swan during
the Swan Upping ceremony

but want to see them in the flesh,
there are a number of guaranteed
opportunities throughout the year.

Trooping the Colour is perhaps
the best. This event marks the
monarch's official birthday, which
is usually designated as the second
Saturday of June.

During the ceremony, the Queen
is escorted by the Household Cavalry
down The Mall from Buckingham
Palace, and around St James's Park to
Horse Guards Parade. After receiving
a salute, she inspects all the troops
of the Household Division (the 'Foot
Guards' and the cavalry or 'Horse
Guards'). One of the Foot Guards'
regiments is selected to troop their
colour through the ranks of guards.
Then the division parades past the
Queen to the music of the massed

The Royal Family

Swan upping

The Crown has claimed ownership of all
mute swans in Britain since the 12th
century, when they were considered
a delicacy at royal banquets. Today,
although the swans are no longer eaten,
the Queen still exercises her right of
ownership on certain stretches of the
River Thames. Each year, a 'Swan Upping'
ceremony takes place, whereby a census
of the swan population is taken on those
stretches of river. It usually takes place in
the third week of July; you can consult the
listings of royal events and ceremonies on
www.royal.gov.uk for precise dates.

The Swan Uppers use six traditional
skiffs to row up-river on their five-day
journey. The Queen's Swan Uppers wear
scarlet uniforms and each boat is identified
with its own flag and pennant. Perhaps
the best place to observe them is as they
pass Windsor Castle. Here, as a mark of
respect, the rowers raise their oars, stand
to attention and salute 'Her Majesty The
Queen, Seigneur of the Swans'.

Nowadays, the ceremony's aim is
primarily swan welfare. When cygnets
are caught, the Swan Uppers weigh and
measure them, and give them a health
check. The Queen's Swan Warden – a
Professor of Ornithology at Oxford
University – rings them with identification
tags and then sets them free again.

bands, comprising around 400 musicians. Finally, the Queen rides in a carriage back to Buckingham Palace at the head of her Guards, before taking another salute. Following a 41-gun salute by the King's Troop in Green Park, she leads the Royal Family onto the palace balcony for a fly-past by the Royal Air Force.

In order to watch the spectacle, visitors should assemble on pavements in The Mall or on the edge of St James's Park facing Horse Guards Parade by around 9am. The proceedings begin at about 10am, and the fly-past takes place at 1pm. There are seated stands around Horse Guards Parade, but tickets must be applied for in writing, and are allocated by ballot in March (see www.royal.gov.uk for details).

Also in June – usually in the third week – is **Royal Ascot** (tel: 0870-727 1234; www.ascot.co.uk), a five-day race meeting. Commencing on a Tuesday, the horseracing is preceded each day by a royal procession. The Queen and the royal party are brought along the track in front of the stands in a parade of horse-drawn landaus. The Queen is a keen race-goer, and owns many horses herself, including 20 winners at Royal Ascot. There are three stands or 'enclosures' at Ascot for spectators. The most prestigious is the Royal Enclosure; it is difficult to secure tickets for this, and a dress code is strictly enforced. Women must wear a dress of a certain length (with no bare midriffs or shoulders), and men are obliged to wear morning dress with top hat.

The Royal Enclosure is the most prestigious stand at Ascot

A little earlier in the calendar is the **Chelsea Flower Show** (tel: 0844-338 7528; www.rhs.org.uk), which takes place in late May at the Royal Hospital, Chelsea. The Queen, as patron of the Royal Horticultural Society, usually opens the show on the first Monday. You may be fortunate enough to catch a glimpse of her as she arrives.

If your visit to London takes place later in the year, you can get a better sighting at the **State Opening of Parliament**. The ceremony usually takes place in October, November or December, but, if a general election has taken place that year, it can be at a different time. As Head of State, it is the Queen's duty to open each new session of Parliament. She travels from Buckingham Palace in a state coach to Westminster, with the Imperial State Crown being conveyed in its own carriage ahead of the Queen. Spectators can watch the procession as it travels down The Mall and along Whitehall. On arrival, the Queen puts on the crown and her parliamentary robe, and enters the House of Lords. No monarch has set foot in the House of Commons (where the MPs sit) since the ill-fated Charles I in 1642.

In Scotland, the **Royal Highland Gathering** (tel: 01339-741 098; www.braemargathering.org) takes place at Braemar on the first Saturday in September. The Queen and other members of the Royal Family often attend. The event features traditional Scottish tests of strength such as the tug of war, tossing the caber and throwing the hammer, as well as displays of Highland dancing and bands of bagpipers.

While 2011 saw the wedding of Prince William and Kate Middleton, 2012 will also see its fair share of pomp and pageant. The **Queen's Diamond Jubilee** (see www.culture. gov.uk/diamondjubilee), marking 60 years on the throne, will be celebrated from 2–5 June. Events will include a pageant on the Thames, a concert at Buckingham Palace and the lighting of beacons throughout the United Kingdom.

You might be lucky enough to see the Queen at the Chelsea Flower Show

The Royal Family

On the water

Sailing and surfing, punts and pedaloes, boats and barges: Britain offers plenty of ways to enjoy being out on the water. But if you prefer to keep your feet on solid ground, there are also spectator opportunities at Cowes Week, the Oxford and Cambridge Boat Race and Henley Regatta.

As the water vole said in Kenneth Grahame's children's classic, *The Wind in the Willows*, there's nothing better than 'simply messing about in boats'. And as an island nation famed for its seafaring history, it's something the British do a lot of. Whether you want to paddle about in a rowing boat on the pond in London's Regent's Park or charter a yacht to check out some of the uninhabited Hebridean islands, there's something to satisfy every ambition.

The National Maritime Museum is the best place to engage with Britain's watery past

If, on the other hand, you are content simply to ponder over Britain's past seafaring glories, there are numerous museums – from the Royal Navy's **Submarine Museum** (tel: 023-9251 0354; www.submarine-museum.co.uk) in Gosport to the **National Maritime Museum** in Greenwich (tel: 020-8858 4422; www.nmm.ac.uk) to the **Aberdeen Maritime Museum** (tel: 01224-337 700; www.aagm.co.uk) in Scotland.

Boat trips

If you're looking for a relaxing time, then a river cruise or a short sea excursion may be in order. In **London**, there are boat trips **between the Houses of Parliament and Greenwich** (tel: 020-7930 4097; www.thamesriverservices.co.uk), and on the **Tate-to-Tate** catamaran (tel: 020-7887 8888; www.tate.org.uk/tatetotate) that shuttles between the Tate art galleries: Tate Modern on the South Bank and Tate Britain in Pimlico.

In **Bristol**, you can enjoy a circuit of the harbour on an old **Bristol Packet** (tel: 0117-926 8157; www.bristolpacket.co.uk), before paying a visit to the museum ship, the **SS Great Britain** (tel: 0117-926 0680; www.ssgreatbritain.org) designed

Cowes Week is Britain's most famous sailing event

see seals, dolphins, whales and bird-life. From Elgol on the Isle of Skye, for example, **Bella Jane Boat Trips** (tel: 01471-866 244; www.bellajane.co.uk) will take you along the rugged coastline on the far side of the Cuillin Hills. **Sea Life Surveys** (tel: 01688-302 916; www.sealifesurveys.com) depart from Tobermory on the Isle of Mull for all-day whale-watching cruises.

Sailing

Britain's most famous sailing event is **Cowes Week** (www.cowes.co.uk) at the beginning of August each year. Over a thousand yachts and some 8,500 competitors participate in the dozens of races each day on the **Solent** (the channel between the south coast and the Isle of Wight). Many people enjoy the associated onshore festivities as much as the sailing. Live music and innumerable cocktail parties are on offer every day in the town of Cowes itself, and on the final Friday a spectacular fireworks display is launched from barges out on the Solent.

If you fancy taking the helm yourself, there are countless places both around the coast and on inland bodies of water where you can try your hand. For yachting, you can take a course with **Elite Sailing** (tel: 01634-890 512; www.elite-sailing.co.uk) on the **Medway Estuary** in north Kent (less than an hour on the train from central London). There is also the opportunity here to gain Royal Yacht Association qualifications (www.rya.org.uk), with which you can then charter a yacht yourself. Meanwhile, **Classic Sailing** (tel: 01872-580 022; www.classic-sailing.co.uk) offers the chance to crew a tall ship or a pilot

by the famous Victorian engineer Isambard Kingdom Brunel. Cruises up the River Ouse in **York** (tel: 01904-628 324; www.yorkboat.co.uk) are accompanied by a running commentary on the historic sights you are sailing past.

In **Norfolk**, pleasure boats such as the **Electric Eel** (tel: 01603-756 096) offer cruises around the Norfolk Broads, one of Britain's National Parks. Blakeney, on the north coast, is the departure point for **Beans Boat Trips** (tel: 01263-740 505; www.beansboattrips.co.uk) to see the colonies of seals in the Wash.

Off the west coast of **Scotland**, ferries run from Kennacraig, Oban, Mallaig and Ullapool out to the Hebridean Islands (see www.calmac.co.uk). At many of the island ports, smaller boats offer round trips to cutter around **Cornwall** and the Isles of Scilly. Up on the western coast of Scotland, there is challenging sailing and spectacular scenery around the **Hebrides**. Consult the website www.sailscotland.co.uk to find details of sailing holidays, schools and yacht charters.

Inland, the **Norfolk Broads** provide one of the most peaceful and picturesque places for sailing. **Hunter's Yard** (tel: 01692-678 263; www.huntersyard.co.uk) offers a range of sailing trips, courses and holidays on their fleet of traditional cabin yachts and wooden half deckers. One of their boats was even used in the BBC adaptation of the famous children's book, *Swallows and Amazons* by Arthur Ransome. The story itself was actually set in the **Lake District**, in the northwest of England. Many of the larger bodies of water there are used for watersports. Derwent Water, Ullswater and Windermere, for example, are used for sailing as well as for canoeing, diving, water-skiing and windsurfing.

Punting

Nowadays, punting is most associated with languid summers on the river in the university cities of Oxford and Cambridge. The calm and shallow waters on the Cherwell and the Cam are ideally suited to the flat-bottomed punts, which are propelled by someone standing at the back of the boat and pushing a pole against the riverbed. Cambridge and Oxford differ over which should be considered the back end and which the front. In Cambridge, the tradition is for the punter to stand on the boat's short deck (the 'counter' or 'till'), whereas in Oxford, you stand at the other end, with the till at the front.

In **Oxford**, you can hire punts at the **Cherwell Boathouse** (tel: 01865-515 978; www.cherwellboathouse.co.uk) on the River Cherwell, which flows through fields and woods before joining the Thames at Christ Church Meadow. Alternatively, there is the peaceful trip on the Isis alongside Port Meadow to the west of the town.

The flat beauty of the Norfolk Broads makes for a wonderful spot to try sailing

Punting is one of Cambridge's most appealing pastimes

In **Cambridge**, punts can be hired at the bottom of Mill Lane (tel: 01223-359 750; www.scudamores. com) or from outside the nearby Granta pub on Newnham Road (tel: 01223-301 845; www.punting incambridge.com). From here, you can glide along the Backs and under the bridges behind Trinity, King's and several other colleges, though this stretch of river does become congested in summer. Those in the know prefer to punt along the lower reaches of the river through the meadows to Grantchester, where you can stop for a picnic.

Lesser-known places for punting include the **River Wear** in **Durham**, where the university owns punts (and rowing boats too). It is also possible to hire punts on the River Avon in the centre of **Bath** and on another river

On the water

Canal boats

Britain has more than 2,000 miles (3,220km) of canals, and, famously, Birmingham on its own has more canals than Venice. Much of the network was built during the Industrial Revolution, and the brightly painted narrowboats that were originally used for transporting goods are today used for recreation or even as homes. You can see some fine examples, and learn about their history, at the **National Waterways Museum** (tel: 0151-355 5017; www.nwm.org.uk) in Ellesmere Port, Cheshire, and at the **Gloucester Waterways Museum** (tel: 01452-318 200; www.gloucesterwaterwaysmuseum.org.uk).

Probably the most impressive canal in the country is the **Kennet and Avon Canal** (www.katrust.co.uk), which takes you from Bristol to Reading via 105 locks and some beautiful countryside. You can hire a narrowboat for the day or for several weeks to navigate some or all of it. See, for example, Kennet Cruises (tel: 0118-987 1115; www.kennetcruises. co.uk). In Scotland, the most famous canal is the **Caledonian Canal** (www. scottishcanals.co.uk), which links the east coast at Inverness with the west coast at Corpach near Fort William, taking in Loch Ness along the way.

Oxford and Cambridge Boat Race – probably the most famous rowing event in the world

of the same name in **Stratford-upon-Avon**. On the **Thames**, above the tidal limit at Teddington, there are punting clubs at Walton, Thames Ditton and Sunbury, which organise punt races during the summer. This recondite sport is governed by the Thames Punting Club, which sets the rules. Races are one punt against another, and are contested over a distance of up to 880yds (805m) along straight stretches of the river. The annual **Thames Punting Championships**

are held at **Maidenhead** (see www. maidenheadrc.org.uk).

Rowing

The major rowing competitions in Britain are popular spectator events. Over the first weekend of July, **Henley Royal Regatta** (tel: 01491-572 153; www.hrr.co.uk) offers 5 days of 'head-to-head' races on the Thames, where two crews compete side by side in each round of a knock-out tournament. Henley is also a major social

The Loch Ness monster

Loch Ness, the second largest loch in Scotland after Loch Lomond, is famous for its elusive monster. Despite many claims of sightings, numerous blurred photographs and even some film footage, the evidence remains inconclusive about the existence of this prehistoric survivor. A research team from the Academy of Applied Science in Massachusetts maintains a year-round vigil with sonar-triggered cameras and

strobe lights suspended from a raft in Urquhart Bay. In the summer, visitors can take **boat cruises** across Loch Ness from Fort Augustus and Inverness. In the nearby village of Drumnadrochit there is also the **Loch Ness Exhibition Centre** (tel: 01456-450-573; www.lochness.com), which features a scale replica of Nessie, as well as the sonar research vessel, the *John Murray*.

event, where spectators dress for show and over-indulge in champagne.

Perhaps the most famous rowing fixture in the world is the annual **Oxford and Cambridge Boat Race** (www.theboatrace.org) held on either the last Saturday of March or the first Saturday of April. The competitors are all students at Oxford and Cambridge universities, though the large number of international oarsmen has given rise to suspicions that many crew members are admitted to their university on account of their rowing, rather than academic, abilities. The race runs from Putney to Chiswick Bridge in London, and spectators can watch for free from many vantage points along the course. There are also large screens at Bishops Park, Fulham and Furnival Gardens, Hammersmith, which enable you to watch the whole race. Since the first race in 1829, Cambridge (the light blues) have won the event more times than Oxford (the dark blues), though the tally remains close.

Surfing

While Britain receives swell on its entire coastline, the best place in the country for surfing is **Cornwall** in the southwest. **Fistral Beach** (tel: 01637-850 584; www.fistralbeach.co.uk) in **Newquay** is probably the most popular surfing spot, though there are plenty of places nearby – such as **Watergate Bay** – that offer excellent conditions for both beginners and professionals, as well as surfing schools and surfer-friendly hotels. The other coastal region that is highly rated by aficionados is the north coast of Scotland – **Thurso East**, for example. Temperatures here can be icy, so a wetsuit is essential all year round.

The surfing season in Britain runs from autumn to spring, during which time there are periods when the surf is consistently between 4 and 12ft (1.2–3.7m). The best time for surfing is perhaps the autumn – especially late September to mid-November, when relatively mild air and water temperatures combine with regular swells and less crowded beaches. Tides can make the sea rise and fall up to 15ft (4.6m) at times, making conditions quite variable and often challenging. Swells in summer are much smaller, averaging between 1 and 4ft (0.3–1.2m).

On the water

Newquay surfers

Literary trails

Whether your literary taste is for the grandiloquence of Shakespeare, the lyrics of Wordsworth or the whodunnits of Agatha Christie's page-turners, you'll find plenty to feed your enthusiasm on your favourite author's home turf.

Britain is blessed with a particularly rich literary heritage. From Chaucer's *Canterbury Tales* to Martin Amis's *London Fields*, much of Britain's literature draws from the country's landscape and its people for its inspiration. Many visitors' only previous experience of its cities and countryside is from the pages of Thomas Hardy, or a film version of one of Jane Austen's novels. Some visitors express disappointment that, contrary to the descriptions in Sherlock Holmes stories, London's streets are no longer cobbled or foggy. But if you know where to look, you can still find unmodernised enclaves of the capital that transport you back to scenes from Charles Dickens, or unspoilt villages in Yorkshire that seem straight from the pages of Charlotte Brontë's *Jane Eyre*.

Of course, Britain also has a thriving contemporary literary culture. There are theatres in most large towns, and some small ones. The **West End** in London (particularly around Charing Cross Road, St Martin's Lane and Shaftesbury Avenue) has a concentration of grand Victorian theatres. There are countless gems, though, throughout the country, from the outdoor **Minack Theatre** (tel: 01736-810 181; www.

Cornwall's outdoor Minack Theatre occupies a stunning natural setting

minack.com) in Cornwall, to the 43-seat **Mull Little Theatre** (tel: 01688-302 673; www.mulltheatre. com) in the Hebrides.

Second-hand bookshops are also a quintessential part of British literary life. London's **Charing Cross Road** has traditionally been the centre of the trade, though shops are gradually being forced elsewhere owing to high rents. **Cecil Court**, just nearby, remains a secure haven. Elsewhere, **Hay-on-Wye** (www.hay-on-wye. co.uk) in Herefordshire, on the borders of Wales, is a magnet for book collectors, with umpteen bookshops. At the end of May and beginning of June, the village also hosts a literary festival (tel: 01497-822 629; www. hayfestival.com), which attracts many famous writers, as well as the world's media. The village of **Wigtown** (www.wigtown-booktown. co.uk) in the Scottish Borders operates in a similar way. It has over 20 bookshops, and also runs the **Wigtown Book Festival** (tel: 01988-402 036; www.wigtownbookfestival.com) in the last week of September.

Hay-on-Wye is a bibliophile's paradise, and hosts a yearly literary festival

Literary trails

Shakespeare

William Shakespeare is unquestionably Britain's greatest playwright. He was born in Stratford-upon-Avon in 1564, spent his working life in London, and then retired back to Stratford. There are a number of sites relating to his life that you can visit. Those in Stratford include **Shakespeare's Birthplace** (tel: 01789-204 016; www.shakespeare. org.uk); **Anne Hathaway's Cottage** (tel: 01789-292 100), which was the family home of Shakespeare's wife just to the west of Stratford in the village of Shottery; **Nash's House** (tel: 01789-292 325), in the gardens of which are the remains of New Place, the grand house Shakespeare bought upon his retirement; and **Holy Trinity Church** (tel: 01789-266 316; www.stratford-upon-avon. org), where the playwright was finally laid to rest in 1616.

If you would like to see a play, the Royal Shakespeare Company performs daily at the **Royal Shakespeare Theatre** (tel: 0844-800 1110; www.rsc.org.uk) – where you can also enjoy backstage tours – and the galleried **Swan Theatre**. Afterwards, you can repair to the Dirty Duck pub (www.dirtyduck-pub-stratford-upon-avon.co.uk), which is where many of the actors also like to go for a post-performance drink.

In the capital, the Globe Theatre is the best place to see a Shakespeare play

In London, the major Shakespeare attraction is the replica of the 1599 **Globe Theatre** (tel: 020-7902 1400; www.shakespearesglobe.com) on the South Bank. This open-roofed theatre-in-the-round stages his plays during the summer. There are also behind-the-scenes guided tours every half hour and an exhibition on the history of the theatre.

Dickens

If Shakespeare is Britain's most famous playwright, then Charles Dickens (1812–70) is its best known novelist. His books, full of detailed descriptions, provide a panorama of Victorian England, from the dingiest slums to the grandest aristocratic mansions. The house in which he was born in Portsmouth is now the **Charles Dickens Birthplace Museum** (tel: 023-9282 7261; www.charlesdickensbirthplace.co.uk). It has been re-furnished in the style of the time and displays Dickens memorabilia.

It is London, however, with which Dickens is perhaps most associated – although only one of his London homes survives. It can be found at 48, Doughty Street in the Bloomsbury area of town, and is now the **Charles Dickens Museum** (tel: 0207-405 2127; www.dickens museum.com). Although he lived here for only two years in the 1830s, it was the place where he wrote *The Pickwick Papers*, *Oliver Twist* and *Nicholas Nickleby*. Inside you can see manuscripts, original furniture and other personal effects.

Not far away, in Holborn, behind the Royal Courts of Justice, is the **Seven Stars** pub (tel: 020-7242 8521), set alongside wigmakers and barristers' chambers on Carey Street. Dickens used to be a regular customer here during the years he worked as a court reporter for a newspaper. Nearby, on Portsmouth Street, you can still find **The Old Curiosity Shop** (tel: 020-7405 9891), which provided the title for one of his novels; it now sells expensive shoes.

Kent is the other area of the country particularly rich in Dickens associations. At the pretty seaside resort of **Broadstairs**, there is the **Dickens House Museum** (tel: 01843-861 232; www.dickensfellowship.org/branches/broadstairs), filled with

Dickens-related artefacts. In Dickens's time it was home to the woman who formed the basis for Betsey Trotwood in *David Copperfield*. Dickens himself stayed at Bleak House on the cliff at the other end of the bay, during his regular summer holidays with his family in the town. Nowadays, summers in Broadstairs feature a **Dickens Festival** (tel: 01843-861 827; www.broadstairsdickensfestival. co.uk), held in late June. A week of events includes plays, concerts, guided walks and a Victorian country fair.

The city of Rochester in Kent also has its own **Dickens Summer Festival** (www.rochesterdickensfestival. org.uk), usually held at the end of May or beginning of June. It features street entertainment and parades featuring characters from Dickens's novels, and people compete to win the Best-Dressed Victorian Lady and Gentlemen competitions. Rochester also hosts a **Dickensian Christmas Festival** on the first weekend in December, with a costume ball and other Victorian festivities. Dickens himself lived in the nearby village of Higham, at **Gads Hill Place** from 1857. The house is, unfortunately, not open to the public, and has long been occupied by a school. You can, however, visit the author's Swiss chalet, where he did much of his writing. This two-storey wooden building originally stood opposite Gads Hill Place, but has now been moved to the garden of Eastgate House (tel: 01634-338 106) on the High Street in the centre of Rochester. Eastgate House featured as Westgate House in *The Pickwick Papers* and the Nun's House in his last novel, *The Mystery of Edwin Drood*.

Rochester hosts the Dickens Summer Festival every year

Christ Church dining hall in Oxford doubled as Hogwarts Hall in the Harry Potter series

Dickens died in 1870 and, despite having requested to be buried in Rochester Cathedral, he was actually laid to rest in **Poets' Corner** in **Westminster Abbey** (tel: 020-7222 5152; www.westminster-abbey.org).

The Lakeland Poets

The spectacular scenery of the Lake District in the northwest of England inspired some of the most popular poetry in the English language. The shores of Ullswater provided the setting for Wordsworth's poem 'Daffodils', which famously begins

Harry Potter

Aficionados of Harry Potter may be interested in seeing some of the atmospheric locations used in the films of the books. When Harry sets off for Hogwarts, he departs from Platform 9¾ at **Kings Cross Station** in London. Look out for the platform sign and a luggage trolley disappearing through a wall...
For the actual journey to Hogwarts, film-makers then used Scotland's West Highland Railway Line (www.westcoastrailways.co.uk). Between mid-May and October, a steam train service runs between Fort William and Mallaig. The spectacular **Glenfinnan Viaduct** on this line is also used in the flying car sequence in *Harry Potter and the Chamber of Secrets*.

Several locations are used for Hogwarts itself. The exterior of **Alnwick Castle** (tel: 01665-511 100; www.alnwickcastle.com) in Northumberland

stands in for exterior Hogwarts shots, and the Quidditch match and broomstick lesson are set within the ramparts. At one point, Harry also crash lands a flying car in the castle's bailey.

One of the classrooms inside the school is set within the Chapter House at **Durham Cathedral** (tel: 0191-386 4266; www.durhamcathedral.co.uk), and Harry walks through the cathedral cloisters with his owl, Hedwig. Other scenes were shot among the dreaming spires of **Oxford University**. Oxford's ancient vaulted **Divinity School** (tel: 01865-277 224) became Hogwarts' Sanatorium, while **Duke Humfrey's Library** (tel: 01865-277 162; www.bodley.ox.ac.uk; guided tours only) doubled up as Hogwarts' Library. The magnificent **Great Hall** at **Christ Church** (tel: 01865-276 492; www.chch.ox.ac.uk) was the setting for Hogwarts Hall.

with the line, 'I wandered lonely as a cloud'. In the village of Grasmere, a little way to the south, you can visit the home where the poet lived. **Dove Cottage** (tel: 01539-435 544; www.wordsworth.org.uk) and the adjacent **Wordsworth Museum** (tel: 01539-435 748) contain many of the personal possessions of Wordsworth, as well as those of his sister Dorothy, who penned her famous *Grasmere Journal* about daily life there. Also on show are exhibits relating to a later occupant of the cottage, Thomas de Quincey, who is best remembered for his *Confessions of an English Opium Eater*. He succumbed to his drug addiction whilst in residence.

Hardy Country

Few writers have evoked a sense of place more vividly than Thomas Hardy. Most of the locations and landmarks featured in his novels can be identified in his home county of Dorset – or 'Wessex', as he preferred to call it. The pretty town of Shaftesbury is the Shaston of the novel *Jude the Obscure*. Weymouth features in many of the novels as Budmouth Regis, and the county town of Dorchester was the setting for *The Mayor of Casterbridge*.

Hardy was born in the cottage his great grandfather built at Higher Bockhampton, just north of Dorchester in 1840 (**Hardy's Birthplace**; tel: 01305-262 366; www.nationaltrust.org). It was here that he wrote *Far from the Madding Crowd* and *Under the Greenwood Tree*. On leaving school, Hardy had been apprenticed to an architect in Dorchester, and after he left the practice in 1885, he used his knowledge to design his own house in the town. **Max Gate** (tel: 01297-489 481; www.nationaltrust.org.uk), where he died in 1928, is now open to the public. A few streets away, the **Dorset County Museum** (tel: 01305-262 735; www.dorsetcountymuseum.org) is also worth visiting since it has a reconstruction of Hardy's study.

Agatha Christie

The major destination for fans of Agatha Christie's murder mysteries is the county of Devon, in the

Literary trails

Dove Cottage in Grasmere was once the home of Wordsworth

southwest of England. Just near the little fishing port of Brixham is Christie's summer home, **Greenway** (tel: 01803-842 382; www.national trust.org.uk; open March to October). Only recently been opened to the public, this picturesque country house contains fine furnishings and collections of archaeology, silver and china. The library is perhaps the most important room in the house. It has a mural painted around the walls by one of the American soldiers stationed here during World War II, when the house was requisitioned as an American army base. The mural depicts the soldier's journey from America to Devon. The author used the house as the seting for several of her novels, including *Dead Man's Folly*, *Ordeal by Innocence* and *Five Little Pigs*.

Not far away is the county town of **Torquay**. The local Tourist Information Centre (Vaughan Parade; tel: 01803-211 211) provides a leaflet (which can also be downloaded from www.englishriviera.co.uk) on the Agatha Christie Mile, a walk through the town which takes in various landmarks relating to the author's life. You start at the Grand Hotel on the seafront, where Christie spent her honeymoon, and continue to the **Torquay Museum** (tel: 01803-293 975; www.torquaymuseum. org), where there is a special Agatha Christie exhibition. Then there is the Town Hall, where Christie worked as a nurse during World War I (acquiring useful knowledge on poisons), and the Imperial Hotel, which featured in three of her novels – *Peril at End House*, *The Body in the Library* and *Sleeping Murder*.

In September each year, Torquay hosts a week-long **Agatha Christie Festival** (tel: 0844-474 2233; www. englishriviera.co.uk/agathachristie/ festival) to coincide with Christie's birthday on 15th September. Events include plays, open-air film screenings, flower festivals, walks, talks, book signings, classic car treasure hunts and murder mystery dinners. There's even a tea dance at the grand **Oldway Mansion** (tel: 01803-207

Burgh Island Hotel hosts regular murder mystery weekends

The Brontë Parsonage Museum was formerly the home of the literary sisters

933), where, in her youth, Christie herself attended several balls.

Further west along the coast is **Burgh Island**, where the Hercule Poirot story *Evil Under the Sun* was set. This beautiful island is accessible across the sand at low tide. Its main landmark is the elegant Art-Deco **Burgh Island Hotel** (tel: 01548-810 514; www.burghisland.com), which hosts murder mystery weekends.

As well as in Devon, Agatha Christie also kept a home in London. Over the course of her life, she lived at nine different addresses in the capital. The best known is 58 Sheffield Terrace in Kensington, which has a blue plaque on the outside commemorating her residence there. Another site of pilgrimage in London is **St Martin's Theatre** (tel: 0844-499 1515; www.the-mousetrap.co.uk) in the West End. Christie's murder mystery, *The Mousetrap*, has been playing here since 1952, and with over 24,000 performances, it is the longest running show in modern history.

Literary trails

Top 10 writers' houses

- **Lawrence of Arabia**: Cloud's Hill, Dorset (tel: 01929-405 616; www.nationaltrust.org.uk)
- **Rudyard Kipling**: Bateman's, Burwash, East Sussex (tel: 01435-882 302; www.nationaltrust.org.uk)
- **Sir Walter Scott**: Abbotsford, Melrose, Roxburghshire, Scotland (tel: 01896-752 043; www.scottsabbotsford.co.uk)
- **Dylan Thomas**: Boathouse, Laugharne, Carmarthenshire, Wales (tel: 01994-427 420; www.dylanthomasboathouse.com)
- **Samuel Johnson**: Gough Square, London (tel: 020-7353 3745; www.drjohnsonshouse.org)
- **Brontë sisters**: Brontë Parsonage Museum, Haworth, West Yorkshire (tel: 01535-642 323; www.bronte.org.uk)
- **John Keats**: Keats Grove, Hampstead, London (tel: 020-7332 3868; www.keatshouse.cityoflondon.gov.uk)
- **Jane Austen**: Chawton, Hampshire (tel: 01420-832 62; www.jane-austens-house-museum.org.uk)
- **Henry James**: Lamb House, Rye, East Sussex (tel: 01580-762 334; www.nationaltrust.org.uk)
- **Virginia Woolf**: Rodmell, Lewes, East Sussex (tel: 01323-870 001; www.nationaltrust.org.uk)

Exploring the landscape

Britain may be modest in size, but it musters a surprising variety of landscapes. From the flat-as-a-pancake black-soiled Fenlands of East Anglia to the jagged peaks of the Scottish Highlands, there is something for walkers of all levels of fitness and experience.

Despite the pressures of cramming 60 million inhabitants together on one island, Britain has managed to retain many areas of unspoilt countryside. An important part of such conservation efforts is the system of **National Parks** and **National Trails**. These were established in the decades after World War II, to help offset the effects of an ambitious programme of new towns and housing estates. At the same time, motorways were laid out across the countryside and – much to the regret of many – the rural railway network was slashed, following the notorious Beeching Report.

There are currently 10 National Parks in England, three in Wales, and two in Scotland (www.national-parks.gov.uk). These include **Snowdonia**, the **Lake District**, the **Norfolk Broads** and the recently designated (in 2009) **South Downs**. In addition to these, there are 15 National Trails in England and Wales (www.nationaltrail.co.uk), and a further four 'Long Distance Routes' in Scotland (www.snh.gov.uk). **The Pennine Bridleway**, the **South Downs Way**, and large sections of several other trails can also be navigated by horse riders and cyclists.

Around the coast

If you want to be really ambitious, you can, of course, walk around

The summit of Snake Pass on the Pennine Way

Wild ponies are part
of the Exmoor landscape

are, however, much shorter sections of the coast that make spectacular (well-signposted) walks. There's the **Norfolk Coast Path** which takes in miles of white sand and some of the country's finest bird sanctuaries. Then there's the **Pembrokeshire Coast Path** in South Wales, with its 35,000ft (10,700m) of ascent and descent – said to be equivalent to climbing Everest. Consider also the 630-mile (1,014km) **South West Coast Path** around Dorset, Devon and Cornwall, which takes in the fossil cliffs of **Chesil Beach**, the most southwesterly point of the British mainland at **Land's End**, and **Exmoor National Park**, famous for its herds of wild ponies.

The Lake District

For the ideal combination of water and mountain, rock and vegetation, head up to the northwest of England to the Lake District. The central part of The Lakes is now a national park (www.lakedistrict.gov.uk), and encompasses all of the land in England higher than 3,000ft (914m), including **Scafell Pike**, England's highest mountain at 3,209ft (978m). It also contains towards 100 lakes

Britain's entire coastline. This 4,000-odd mile (6,437km) jaunt is not for the faint-hearted. A teenager who completed the task accompanied by his pet dog in 2008 complained that it had given him a blister the size of a digestive biscuit. Imagine the hardship encountered by another walker, who made the journey even longer (6,500 miles, 10,461km, in total) by not taking ferries across all the estuaries, but walking around them instead. It took him six months and nine sets of shoe soles. In order not to have to carry the 100 different maps required for the trip, his tolerant wife mailed smaller bundles of them to pre-designated post offices along the way.

If you have neither the time to spare, nor a forgiving spouse, there

Five great walks
• Hadrian's Wall (Tyneside and Cumbria)
• Offa's Dyke (the Welsh Borders)
• West Highland Way (from Milngavie, near Glasgow, to Fort William)
• Mount Snowdon (Snowdonia National Park, North Wales)
• Beachy Head (East Sussex)

Exploring the landscape

– although only one, Bassenthwaite Lake, is officially named a lake, the others being meres, waters or tarns.

The aesthetic perfection has long been admired. The so-called Lake Poets – Wordsworth, Coleridge and Southey – took inspiration from the landscape for their romantic conception of man's place in nature. The artist and critic John Ruskin, who championed the cause of naturalism in art, lived in a house facing **Coniston Water**, and some time later, Beatrix Potter bought a farm near **Ambleside**, where she continued working on her beautifully illustrated animal tales for children.

In more recent times, the close observation of the Lakeland landscape has yielded the extraordinary work of Alfred Wainwright (1907–91). His guidebooks detailing the best routes up the fells are comprised of reproductions of his own manuscripts, with beautiful pen-and-ink drawings and immaculate handwriting. Seven volumes cover 214 of the fells, which are now often collectively referred to as 'the Wainwrights', and conquering the complete set of peaks is a popular challenge among walking enthusiasts. Wainwright himself considered the 'finest half-dozen' fells to be Scafell Pike, Bowfell, Pillar, Great Gable, Blencathra and Crinkle Crags.

Another popular route that Wainwright devised for walkers is the **Coast to Coast Walk**, a 192-mile (309km) path which begins at **St Bees** in the Lake District, and stretches across the country horizontally to **Robin Hood's Bay** in North Yorkshire. Walkers are supposed to dip their feet in the Irish Sea at the start and the North Sea at the end. In between, they pass through three contrasting national parks: the Lake District, the Yorkshire Dales, and the North York Moors. The walk splits conveniently into manageable sections, and with overnight stays at guest houses along the way, the

A family walking at Elterwater in the Lake District

entire route can be fitted into a two-week holiday.

The Munros of Scotland

A Munro is a Scottish mountain of over 3,000ft (914m). The name comes from Sir Hugh Munro, who produced the first list of such mountains in 1891. There are 283 Munros, and a further 227 Munro 'tops' (subsidiary peaks on Munros). Perhaps the most famous Munros are **Ben Nevis**, the highest mountain in Great Britain, at 4,409ft (1,344m), **Ben Macdui** (4,295ft/1,309m) in the Cairngorms and **Buachaille Etive Mòr** (3,353ft/1,022m) at the entrance to Glencoe. Other Scottish mountains are categorised as Corbetts, which are between 2,500 and 3,000ft (760–910m) in height, and Grahams, which are between 2,000 and 2,500ft (610–760m).

A popular practice amongst hillwalkers is 'Munro Bagging', the aim being to climb all of the listed Munros. Having climbed all of them, a walker is entitled to be called a Munroist. As of 2009 more than

Buachaille Etive Mòr is one of the most famous of Scotland's Munros

4,000 have reported completing the full list. The first continuous round of the Munros was completed in 1974, whilst the current record for the fastest continuous round is 39 days, 9 hours. One person has completed the full list 13 times. Winter ascents of certain Munros provide challenging ice climbs. Walkers need to be well prepared for the often extreme weather conditions, as there are numerous fatalities every year.

Exploring the landscape

National Cycle Network

The **National Cycle Network** (www. sustrans.org.uk) comprises 12,600 miles (20,278km) of cycle paths. The routes aim to minimise contact with motor traffic, and although some are on minor roads, many others are on disused railway lines, canal towpaths and bridleways. The network is signposted using a white bicycle symbol on a blue background, with a white route number in an inset box.

In addition, there is the **National Byway** (www.thenationalbyway.org), a 4,000-mile (6,400km) cycling route that runs along quiet roads around England and parts of Scotland and Wales. It includes a number of loops so that cyclists can start and finish in the same place. These circular routes range in length from 16 miles (26km) to 50 miles (80km). Signposts have white writing on a brown background.

Art experiences

These days, art in Britain is a very democratic business. Many cities are endowed with grand Victorian museums which grant public access to great art free of charge. A number of artists have bequeathed their studios to the nation. And auction houses and commercial galleries are only too happy to display their wares.

Centuries of artistocratic and royal collectors have ensured that Britain is rich in artistic treasures. Wealthy patrons have long displayed their trophies in galleries in their country houses. **Holkham Hall** in Norfolk (tel: 01328-710 227; www.holkham.co.uk) and **Castle Howard** in North Yorkshire (tel: 01653-648 333; www.castlehoward.co.uk) have particularly fine examples. Unlike in France and Italy, however, the collections of the ruling class were never nationalised, and the first public museums in Britain were based around antiquarian collections of curiosities, prints, drawings and books. The **Ashmolean Museum** (tel: 01865-278 000; www.ashmolean.org) in Oxford opened in 1683, and the **British Museum** (tel: 020-7323 8299; www.britishmuseum.org) in 1759. Both subsequently acquired large collections of art and archaeological treasures, and moved into sprawling neoclassical buildings in the first half of the 19th century. The **Fitzwilliam Museum** (tel: 01223-332 900; www.fitzmuseum.cam.ac.uk) in Cambridge was founded during this period, and was similarly housed.

The very first purpose-built art gallery, however, was the **Dulwich Picture Gallery** (tel: 020-8693 5254; www.dulwichpicturegallery.org.uk) in South London. It was completed in 1817 to designs by Sir John Soane. His use of skylights to provide natural light from above has been adopted by architects of art galleries ever since. A few years later, in 1824, the **National Gallery** (tel: 020-7747 2885; www.nationalgallery.org.uk) in London was established from the legacy of a wealthy banker.

The 19th century also brought a new breed of museum, founded on

The elegant curves of the main gallery at Tate St Ives

The National Gallery in Trafalgar Square is one of the world's great art collections

Art experiences

the great wealth that was accruing to the entrepreneurs of the Industrial Revolution. Most notable of all was Henry Tate, who made his fortune from sugar lumps and gave his name to the museum of British art now known as **Tate Britain** (tel: 020-7887 8888; www.tate.org.uk). The Tate foundation subsequently established several other galleries including **Tate Liverpool** (tel: 0151-702 7400), **Tate St Ives** (tel: 01736-796 226) in Cornwall, and **Tate Modern** (tel: 020-7887 8888) on London's South Bank. The **Victoria and Albert Museum** (tel: 020-7942 2000; www.vam.ac.uk) in South Kensington was also founded on Britain's industrial prosperity. It was originally devoted to the applied arts and science, but the collection has evolved to encompass a wide variety of decorative art and design, from costume to ceramics and from furniture to photography.

The Royal Academy of Arts

Ever since its founding in 1768, the **Royal Academy** (tel: 020-7300 8000; www.royalacademy.org.uk) on London's Piccadilly has been governed by practising artists, who are elected to its membership. Its main function today is the putting on of large-scale exhibitions, which include a **Summer Exhibition**, held from early June to mid-August each year. Anyone can submit their own handiwork for this, and a panel of academicians selects which works are included. Most of the paintings and sculptures exhibited are for sale, and dealers try to get in early in the hope of spotting some bargains.

Scotland has the **Royal Scottish Academy** (tel: 0131-225 6671; www.royalscottishacademy.org), which was founded in 1826, and is run along similar lines. It is located on The Mound, on Princes Street in Edinburgh.

conservatism of the British nation, and the stability and relative prosperity that have characterised its history. However, the 1990s brought the closest thing yet to a home-grown avant garde. The so-called Young British Artists (or YBAs) – Damian Hirst, Tracey Emin, Sarah Lucas, Michael Landy and Gary Hume, among others – were graduates of the same art school and exhibited together just after leaving. Their work, however, is varied in form and content. Hirst, for example, is famous for pickling sharks in formaldehyde, while Emin exhibited her own unmade bed (complete with dirty clothes and used condoms).

Your best opportunities for seeing the YBAs' work, as well as that of other leading contemporary artists, are at **Tate Modern** (tel: 020-7887 8888; www.tate.org.uk) on the banks of the Thames across from St Paul's Cathedral, and the **Saatchi Gallery** (tel: 020-7823 2363; www.saatchi-

The contemporary art scene

Art historians have long held that Britain – unlike France, Germany, the United States and many other developed countries in the western world – has never given birth to an avant-garde art movement. This is often attributed to the essential

Ten great art museums outside London

- **Barbara Hepworth Museum**, St Ives, Cornwall (tel: 01736-796 226; www.tate.org.uk/stives/hepworth)
- **Gainsborough's House**, Suffolk (tel: 01787-372 958; www.gainsborough.org)
- **Kettle's Yard**, Cambridge (tel: 01223-748 100; www.kettlesyard.co.uk)
- **Sainsbury Centre for Visual Arts**, near Norwich (tel: 01603-593 199; www.scva.org.uk)
- **Barber Institute of Fine Arts**, Birmingham (tel: 0121-414 7333; www.barber.org.uk)

- **The New Art Gallery**, Walsall (tel: 01922-654 400; www.thenewartgallerywalsall.org.uk)
- **The Lowry**, Salford, Manchester (tel: 0843-208 6000; www.thelowry.com)
- **Whitworth Art Gallery**, Manchester (tel: 0161-275 7450; www.whitworth.manchester.ac.uk)
- **Henry Moore Institute**, Leeds (tel: 0113-246 7467; www.henry-moore.org)
- **The Bowes Museum**, County Durham (tel: 01833-690 606; www.thebowesmuseum.org.uk)

gallery.co.uk) in a former army barracks on the King's Road in Chelsea. Each year, the Tate also hosts the Turner Prize, Britain's most prestigious competition for contemporary artists. Works by the shortlisted artists are usually displayed at **Tate Britain**, though recently, **Tate Liverpool** has also been used as a venue *(see p.51 for contact details)*.

Important exhibitions of contemporary art are also held at the **Whitechapel Gallery** (tel: 020-7522 7888; www.whitechapelgallery.org), the **Hayward Gallery** (tel: 020-7921 0813; www.haywardgallery.org.uk) and the **Serpentine Gallery** (tel: 020-7402 6075; www.serpentinegallery. org) in London, the **MK Gallery** (tel: 01908-676 900; www.mkgallery.org) in Milton Keynes, the **Ikon Gallery** (tel: 0121-248 0708; www.ikon-gallery. co.uk) in Birmingham, and the **BALTIC Centre for Contemporary Art** (tel: 0191-478 1810; www.baltic mill.com) in Newcastle.

The art market

London is the centre of the European art market. It is home to over 200 commercial galleries, as well as the headquarters of all the major auction houses. You can go and see an auction in progress – or at least view the artworks that are about to be sold – at **Sotheby's** (tel: 020-7293 5000; www.sothebys.com) on Bond Street. There is also a chic, and not overly pricey café on the premises. **Christie's** (tel: 020-7839 9060; www. christies.com) have their main auction rooms not far away on King Street in the St James's district, as well as salerooms for more less expensive items at 85 Old Brompton Road in South Kensington (tel: 020-7930 6074).

London's Mayfair district is the location of many of the smartest galleries. It may seem intimidating, but you are welcome to go inside these showrooms and look at what's on display. The **Waddington Custot**

Art experiences

The Hayward Gallery is a significant exhibition centre

Galleries at 11 Cork Street (tel: 020-7851 2200; www.waddington custot.com) are good for paintings by established 20th-century figures, while **Sadie Coles HQ** (tel: 020-7493 8611; www.sadiecoles.com) at 69 South Audley Street shows recent work by cutting-edge contemporary artists. **The Fine Art Society** (tel: 020-7629 5116; www.faslondon. com) at 148 New Bond Street is worth a visit for its historic premises and exhibitions of 19th- and 20th-century British art.

The grittier East End is home to many of Britain's younger generation of artists, and a number of gallerists have set up shop there to show their work. The best known is **White Cube** (tel: 020-7930 5373; www.whitecube. com) on Hoxton Square, which represents a number of the so-called YBAs *(see p.52)*. **Vyner Street** is lined with less established galleries run on tiny budgets in old shops and post-industrial buildings.

White Cube on Hoxton Square houses works by many contemporary artists

Art in Scotland

Scotland has a distinguished art history all of its own. While many of its more ancient treasures, such as the Lewis Chessmen, are now housed at the British Museum in London, there is much else on display at the **National Museum of Scotland** (tel: 0300-123 6789; www.nms.ac.uk) in Edinburgh. For paintings and sculpture from the early Renaissance to the late 19th-century, the country's foremost collection is at the **Scottish National Gallery** (tel: 0131-624 6200; www.national galleries.org), also in Edinburgh.

Scotland is particularly rich, however, in museums for more recent art. Since its industrial heyday in the 19th century, Glasgow has been a major centre for artists. It nurtured the group of anti-academic painters known as the Glasgow Boys, who brought the naturalism and symbolism of modern French painting to bear on everyday subjects in rural Scotland. The work of its leading members – such as Sir James Guthrie (1859–1930), Sir John Lavery (1856–1941) and William George Macgregor (1855–1923) – can be seen at the city's **Kelvingrove Art Gallery** (tel: 0141-276 9599; www.glasgowlife. org.uk). This exuberantly designed Spanish-Baroque-style building also contains fine collections of Old Masters and French Impressionists.

Glasgow is also famously associated with the artist and designer Charles Rennie Mackintosh. One of his most important creations is the **Glasgow School of Art** (tel: 0141-353 4500; www.gsa.ac.uk), designed (outside and in) with his idiosyncratic fusion of the Arts and Crafts and Art Nouveau

Kelvingrove Art Gallery

many other artists, most notably James McNeill Whistler.

In Edinburgh, the **Scottish National Gallery of Modern Art** (tel: 0131-624 6558; www.nationalgalleries.org) presents a good survey of the art movements of the last century. Just across the road, its sister collection, the **Dean Gallery** (contact details as above), is notable for its collection of Dada and Surrealist art. It also houses many of the works of locally born Edouardo Paolozzi (1924–2005), as well as a recreation of his studio.

Elsewhere in Scotland, the **Aberdeen Art Gallery** (tel: 01224-523 700; www.aagm.co.uk), has particular strength in 19th-century art and the Scottish Colourists. The latter – four or five artists who were inspired by the French Fauvists – can also be seen in force at **Kirkcaldy Museum and Art Gallery** (tel: 01592-583 213; www. museumsgalleriesscotland.org.uk). Perhaps the most famous of the Scottish Colourists, J.D. Fergusson (1874–1961), has a whole museum – the **Fergusson Gallery** (tel: 01738-783 425; www.pkc. gov.uk) – devoted to him in Perth.

styles. The Mackintosh Building at the heart of the campus houses an exhibition gallery. The other areas of the school can be viewed on a guided tour. Also important for Mackintosh enthusiasts is the **Hunterian Museum** (tel: 0141-330 4221; www.hunterian. gla.ac.uk) at the University of Glasgow, which holds a large collection of his watercolours, in addition to works by

Art experiences

Constable country

John Constable (1776–1837) is noted for his paintings of the landscape of his native Suffolk. His most famous work, *The Hay Wain (see picture p.145)*, depicts **Flatford Mill**, which is situated near the village of East Bergholt and was owned by his father. Visitors today will find that remarkably little has changed from the scenes depicted by Constable. Just along the riverside footpath from the mill is **Flatford Bridge Cottage** (tel: 01206-298 260; www.nationaltrust.

org.uk), where an exhibition documents the painter's life and work. From there you can either hire a rowing boat and glide along the river, or follow the **Constable Walk** which takes you to Manningtree Railway Station (from where there are direct trains to London). In **East Bergholt** itself, the sites of the painter's birthplace (between the church and the village shop), and his studio (on Cemetery Lane) are both indicated with commemorative plaques.

Sporting passions

Whether you like watching or playing, are into boxing or bowls, and are expert or novice, Britain's healthy obsession with sport should mean that you'll find what you're looking for. And while tickets for Manchester United games or the British Grand Prix may be expensive, there are plenty of quite affordable events, from Test matches to horse racing meetings.

The British have often been portrayed as preferring sport to art and culture. It's probably true, though it's not something you'll find many people apologising about. The British are responsible for inventing – or at least playing a crucial role in developing – a wide range of sports that are now popular around the world. Football, rugby (both union and league versions), cricket, golf, tennis, boxing and snooker all trace their histories back to these shores. And although British nationals may no longer dominate the first ranks of many of these sports, the country does still host some of the world's most prestigious tournaments, and levels of amateur participation remain as high as ever.

Football

In the last few decades, professional football has undergone a remarkable transformation in Britain. Even 25 years ago, its fanbase was largely male, stadiums offered standing room only (with no toilet facilities for women), and matchdays were plagued with pitched battles between gangs of hooligans. Things are very different today, in large part because of the enormous cash injection from satellite television fees. Premier League

Tennis

The main fixtures for tennis enthusiasts are the tournaments at **Wimbledon** (tel: 020-8971 2473; www.wimbledon.com) in the second half of June and the 'warm-up' event at **Queen's Club** (tel: 020-7386 3400; www.queensclub.co.uk) just before. Wimbledon also has a **Lawn Tennis Museum** (tel: 020-8946 6131) where you can see the club's famous trophies as well as video footage of great sporting moments.

If you fancy a knock-about yourself, there are courts available at municipal parks in towns up and down the country. To find a court, consult www.tennisforfree.com.

clubs can now afford the best players in the world, most grounds have been completely revamped with seating and modern amenities, and the fanbase is far wider and more family-orientated. But although hooliganism is largely a thing of the past, the passion of the crowd and the quality of their singing and swearing is as robust as ever.

Tickets to see the top Premiership teams – Manchester United, Arsenal and Chelsea, for example – are expensive (ranging from about £30 to £100) and must be purchased well in advance. Tickets for lower-ranking teams are more affordable, and may even still be available on matchday itself.

If you want to play football yourself, there is no shortage of opportunities. Amateur games for all ages and for both men and women take place at local parks, all-weather pitches and leisure centres across the country. To find a team to join near where you are, consult www.wantto playfootball.co.uk.

Cricket

Silly mid-off, LBW, googly, square leg and golden duck: cricket is a funny old game, with arcane terminology and matches up to five days long. Those in the know, however, swear that once you understand the basics, it's an engrossing sport that will have you rejoicing in the sound of leather on willow (or, to the uninitiated, ball on bat). As with a number of traditional British sports, cricket is also played in many of the Commonwealth countries. Over the last hundred years, several of these – India, Australia and South Africa, for example – have outdone the former colonial power in developing their fanbases and often in the skill of their teams too.

Purists assert that the 'Test' series is the most sublime version of the

Lord's is a great place to catch a cricket match while in London

game. It consists of five matches lasting five days each played between different national teams. The most famous of such contests is **The Ashes** series between England and Australia. It is played every other year, with each country taking turns to host the event. Each of the five matches in the series is played at a different ground, with the most commonly used venues in England being **Edgbaston** (Birmingham; www. edgbaston.com), **Lord's** (London; www.lords.org), **Headingley** (Leeds; www.yorkshireccc.com), **Old Trafford** (Manchester; www.lccc.co.uk), **The Oval** (London; www.kiaoval. com) and **Trent Bridge** (Nottingham; www.trentbridge.co.uk). Tickets for Test matches usually cost

between £5 and £70, depending on where you sit, and how many days you attend.

Alongside the international matches, Britain has its own domestic competitions. A league of 18 'first-class' counties play each other in 'limited overs' matches. Between 20 and 50 overs (an over consists of six balls) are bowled by each side, so that a match can usually be completed in one day. Each county has its own ground. The six grounds used for Test matches are also county grounds; Lord's, for example, is the home of Middlesex County Cricket Club. Tickets for county matches usually cost between £5 and £20; see www.ecb.co.uk for details.

Horse racing

Horse racing in Britain is either flat racing – unobstructed runs over varying distances – or National Hunt (steeplechase) racing, where the horses have to jump over hurdles or fences along the course. There are courses all over the country. Perhaps the most famous is **Newmarket** (tel: 0844-579 3010; www.newmarketracecourses.co.uk), which is also a centre for stud farms and horse training, and is home to the **National Horseracing Museum** (tel: 01638-667 333; www. nhrm.co.uk).

Among the biggest events in the racing calendar are **Royal Ascot** (tel: 0870-727 1234; www.ascot.co.uk), a five-day race meeting attended by the Queen in the third week of June; the **Cheltenham Festival** (tel: 0844-579 3003; www.cheltenham.co.uk), a four-day National Hunt meeting in mid-March; **The Grand National**

Royal Ascot is one of the key events in the horse racing calendar

(tel: 0844-579 3001; www.aintree.co.uk) at Aintree in April – the longest and most gruelling National Hunt race in the calendar; and the richest flat race, **The Derby** (tel: 01372-726 311; www.epsomderby.co.uk), held at Epsom in early June.

Tickets for events can be bought online from racecourse websites. The most expensive tickets grant entrance to the stand or 'enclosure' with the best views and facilities; there is often a dress code for these areas. On-course betting is a part of the experience, and is conducted in hard cash only.

St Andrews in Scotland is home to one of Britain's most iconic golf courses

Golf

The game we recognise as golf originated in Scotland, where the first written record – from 1457 – is of James II banning the game because it distracted people from the more useful pursuit of archery. Today, while Scotland remains the game's spiritual home, there are fine courses all over the country. For information on watching tournaments, see www.pga.info and www.europeantour.com. For listings of golf courses you can play, see www.englishgolf-courses.co.uk.

Motor racing

The main fixture in the motor racing calendar is the **British Grand Prix**, usually held on the second weekend in July. The current venue for the event is the Silverstone Circuit (tel: 0844-3750 740; www.silverstone.co.uk) in Northamptonshire. Tickets for the race itself cost from £130 upwards and must be booked well in advance. There is a wide range of

types of race at Silverstone at other times in the year, when tickets are much more affordable.

For retro enthusiasts, the **Goodwood Festival of Speed** (tel: 01243-755 000; www.goodwood.co.uk) is an absolute must at the beginning of July. Held at the circuit in the grounds of a stately home in West Sussex, the four-day event features historic racing cars and motorbikes, appearances (and demonstration drives) from famous champions of the recent past, and a hillclimb competition.

Sporting passions

Top five golf courses

- **Royal St George's**, Kent (tel: 01304-613 090; www.royalstgeorges.com)
- **Royal Lytham and St Annes**, Lancashire (tel: 01253-724 206; www.royallytham.org)
- **Nefyn**, Wales (tel: 01758-720 218; www.nefyn-golf-club.com)
- **Turnberry**, Scotland (tel: 01655-331 550; www.turnberrygolfclub.net)
- **St Andrews**, Scotland (tel: 01334-466 666; www.standrews.org.uk)

PLACES

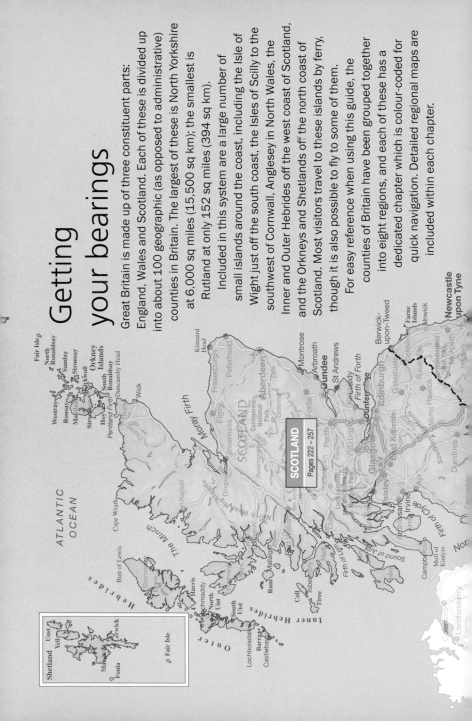

Getting
your bearings

Great Britain is made up of three constituent parts:
England, Wales and Scotland. Each of these is divided up
into about 100 geographic (as opposed to administrative)
counties in Britain. The largest of these is North Yorkshire
at 6,000 sq miles (15,500 sq km); the smallest is
Rutland at only 152 sq miles (394 sq km).

Included in this system are a large number of
small islands around the coast, including the Isle of
Wight just off the south coast, the Isles of Scilly to the
southwest of Cornwall, Anglesey in North Wales, the
Inner and Outer Hebrides off the west coast of Scotland,
and the Orkneys and Shetlands off the north coast of
Scotland. Most visitors travel to these islands by ferry,
though it is also possible to fly to some of them.

For easy reference when using this guide, the
counties of Britain have been grouped together
into eight regions, and each of these has a
dedicated chapter which is colour-coded for
quick navigation. Detailed regional maps are
included within each chapter.

SCOTLAND

Pages 222 – 257

ATLANTIC
OCEAN

Fair Isle
North
Ronaldsay
Sanday
Westray Rousay Stronsay
Mainland **Orkney**
Stromness Kirkwall South Islands
Hoy
Pentland Firth Duncansby Head
Wick
Thurso

Cape Wrath

The Minch

Butt of Lewis

Stornoway

Kinnaird
Head

Moray Firth

Ullapool

Dingwall

Inverness
Elgin
Fraserburgh
Peterhead

Cairngorms
National
Park

Dee
Braemar

SCOTLAND

Aberdeen

Montrose
Arbroath
Dundee
St Andrews
Forfar

Kirkcaldy
Firth of Forth
Perth

Stirling

Dunfermline
Edinburgh

Berwick-
upon-Tweed

Galashiels

Glasgow
East Kilbride

Hawick
Moffat

Dumfries

Firth of Clyde

Ayr
Irvine

Campbeltown
Mull of
Kintyre

Sound of Jura

Firth of Lorn

Oban

Mull
Tobermory
Coll
Tiree

Inner Hebrides

Rum

Mallaig

Fort William

Loch Lomond
& the Trossachs
National
Park

Paisley

Loch
Katrine

Firth of Forth

Loch
Earn

Loch
Lomond

North West Highlands

Hebrides

Harris

North
Uist

South
Uist

Barra
Castlebay

Lochboisdale

Lochmaddy

Outer Hebrides

Newcastle
upon Tyne

Farne
Islands
Alnwick
Morpeth
Hexham
Northumberland
Nat. Park

Londonderry
Coleraine

Shetland
Unst
Yell
Foula
Mainland
Lerwick

Fair Isle

SCOTLAND

3

NORTH

Pages 190 – 221

CENTRAL

Pages 150 – 171

EAST ANGLIA

Pages 136 – 149

LONDON

Pages 64 – 101

SOUTHEAST

Pages 102 – 117

WALES

Pages 172 – 189

SOUTHWEST

Pages 118 – 135

NORTH SEA

IRISH SEA

CELTIC SEA

REPUBLIC OF IRELAND

ENGLAND

English Channel

Strait of Dover

FRANCE

St George's Channel

Bristol Channel

Cardigan Bay

London

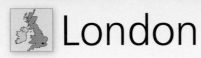

Fire, plague, population explosions, aerial bombing, economic recessions, urban blight, terrorism… London has taken everything history could throw at it, and this has made it one of the world's most complex and fascinating cities. Indeed, as Samuel Johnson famously declared, 'when a man is tired of London, he is tired of life; for there is in London all that life can afford'.

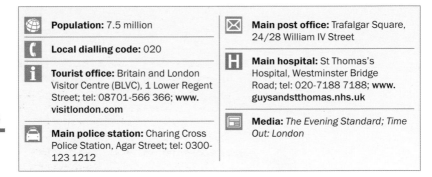

Population: 7.5 million

Local dialling code: 020

Tourist office: Britain and London Visitor Centre (BLVC), 1 Lower Regent Street; tel: 08701-566 366; www.visitlondon.com

Main police station: Charing Cross Police Station, Agar Street; tel: 0300-123 1212

Main post office: Trafalgar Square, 24/28 William IV Street

Main hospital: St Thomas's Hospital, Westminster Bridge Road; tel: 020-7188 7188; www.guysandstthomas.nhs.uk

Media: *The Evening Standard*; *Time Out: London*

There must be something special about London to attract more than 27 million overnight visitors each year. And it is not the weather. There are, however, wonderful palaces and cathedrals, theatres and museums, parks and gardens, restaurants serving cuisine from all parts of the world, a thriving nightlife, and a refreshingly cosmopolitan and open attitude towards diversity in all things, especially its own inhabitants.

When people talk about London, they are usually referring to the area covered by Greater London. This administrative organisation was imposed on the city in 1965. It comprises the City of London and 32 London boroughs.

Originally, there were two cities here: the City of Westminster (centred on the Houses of Parliament and Westminster Abbey) and the City of London (often referred to simply as 'the City', and covering what is now the financial district – the historic square mile between St Paul's Cathedral and the Tower of London). Westminster is now a borough just like any other, governed by a borough council. The City of London, on the other hand, has its own unique institutions of local government dating back to the 12th century, with the Corporation of London headed up by the Lord Mayor.

Westminster

The City of Westminster was once separated from the City of London to the east by open fields. The space in between has long since been filled by dense development, but Westminster retains a stately character all of its own.

Buckingham Palace

To some, the Queen's home is one of the ugliest buildings in the capital, but it's also held in esteem as the symbol of Britain's royalty. It was built for George IV (the Prince Regent), who commissioned architect John Nash in 1820. The palace wasn't occupied until Victoria became queen in 1837 and made it her official London residence.

Visitors gather in front of **Buckingham Palace** ❶ for the Changing the Guard ceremony *(see p.24)* and perhaps to snatch a glimpse of the Queen, who is in residence when the

Catching some rays in sunny St James's Park

Buckingham Palace is an enduring symbol of Britain's royalty

Royal Standard is flying. The more dedicated may pay a visit to the **State Rooms** (tel: 020-7766 7300; www. royalcollection.org.uk; late July–Sept daily 9.30am–6.30pm; charge), which are open in the autumn when the Queen is Scotland. Otherwise, you can visit the **Royal Mews** (tel: 020-7766 7302; www.royalcollection.org. uk; Apr–Oct daily 10am–5pm, Nov–Dec Mon–Sat 10am–4pm; charge), which contain royal vehicles from horse-drawn coaches to Rolls-Royces. There is also the **Queen's Gallery** (tel: 020-7766 7301; www.royalcollection.org.uk; daily 10am–5.30pm; charge), which displays artworks from the Royal Collection.

Bounding Buckingham Palace to the north and east are **St James's Park** and **Green Park**. St James's Park provides a haven for water birds, and civil servants on their lunchbreaks. Green Park is where Charles II used to take his daily stroll in the 17th century.

In front of the palace is **the Mall**, a broad ceremonial avenue that leads to Admiralty Arch and Trafalgar

London

↑ London Zoo ↑ Camden Town

SOMERS TOWN

St Pancras International Station

King's Cross Station

KING'S CROSS & ST PANCRAS

REGENT'S PARK

REGENT'S PARK

QUEEN MARY'S GARDENS

Open Air Theatre

ST JAMES'S GARDENS

Euston Station

EUSTON

British Library

Shaw Theatre

ST PANCRAS

ST ANDREW GARDENS

Foundling Museum

CORAM'S FIELDS

Charles Dickens Museum

Madame Tussauds **14**

Royal Academy of Music

REGENT'S PARK

EUSTON SQUARE

WARREN STREET

St Marylebone

Marylebone Road

GT PORTLAND STREET

Park Cres.

University College

Brunswick Shopping Centre

Guildford

RUSSELL SQUARE

Great Ormond Hospital for Children

MARYLEBONE

Marylebone High St.

BT Tower

GOODGE STREET

University of London

BLOOMSBURY

BBC Broadcasting House

Wallace Collection

Wigmore Hall

Wigmore Street

John Lewis

GOODGE ST

St Giles High St

British Museum **15**

Gt. Russell St

Bloomsbury Way

HOLBORN

Sir John Soane's Museum

Lincoln's Inn Ha

LINCOLN'S INN FIELDS

Royal Courts of Justice

Gray's Inn

Selfridges

OXFORD CIRCUS

TOTTENHAM COURT ROAD

New Oxford St

ST GILES

Holborn

Oxford Street

Soho Sq.

BOND STREET

Handel House Museum **12**

13

St George

Palladium Theatre

Liberty

Hamleys

Ronnie Scott's Jazz Club

SOHO **9**

Chinatown **10**

Cambridge Circus

COVENT GARDEN Acre

Royal Opera House

Theatre Royal Drury Lane

London Transport Museum

Bush House

Courtauld Gallery

Somerset House **16**

Kensington and Chelsea map on page 86

Roosevelt Memorial

Grosvenor Square

Sotheby's

Faraday Museum

Royal Academy of Arts

PICCADILLY CIRCUS

Piccadilly Circus **11**

↑ Eros

Leicester Square

LEICESTER SQUARE **7**

Long Acre

Covent Garden Market

COVENT GARDEN **8**

STRAND

MAYFAIR

MOUNT ST GARDENS

Grosvenor Chapel

The Ritz

Fortnum & Mason

National Gallery

Trafalgar Square **6**

Nelson's Column

St Martin-in-the-Fields

CHARING CROSS

Charing Cross Station

Cleopatra's Needle

EMBANKMENT

Haywa Galle

(British Fi Instit

Institute of Contemporary Arts **5**

Admiralty Arch

Northumberland Ave

Wellington Museum, Apsley House

Wellington Monument

HYDE PARK CORNER

GREEN PARK

St James's Palace **2**

Clarence House

Pall Mall

ST JAMES'S

Duke of York Memorial

The Mall

HORSE GUARDS PARADE

Banqueting House

P.S. Tattershall Castle

Southbank Centre

Royal Festival Hall

SOUTH BAN

BFI Londo IMAX Cinem

Constitution Hill

GREEN PARK

BUCKINGHAM PALACE GDNS

Buckingham Palace **1**

Queen Victoria Memorial

ST JAMES'S PARK

St James's Park Lake

Duck Island

Birdcage Walk

No. 10 Downing St

Foreign Office

Churchill War Rooms

Parliament

WESTMINSTER

London Eye **26**

JUBILEE GDNS

London Aquarium

Waterl Statio

County Hall

Queen's Gallery

Royal Mews

Westminster Chapel

Queen Elizabeth Conference Centre

New Scotland Yard

ST JAMES'S PARK

Westminster Abbey **3**

Parliament Square

Big Ben

Houses of Parliament **4**

Westminster Bridge

Nightingale Museum

St Thomas's Hospital

Belgrave Square

Belgrave Pl.

Eaton Square

Eccleston Street

VICTORIA

Victoria Station

Victoria Coach Station

BELGRAVIA

Westminster Roman Catholic Cathedral

Victoria Street

Westminster

St John's Concert Hall

VICTORIA TOWER GARDENS

ARCHBISHOP'S PARK

Lambeth Palace

Lambeth Bridge

Tate Britain **5** ↓

Thames

Central London

Airports: Heathrow (tel: 0844-335 1801; **www.heathrowairport.com**) is 15 miles (24km) west of the city centre. The fastest route into town is the Heathrow Express train (**www.heathrowexpress.com**) to Paddington Station, which runs every 15 minutes (journey time: 20 minutes) between 5.10am and about 11.30pm. Fare: £16.50 single. Alternatively, take the Tube (**www.tfl.gov.uk**) on the Piccadilly line (journey time: 50 minutes). Fare: £5 single. National Express (**www.nationalexpress.com**) run coaches to Victoria Coach Station (journey time: 50–90 minutes). Fare: from £5 single. By taxi, a black cab fare is £60–80 plus a 10 percent tip; a pre-booked minicab should cost less. Gatwick (tel: 0844-335 1802; **www.gatwickairport.com**) is 28 miles (45km) south of the city centre. Gatwick Express trains (**www.gatwickexpress.com**) run to Victoria Station every 15 minutes between 4.30am and 12.30am (journey time: 30 minutes). Fare: £18 single. easyBus (**www.easybus.co.uk**) run services to West London day and night (journey time: 65 minutes). Fare: from £2 single. Stansted (tel: 0844-335 1803; **www.stanstedairport.com**) is 40 miles (64km) northeast of the city centre. Stansted Express trains (**www.stanstedexpress.com**) run to Liverpool Street Station every 15 minutes between 5.30am and 12.30am (journey time: 45 minutes). Fare: £20 single. easyBus (**www.easybus.co.uk**) run services to West London day and night (journey time:

75 minutes). Fare: from £2 single. Luton (tel: 01582-405 100; **www.london-luton.co.uk**) is 32 miles (51km) north of the city centre. easyBus (**www.easybus.co.uk**) run services to Victoria day and night (journey time: 65 minutes). Fare: from £2 single. London City Airport (tel: 020-7646 0000; **www.londoncityairport.com**) is east of the city centre. Docklands Light Railway (**www.tfl.gov.uk**) connects with the Tube to take you to Central London (journey time: 30 minutes). Fare: £4. By taxi, a black cab fare to the West End is £30 plus a 10 percent tip; a pre-booked minicab should cost less

Tube: The Tube network (**www.tfl.gov.uk**) runs from 5.30am to around midnight. Buy tickets from stations (prices from £4 upwards); or use a pre-paid Oystercard on Tube, rail and buses. Fares with Oystercards are cheaper. Order cards ahead of your visit at **www.visitbritaindirect.com**

Buses: Buses run throughout the city (**www.tfl.gov.uk**). The flat fare in Central London is £2 (or £1.20 with an Oystercard); tickets can be purchased at bus stops or from the driver. At night there is a reduced service

Taxis: Licensed taxis ('black cabs') can be hailed on the street; they display the regulated charges on the meter. Minicabs are cheaper, but can only be hired by calling ahead. Try Addison Lee, tel: 0844-800 6677, **www.addisonlee.com**

Square beyond. Overlooking the Mall is the **Institute of Contemporary Arts** (tel: 020-7930 3647; www.ica.org.uk; Wed–Sun noon–7pm; charge), which is an exhibition space for modern art. It also contains a cinema for art-house films.

St James's Palace

A different atmosphere is found on **Pall Mall**, which runs through the heart of the St James's district on the west side of Trafalgar Square. This is London's 'Club Land'; the grand buildings lining the road are the

The imposing French-Gothic exterior of Westminster Abbey

exclusive meeting places of Great and Good. The street takes its name from *paille maille*, a French lawn game imported to England in the 17th century and played by Charles I on a long green which once occupied this site.

Wedged between Pall Mall and Green Park are a number of stately homes. The most impressive of these, built by Henry VIII in the 1530s, is **St James's Palace ➋**, which is now occupied by royal offices. Nearby is **Clarence House** (tel: 020-7766 7303; www.royalcollection.org.uk; Aug Mon–Fri 10am–4pm, Sat–Sun 10am–5.30pm; charge), the London residence of Prince Charles. Guided tours of some of the rooms are offered daily during August and September.

Westminster Abbey

A short walk from the southeast corner of St James's Park is Westminster, the seat of government for nearly 750 years. Westminster is also a holy place – the burial ground of English monarchs and the site of one of the greatest monasteries of the Middle Ages.

Westminster Abbey ➌ (tel: 020-7222 5152; www.westminster-abbey.org; Mon–Tue and Thur–Fri 9.30am–4.30pm, Wed until 7pm, Sat until 2.30pm; charge) was founded by Edward the Confessor, who is buried in front of the high altar. In December 1066, the ill-fated Harold (soon to lose his throne to William the Conqueror) was crowned as the new

king in the Abbey. Since that day, all but two English monarchs have been crowned here.

Little remains of Edward's Saxon abbey; it was completely rebuilt under the Normans and then redesigned in flamboyant French-Gothic style 200 years later. The Henry VII Chapel is a 16th-century masterpiece of fan-vaulted ceilings, decked out in colourful medieval banners. Poets' Corner contains the graves of Chaucer, Tennyson and Dryden, plus monuments to Shakespeare, Milton, Keats and Wilde among others. The abbey also houses the English Coronation Chair, built in 1300 for Edward I and still used for the crowning of monarchs.

The Houses of Parliament

On the riverside of Westminster Abbey rise the **Houses of Parliament** ❹, a Gothic structure designed in the 1830s by Charles Barry and August Pugin to replace the old Westminster Palace built by Edward the Confessor. The building contains 2 miles (3km) of passages and more than 1,000 rooms.

At the south end is Victoria Tower, from which a Union flag flies whenever Parliament is in session, while on the north side rises the Clock Tower, commonly known as **Big Ben** after the massive bell, cast in 1858, that strikes the hours. Facing Big Ben is Portcullis House, a modern office block for members of parliament.

Within Parliament convene the two governing bodies of Great Britain, the House of Commons and the House of Lords, which moved into the old Palace of Westminster after Henry VIII vacated the premises in the 16th century. The Commons, comprised of the elected representatives of various political parties, is the scene of lively debate. You can watch proceedings from the safety of the **Visitors' Gallery** (see www.parliament.uk for details).

One of the few relics of the old Westminster Palace to withstand a devastating fire in 1834 is **Westminster Hall**, built in 1099 with a hammerbeam roof of ancient oak. The hall has seen some of English history's most dramatic moments – from the trial of Sir Thomas More in 1535 to the investiture of Oliver Cromwell as Lord Protector in 1653.

Whitehall is the avenue that runs north from the Houses of Parliament to Trafalgar Square. It is the location of numerous government ministries, as well as the Prime Minister's residence at No. 10 Downing Street.

At the end of King Charles Street, down Clive Steps, a small wall of sandbags identifies the **Churchill War Rooms** (tel: 020-7930 6961; http://cwr.iwm.org.uk; daily 9.30am–6pm; charge), the underground nerve-centre from which Churchill directed Britain's war effort. Now a museum, the rooms have been restored to their 1940s state.

On the other side of Whitehall is **Banqueting House** (tel: 0844-482 7777; www.hrp.org.uk; Mon–Sat 10am–5pm; charge), a remnant of the old Whitehall Palace and a masterpiece of the English Baroque.

Big Ben lies at the south end of the Houses of Parliament

Hanging out on Trafalgar Square

Inigo Jones built the hall in 1622 at the request of James I. A decade later Peter Paul Rubens added the allegorical ceiling.

Victoria and Pimlico

Victoria Street runs southwest from Parliament Square. Set back from the street is **Westminster Cathedral** (tel: 020-7798 9055; www.westminster cathedral.org.uk; Mon–Fri 7am–7pm; free), England's most important Roman Catholic church, built in the 1890s in a bizarre Italo-Byzantine style.

Millbank follows the gentle curve of the Thames to the south of Parliament Square, sweeping round to the neoclassical home of **Tate Britain ❺** (tel: 020-7887 8888; www.tate.org. uk; daily 10am–6pm; free). Inside is the national collection of British art. Among the outstanding artworks are landscapes by John Constable and impressionistic seascapes by J.M.W. Turner.

The West End

London's West End includes Covent Garden, Soho, Piccadilly, Bond Street and Oxford Street. It provides visitors not only with a wealth of fine buildings, art galleries and theatres, but also with almost every type of shopping emporium imaginable.

Trafalgar Square

At the heart of London is **Trafalgar Square ❻**, laid out in the 1830s and '40s by Sir Charles Barry and dedicated to the memory of Admiral Lord Nelson and his decisive victory over Napoleon's fleet off Cape Trafalgar in 1805. The square is dominated by the 162ft (50m) Nelson's Column and four sculpted lions.

The square has long been the site of public gatherings, political demonstrations and New Year celebrations. Every Christmas a 70ft (20m) Norwegian spruce is erected in the square, a gift from the city of Oslo in recognition of the protection given by Britain to members of the Norwegian Royal Family in World War II.

The National Gallery

Running along the north side of Trafalgar Square is the **National Gallery** (tel: 020-7747 2885; www.national gallery.org.uk; daily 10am–6pm, Fri until 9pm; free). Founded in 1824, it has grown into one of the most outstanding collections in the world, with paintings by da Vinci, Rembrandt and Van Gogh.

Around the corner, established in 1856, is the **National Portrait Gallery** (tel: 020-7312 2463; www.npg. org.uk; daily 10am–6pm, Thur and Fri until 9pm; free). It contains the faces of the nation's illustrious men and women by the nation's illustrious artists and photographers.

To the right of the National Gallery is the church of **St Martin-in-the-Fields** (tel: 020-7766 1100; www.st martin-in-the-fields.org; daily 8am–7pm; free), the oldest surviving structure on Trafalgar Square, built by James Gibbs in 1722–6. The church became well-known during World War II when its crypt was a refuge from the Blitz.

Leading north from Trafalgar Square is Charing Cross Road, lined with bookshops, including Foyle's, said to be London's largest. On the west side of the street is **Leicester Square ❼**, where the city's main multiplex cinemas stage celebrity-filled film premieres.

Covent Garden

To the east of Charing Cross Road is **Covent Garden ❽**, a maze of narrow streets and tiny alleys. At its centre lies a cobblestone piazza, designed by Inigo Jones, and a steel-and-glass market pavilion constructed in the 1830s to house

Inside Covent Garden's market pavilion

The entrance to Chinatown

flower, fruit and vegetable stalls. The market was moved to new quarters south of the river in 1974, and today the district is full of restaurants and shops. It's also a venue for street entertainers.

Used as a backdrop for the film *My Fair Lady* in 1964, Covent Garden has long been associated with British theatre. Dominating the west end of the piazza, St Paul's Church (1633), by Inigo Jones, is known as the 'actor's church'. On the opposite side of the square is the **Royal Opera House** (tel: 020-7304 4000; www. royaloperahouse.org). Inside, the magnificent Floral Hall contains a bar and restaurant.

Soho

On the western side of Charing Cross Road, across from Covent Garden, is the district of **Soho** ❾, long known for its low-life bars and sex clubs – though the sleazy side has largely gone, with only a few strip shows remaining. Instead, the area is a now a fashionable quarter for restaurants, bars and media companies. The southern part of the district – to the south of Shaftesbury Avenue – is known as **Chinatown** ❿, and is packed with Chinese restaurants.

The western boundary of Soho is marked by **Regent Street**, with upmarket shops that include Liberty, Hamleys and the Apple Store. This elegant thoroughfare divides Mayfair from Soho as effectively as if there were an ocean between the two. The Britain and London Visitor Centre is at 1 Regent Street, and is the central source of tourist information.

At the southern end of Regent Street is **Piccadilly Circus** ⓫, a busy junction crowded with black cabs, red buses and awestruck tourists. At its centre stands the bronze statue of Eros atop a fountain.

Piccadilly and Mayfair

Piccadilly itself is the bustling road that runs southwest from Piccadilly

---

All aboard

On the southeastern corner of Covent Garden, the old flower market now houses the **London Transport Museum** (tel: 020-7565 7299; www.ltmuseum. co.uk; daily 10am–6pm, Fri from 11am; charge). Children in particular enjoy the collection of buses, trams and trains.

Circus towards Hyde Park Corner. Along the way are many smart shops, such as high-class grocer Fortnum and Mason. There are also several Victorian arcades – covered streets lined with unusual emporia. **Burlington Arcade**, with its uniformed doormen, is the most famous.

A few doors from Burlington Arcade is the **Royal Academy of Arts** (tel: 020-7300 8000; www.royalacademy.org. uk; daily 10am–6pm, Fri until 10pm; charge), which stages blockbuster exhibitions of major artists.

To the north of Piccadilly is the exclusive district of Mayfair, the preserve of many of Britain's wealthiest residents. Mayfair's most famous thoroughfare is **Bond Street** ⓬, lined with expensive shops. Here you can find all the big names: Chanel, Gucci, Bulgari and many others. Mayfair is also renowned as a centre of the European art market. It is the home of all the country's top antiques dealers as well as numerous art galleries and the top auction houses.

Oxford Street

The northern limits of Mayfair are defined by **Oxford Street** ⓭, which is often referred to as London's high street. The western half contains most of London's top department stores, including Selfridges; the eastern end is not as smart and accommodates a mixture of souvenir shops and uninspiring chain stores.

To the north of Oxford Street is the district of Marylebone (pronounced *marly-bone*), which continues up to the southern edge of Regent's Park. Infamous in the 18th century for its

The Wallace Collection is Marylebone's star attraction

taverns, boxing matches and cockfights, its main attraction nowadays is the **Wallace Collection** in Manchester Square (tel: 020-7563 9500; www.wallacecollection.org; daily 10am–5pm; free). This treasure trove of 17th- and 18th-century fine and decorative arts includes Sèvres porcelain, French furniture and works by Titian, Rubens and Holbein.

On the northern edge of Marylebone, near Baker Street tube station, is the waxworks exhibition of **Madame Tussauds** ⓮ *(see box, right)*.

Bloomsbury

Beyond the eastern end of Oxford Street lies Bloomsbury, which has quite a different feel again. This is the city's traditional university district, and accommodates numerous colleges and research institutes. Bloomsbury was once also home to intellectual giants such as John Maynard Keynes and Virginia Woolf.

Charles Dickens was another resident. He lived with his family at 47 Doughty Street in the late 1830s, during which time he wrote parts of *Oliver Twist* and *Pickwick Papers*. His home, now the **Dickens House Museum** (tel: 0207-405 2127; www.dickensmuseum.com; daily 10am–5pm; charge), is filled with portraits, letters, furniture and his other personal effects.

Bloomsbury's main visitor attraction, however, is the **British Museum** ⑮ (tel: 020-7323 8299; www.britishmuseum.org; daily 10am–5.30pm; free), one of the world's greatest collections of art and archaeology. Its Great Court, a large covered square

Madame Tussauds

Madame Tussauds (tel: 020-7935 6861; www.madame-tussauds.co.uk; daily July–Sept 9am–5.30pm, Oct–June 10am–5.30pm, from 9.30am at weekends; charge) was first established in 1802 by Marie Tussaud, who learned her craft in post-Revolution Paris, making wax effigies of the heads of guillotine victims. Today's waxworks are of celebrities, from pop stars to sports heroes – though anyone who fades from the headlines is soon melted down.

containing the majestic Lion of Knidos and an Easter Island statue, is worth a visit in itself. Don't expect to see everything in a day; a month wouldn't be time enough *(see box p.78)*.

Holborn

To the south of Bloomsbury is Holborn, London's legal district. Here you can find the historic Inns of

The Great Court at the British Museum

★ 2012 OLYMPIC SITES

Britain is concentrating extraordinary efforts and money – over £9 billion – on the 2012 Olympics, and with immense public pressure for results, the investment looks set to achieve spectacular returns in both venues and entertainment.

The 2012 Olympic Games (www.london 2012.com) will take place from 27 July to 12 August, with the focus of attention on Olympic Park in Stratford, East London. There are in addition numerous other venues across the capital and across the country. After the main Games, the Paralympic Games will take place from 29 August to 9 September. Thereafter, most of the venues will remain in use as part of the Olympics' legacy, and can still be visited, whether for sports activities or just to view the spectacular architecture and design.

The Olympic Park itself is a vast site accommodating nine sporting venues: the Olympic Stadium, Aquatics Centre, Water Polo Arena, Basketball Arena, Handball Arena, Velodrome, BMX Track, Hockey Centre and Eton Manor

(wheelchair tennis). Visitors can travel there from central London by public transport, with Stratford and Stratford International stations on the east side of the park and West Ham Station to the south. Overground trains will run from London Liverpool Street, tube trains on the Jubilee and Central lines, and Docklands Light Railway (DLR) trains from Tower Gateway.

The centrepiece is the 80,000-capacity Olympic Stadium in the south of the Olympic Park, where the main track events will be staged. Sweeping away from the stadium are gardens that celebrate the tradition of British horticulture. In the park's southeast corner is the Aquatics Centre, designed by Zaha Hadid. Another architectural feat is the Velodrome at the northern end of the

An artist's impression of the vast Olympic Stadium in Stratford

site; this eco-friendly structure is clad in wood, and is entirely naturally ventilated.

Elsewhere in London, the ExCeL exhibition centre in the Docklands (DLR to Custom House) will accommodate five arenas for sports including boxing, fencing, judo, table tennis, weightlifting and wrestling. Just across the river, the equestrian events benefit from the glorious setting of Greenwich Park. Not far away, the North Greenwich Arena, formerly the Millennium Dome (on the Jubilee line), is hosting gymnastics.

In central London, there will be beach volleyball on Horse Guards Parade in Westminster, and nearby, the marathons and cycling road races will start and finish in grand style on The Mall in front of Buckingham Palace. Fifteen minutes' walk north in Hyde Park, spectators can watch the triathlon. A short underground ride west from Hyde Park Corner conveys volleyball fans to the exhibition centre outside Earl's Court Tube station.

The Jubilee line will ferry passengers northwest to Lord's Cricket Ground, where the archery tournament is to be held. The same tube line (and the Metropolitan one too) extends still further north to Wembley Arena for the badminton and rhythmic gymnastics events. Next door, the 120,000-seat Wembley Stadium will stage the gold medal matches in the football competition.

While the London Underground is the easiest transport option, it may also be the most crowded. Consider overground trains, buses and park-and-ride schemes. Beware that London is likely to be very crowded during the Games. Book ahead as far as possible.

Medals emblazoned with the distinctive London 2012 logo

British hopeful Tom Daley is aiming to win big on his home turf

Court. There were originally 12 inns, founded in the 14th century for the lodging and education of lawyers on 'neutral' ground between the merchants of the City and the monarchs of Westminster. Today only four remain, and no one can become a barrister in London without being accepted into one of them.

Perhaps the most impressive is **Lincoln's Inn** (tel: 020-7405 1393; www.lincolnsinn.org.uk; guided tours only, booking ahead essential; charge), which has a medieval hall and a 17th-century chapel by Inigo Jones. Outside is a leafy expanse known as Lincoln's Inn Fields. It was once a notorious venue for duels and executions, but today attracts summer picnickers and sunbathers.

On the north side of the park square

is the **Sir John Soane's Museum** (tel: 020-7405 2107; www.soane.org; Tue–Sat 10am–5pm; free), an eccentric town house which is a sort of British Museum in miniature. It was once the home of a celebrated 19th-century architect, and his remarkable collection of antiquities and paintings remain *in situ* for visitors to enjoy.

The Strand and Fleet Street

The southern edge of Holborn is defined by the Strand, a broad street that links Trafalgar Square in the west with the City in the east. Here, by Waterloo Bridge, is the neoclassical **Somerset House** ⑯ (tel: 020-7845 4600; www.somersethouse.org.uk). It now houses the **Courtauld Gallery** (tel: 020-7848 2526; www.courtauld. ac.uk; daily 10am–6pm; charge), which is particularly noted for its collection of paintings by Van Gogh, Gauguin and Cézanne. In the winter, the courtyard of Somerset House is the setting for a temporary ice rink. In summer, there are sometimes outdoor film screenings.

As you continue going east, the Strand becomes Fleet Street and you enter what was – until the 1980s – the

Fleet Street's historic buildings now house modern businesses

St Paul's Cathedral was the first cathedral dedicated to Protestantism

the domain of merchants and craftsmen, a powerful coalition of men who helped force democracy upon the English monarchy and then built the world's largest mercantile empire. Despite the encroachment of modern office blocks and computers, the area retains something of its medieval ways: the square mile is still governed separately from the rest of London, by the ancient City Corporation and its Court of Common Council – relics of the medieval trade and craft guilds. It also has its own separately elected Lord Mayor, who rides through the City each November in a golden coach.

St Paul's Cathedral

Dominating the skyline of the City like no other structure is **St Paul's Cathedral** ⑰ (tel: 020-7246 8357; www.st pauls.co.uk; Mon–Sat 8.30am–4pm; charge). It was designed by Christopher Wren after its predecessor was destroyed in the Great Fire of 1666, and became the first cathedral to be built and dedicated to the Protestant faith.

Its most famous feature is of course its dome, which is second in size only to St Peter's in Rome. Inside the dome is the Whispering Gallery, so called because you can easily comprehend the voices of anyone standing on the opposite side of the void. A winding stairway leads outside, where you can enjoy panoramic views of London.

The Barbican

To the north of St Paul's is the **Barbican Centre** ⑱ (tel: 020-7638 4141; www.barbican.org.uk), its 1960s Brutalist architecture contrasting starkly with the stately forms of the cathedral.

centre of the national newspaper industry. Just north of Fleet Street at 17 Gough Square is the former home of Samuel Johnson, the noted scribe who compiled the first English dictionary. **Dr Johnson's House** (tel: 020-7353 3745; www.drjohnsons house.org; Mon–Sat 11am–5.30pm; charge) is a museum containing memorabilia relating to his life.

The City of London and the East End

The City of London (generally known simply as 'The City') was for centuries

Inside the Barbican Arts Centre

This urban renewal project arose from the rubble of an old neighbourhood that had been destroyed in the 1940–41 Blitz. Within the complex is the Barbican Arts Centre, accommodating an art gallery, a theatre, a cinema and a concert hall.

Nearby is the **Museum of London** ⑲ (tel: 020-7001 9844; www.museumoflondon.org.uk; daily 10am–6pm; free), which charts the history of the city. There are reconstructed shop fronts, audio-visual shows and precious exhibits such as the Lord Mayor's coach.

The Guildhall

In the shadows of the Barbican's towers is the **Guildhall** (tel: 020-7606 3030; www.cityoflondon.gov.uk; phone to check opening times; free) one of the few buildings to survive the Great Fire and now the home of the City government. This ornate Gothic structure was built in 1411 with funds donated by various livery companies, the medieval trade and craft guilds that held sway over the City. Inside the Guildhall, the Great Hall is decorated with the colourful banners of the 12 livery companies and the shields of all 92 guilds.

Britain's financial heartland

A short walk east along Gresham Street brings you to a bustling intersection dominated by the **Bank of England**. The Bank still prints and mints all British money, administers to the national debt and also now sets interest rates. Around the corner on Bartholomew Lane is the entrance to the **Bank of England Museum** (tel: 020-7601 5545; www.bankofengland.co.uk; Mon–Fri 10am–5pm; free), where visitors are even allowed to pick up a gold bar.

Nearby stands the old **London Stock Exchange**, founded in 1773.

The trading floor is no longer used as shares are now traded electronically. This computerisation brought demands for office buildings purpose-built for modern communications. One of the first, and most dramatic, is the 1986 **Lloyd's of London building** in Lime Street, designed for the insurance organisation by Richard Rogers. Another impressive piece of architecture is **30 St Mary Axe**, a 40-storey tapering glass tower designed by Lord Foster and known affectionately as 'The Gherkin'.

Gracechurch Street leads south to London Bridge and the Thames. Just before you reach the river, a huge fluted column peers over the rooftops. The 202ft (60m) **Monument** (tel: 020-7626 2717; www. themonument.info; daily 9.30am–5.30pm; charge) is Sir Christopher Wren's memorial to the Great Fire of 1666 which destroyed more than 13,000 houses. You can climb 311 steps to a small platform, from which there is an impressive view.

The Tower of London

Lower Thames Street traces the medieval banks of the river past the old Billingsgate Fish Market and the elegant Custom House. A medieval fortress commands this southeast corner of the City; it is known as the **Tower of London ⓴** (tel: 0870-756 6060; www. hrp.org.uk; Tue–Sat 9am–5.30pm, Sun–Mon 10am–5.30pm; charge).

William the Conqueror built the inner keep (the White Tower) and it remained a royal residence until the 16th century, when the court moved to Westminster. The Tower then

became the storehouse for the Crown Jewels and the most infamous prison and execution ground in London. German spies were executed here in both world wars.

Today, in addition to seeing the **Crown Jewels** *(see also p.27)*, visitors can also enjoy the Royal Fusiliers Museum's display of weaponry from the mid-17th to mid-19th centuries. An added attraction is the sight of the Yeomen Wardens or 'Beefeaters', so-called because they were once the buffetiers or guardians of the king's buffet.

Outside again, there are magnificent views of **Tower Bridge ⓴**, London's most famous river crossing. Up to four or five times a day, its bascules rise to let tall vessels through. The **Tower Bridge Experience** (tel: 020-7403 3761; www.towerbridge.org.uk; Apr–Sept 10am–6.30pm, Oct–Mar 9.30am–6pm; charge) offers a tour of the inside of the bridge.

The Gherkin looms over the City's historic buildings

East London

Back on solid land, you can take one of the Docklands Light Railway trains from Tower Hill tube station to venture further east to the Isle of Dogs. This is the location of the cluster of skyscrapers known as **Canary Wharf**. They are testimony to the continuing ambition of the City's financiers.

Alternatively, staying within the old City of London, you can walk north, up Mansell Street, to where the richest district in the country comes cheek by jowl with what has traditionally been one of the poorest. For centuries, London's East End has been the place where newly arrived immigrants have settled. Huguenots, Jews and now Bangladeshis have all made their mark on the area, and it is one of the most culturally exciting parts of the capital.

On Whitechapel Road, heading east from the Aldgate junction, is the **Whitechapel Art Gallery** (tel: 020-7522 7888; www.whitechapelgallery.org; Tue–Sun 11am–6pm, Thur until 9pm; free), which hosts exhibitions of contemporary art. Heading north on Commercial Road, you come to **Spitalfields Market**, which was once a wholesale fruit and vegetable market, but is now full of antiques and crafts stalls, and surrounded by fashionable boutiques.

The South Bank

Londoners used to perceive the south of London as being off the edge of the world – and even taxi drivers refused go there. Things are very different today; the South Bank now attracts throngs of people to its galleries and museums, entertainment venues and stylish restaurants.

Southwark

On the south side of Tower Bridge is the restaurant-lined **Butler's Wharf**

Examining the produce at Borough Market

A former power station houses **Tate Modern** (tel: 020-7887 8888; www.tate.org.uk; Sun–Thur 10am–6pm, Fri–Sat 10am–10pm; free), a national collection of international modern and contemporary art. The massive turbine hall gives temporary installations room to breathe. Displays in the gallery's main rooms are arranged thematically rather than chronologically, mixing the work of Picasso, Bacon, Pollock, Rothko and Warhol.

Relaxing in the sunshine outside Tate Modern, a former power station

and the **Design Museum** ㉒ (tel: 020-7940 8790; www.designmuseum.org; daily 10am–5.45pm; charge), which presents exhibitions related to architecture, graphic and product design.

The riverside walk between Tower Bridge and London Bridge passes by the World War II battleship **HMS Belfast** (tel: 020-7940 6300; http://hmsbelfast.iwm.org.uk; daily Mar–Oct 10am–6pm, Nov–Feb 10am–5pm; charge). A tour takes you round the cramped accommodation endured by its 950-man crew.

Continuing towards London Bridge, cut through **Hay's Galleria**, a small shopping mall, to reach Tooley Street. Here, the **London Dungeon** ㉓ (www.thedungeons.com; daily 10am–5.30pm with exceptions; charge) provides a gruesome, actor-led account of London's history – children love it, but be prepared for long queues and steep entrance charges.

Just to the south of London Bridge is **Southwark Cathedral** (http://cathedral.southwark.anglican.org), where Shakespeare was a parishioner. Adjacent is **Borough Market**, a historic wholesale fruit and vegetable market. On Thursdays, Fridays and Saturdays crowds flock to a retail market here offering a wide range of gourmet products, not just fruit and veg.

Continuing westwards along the river, you come to a replica of Shakespeare's **Globe Theatre** (tel: 020-7401 9919; www.shakespearesglobe.com). This open-roofed theatre-in-the-round stages performances of the Bard's plays every summer (guided tours every half hour 9.15am–12.15pm).

Next door to the Globe a towering brick chimney identifies **Tate Modern** ㉔ (*see box*).

The Southbank Centre

Further west along the river is the **Southbank Centre** ㉕ (tel: 020-7960 4200; www.southbankcentre.co.uk), London's largest arts complex. The Royal Festival Hall plays host to orchestral concerts, while next door are the Queen Elizabeth Hall and the Purcell Room, used for smaller-scale events, from chamber music to poetry readings. On the upper level of the complex is the Hayward Gallery, which has changing exhibitions of contemporary art. BFI Southbank, in the shadow of Waterloo Bridge, presents a repertory of vintage and foreign-language films as well as the London Film Festival each November. Back by the river is the concrete bulk of the **National Theatre** (www.nationaltheatre.org.uk) – three theatres under one roof. For a peak behind the scenes, you can book a backstage tour (tel: 020-7452 3400).

The London Eye

Continuing westwards, you come to the 450ft (135m) **London Eye** ㉖ (tel: 0870-5000 600; www.londoneye.com; daily Apr–Aug 10am–9.30pm, winter until 8.30pm; charge) observation wheel erected for the millennium. The 32 enclosed capsules take 30 minutes to make a full rotation, and on a clear day, you can see for 25 miles (40km).

Next to it is County Hall, which until 1986 was the seat of the Greater London Council. It now contains two hotels, as well as the **London Aquarium** (tel: 020-7967 8000; www.londonaquarium.co.uk; Mon–Thur 10am–6pm, Fri–Sun until 7pm; charge), which accommodates everything from sharks to stingrays.

The London Eye offers spectacular views over the capital

Downriver to Greenwich

If you return to Westminster Bridge and cross over to the north side, you can catch a boat (tel: 020-7930 4097; www.thamesriverservices.co.uk) from the pier to take you downriver to Greenwich. As you disembark, you are confronted by **The Cutty Sark**, built in 1869 and now being rebuilt after a damaging fire. It was the last of the great China clippers, which ran tea from the Orient to Europe.

Greenwich has been associated with British sea power for the past 500 years, and the impressive Baroque buildings just to the east are the former **Royal Naval College**, which was originally designed by Sir Christopher Wren in the late 17th century. Its highly elaborate chapel, and the Painted Hall (decorated by Sir James Thornhill) are open to the public (tel: 020-8269 4747;

www.oldroyalnavalcollege.org; daily
10am–5pm; free).

Since the Tudor period, Greenwich
has also been the site of a royal palace.
James I had the old palace demolished
and commissioned Inigo Jones to
build a new residence for his queen,
Anne of Denmark. The result is the
Queen's House, completed in 1637, a
masterpiece of the Palladian style and
perhaps the finest piece of Stewart
architecture in England.

Next door is the **National Maritime Museum** (tel: 020-8858 4422;
www.nmm.ac.uk; daily 10am–5pm;
free). Here, the 1805 Battle of Trafalgar is re-lived and the glory of the
nation's maritime tradition unfolds,
with boats, paintings, and memorabilia from heroic voyages. A short
distance up the hill is the **Royal
Observatory** (details as above), built
in 1675 in order to perfect the arts
of navigation and astronomy. Since
that time, the globe's longitude and
time zones have been measured from
the Greenwich Meridian, which
cuts right through the middle of
Flamsteed House, now a museum of
astronomical instruments and time-
pieces.

Kensington and Chelsea

The Royal Borough of Kensington
and Chelsea is one of the most desirable residential areas of London. Its
elegant houses and apartment buildings are interspersed with grand
museums, beautiful parks and upmarket shopping streets.

Looking up through Greenwich Park
to Flamsteed House

The King's Road

Chelsea's main artery is the King's
Road, so called because it was built
to connect St James's Palace and
Hampton Court. More recently, it was
the unofficial centre of the 'Swinging
Sixties'; the miniskirt made its first
appearance in its boutiques. In the
1970s, Vivienne Westwood opened a
shop called 'Sex', and started the punk
phenomenon. Today the street attracts
a well-heeled crowd, but is far more
mainstream.

Running parallel with the King's
Road is Royal Hospital Road, where
you can find Sir Christopher Wren's
Chelsea Royal Hospital (tel: 020-
7881 5298; www.chelsea-pensioners.
org.uk; Mon–Fri, 10am–noon, 2–4pm;
free). This home for veteran soldiers

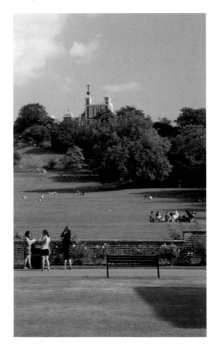

first opened in 1682 and a few hundred army pensioners still reside here. They parade in their famous scarlet frockcoats on Oak Apple Day (29 May). Visitors can see the Great Hall, Octagon and Chapel, the museum and the Ranelagh Gardens.

On Royal Hospital Road, tracing the history of the British military from the 15th century, is the **National Army Museum** (tel: 020-7881 6606; www.nam.ac.uk; daily 10am–5.30pm; free). Further along the same street is the entrance to the **Chelsea Physic Garden** 27 (tel: 020-7349 6458; www.chelseaphysicgarden.co.uk; Apr–Oct, Tue–Fri noon–5pm, Sun until 6pm; charge), a botanical laboratory founded in 1676. It's a pretty place for a stroll and afternoon tea.

Knightsbridge and South Kensington

Heading north from Chelsea up Sloane Street, you come to the bustling neighbourhood of luxury shops and first-class hotels at Knightsbridge. Its main street is Brompton Road,

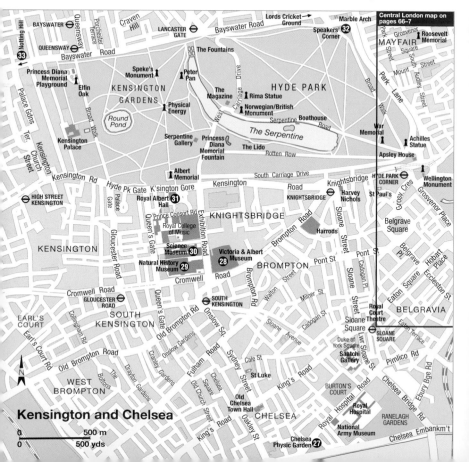

Kensington and Chelsea

0   500 m
0   500 yds

Central London map on pages 66–7

The Central Hall of the Natural History Museum

where **Harrods**, London's most famous department store, is situated. Shoppers are asked to dress 'presentably' and wear shoes.

At the end of Brompton Road is the district of South Kensington, noted for its large museums. The **Victoria and Albert** ㉘ (tel: 020-7942 2000; www.vam.ac.uk; daily 10am–5.45pm, Fri until 10pm; free) is the most famous of these. Its 7 miles (11km) of galleries house 5 million items of fine and applied arts, from Winnie-the-Pooh illustrations to historic costumes.

Just across the road is the **Natural History Museum** ㉙ (tel: 020-7942

Kew Gardens

Further west, upstream from Chelsea, is the quiet suburb of Kew, home of the **Royal Botanic Gardens**, generally known simply as Kew Gardens (tel: 020-8332 5655; www.kew.org; daily 9.30am–6.30pm, winter until 4.15pm; charge). These 300 acres (120 hectares) were first planted in 1759 under the direction of Princess Augusta, but in 1772, George III put Kew in the hands of botanist Sir Joseph Banks, who had just returned from a round-the-world expedition to collect plant specimens with Captain Cook. Kew is now a Unesco World Heritage site.

⬛ HAMPSTEAD WALK

Full of pretty houses on leafy groves, Hampstead seems the quintessence of an English village. In reality, it is not so much rural idyll as exclusive suburb, a haven in a hectic city.

Until not so long ago, Hampstead was the home of artists, writers and anyone with a liberal disposition. At the last count, the suburb had over 90 blue plaques commemorating such famous residents as John Constable, George Orwell, Florence Nightingale and Sigmund Freud. Now, you only need to have deep pockets to live here: its pretty alleys, leafy streets and expansive heath make this villagey suburb a desirable address.

From Hampstead Tube Station, take Heath Street south (past The Horseshoe pub) and turn right at Church

Hampstead Heath is one of London's most attractive green spaces

Row. Follow the sign to John Constable's grave in the bosky graveyard of **St John's Church**, halfway down.

Fenton House
Now head north up Holly Walk, past the one-time home of Scottish writer Robert Louis Stevenson, and turn left up to Hampstead Grove. On your left is **Fenton House** (tel: 020-7435 3471; www.nationaltrust.org.uk; Mar–Oct Wed–Sun 11am–5pm; charge), a William-and-Mary-period merchant's house. Behind the gilded gates, the walled garden, with its apple orchard and rose garden, has hardly changed for 300 years. Inside are paintings, furniture, porcelain and a collection of harpsichords. In spring, concerts here re-create 18th-century parlour parties.

Burgh House
Back on Hampstead Grove, turn right and descend to Heath Street again, then cross over to New End. At the far end is New End Square and **Burgh House** (tel: 020-7431 0144; www.burghhouse.org.uk; Wed–Fri and Sun noon–5pm; free). Built in 1704, it contains the local history museum, with a permanent display on painter John Constable.

Tips
• Distance: 2¾ miles (4.5km)
• Time: Half a day
• The best days to walk this route are Thursday, Friday and Saturday, when all the museums are open.

Willow Road

Returning to New End, continue on to Willow Road. At the far end, overlooking the heath, is the Modernist **2 Willow Road** (tel: 020-7435 6166; www.nationaltrust.org.uk; Mar–Oct Wed–Sun 11am–5pm; charge), designed by Erno Goldfinger for himself. Inside is his art collection, with works by Henry Moore, Max Ernst and Marcel Duchamp.

Keats House

Turning right on Downshire Hill, Keats Grove is off to the left. **Keats House** (tel: 020-7435 2062; www.keats house.cityoflondon.gov.uk; May–Oct Tue–Sun 1–5pm, Nov–Mar Fri–Sun only; charge), the Regency villa where the consumptive poet lodged before departing for Rome, where he died a year later, in 1821, aged 25. Under a plum tree in the garden he penned one of his best-loved poems, *Ode to a Nightingale*. Inside are his keepsakes of Fanny Brawne, the neighbour with whom he fell in love.

Keats House was formerly the home of the Romantic poet

Hampstead Heath

At the end of Keats Grove, turn left on to South End Road and take one of the paths on your right on to the heath. The heath is criss-crossed with paths, but bear north for the top of the hill and **Kenwood House** (tel: 020-8348 1286; www.english-heritage.org.uk; daily 11am–4pm; free). This mansion houses the art collection of brewing magnate, Edward Guinness, and includes works by Rembrandt, Vermeer and Turner. There are also fine Robert Adam interiors.

Outside again, stroll through the gardens and the heath beyond to return to Hampstead Tube Station.

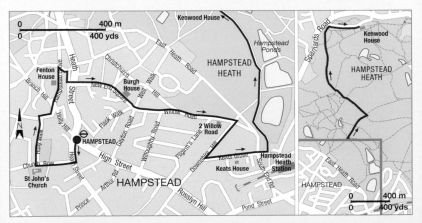

The ornate Albert Memorial stands on the edges of Hyde Park

circular 8,000-seat auditorium stages the BBC-sponsored summer Promenade Concerts, an annual showcase of classical music. Just opposite, on the edge of Hyde Park is the **Albert Memorial**, an extravagant Gothic monument to Prince Albert, the consort of Queen Victoria, and the man who did so much to establish South Kensington's museums.

Kensington Gardens and Hyde Park

A short walk westwards through the park brings you to **Kensington Palace** (tel: 0844-482 7777; www.hrp.org.uk; daily 10am–6pm; charge), where you can view the State Apartments and the Royal Dress Collection, which includes gowns that belonged to Princess Diana, who once lived here. To the north of the palace is the **Princess Diana Memorial Playground**, where children can let off steam.

To the east, Kensington Gardens merges into Hyde Park. In the

5000; www.nhm.ac.uk; daily 10am–5.50pm; free). It has one of the best dinosaur collections anywhere. The highlight is a full-scale animatronic T-Rex that roars and twists convincingly. Adjacent is the **Science Museum** ③⓪ (tel: 0870-870 4868; www.sciencemuseum.org.uk; daily 10am–6pm; free), with attractions such as an IMAX cinema, the world's oldest surviving steam locomotive and the Apollo 10 command module (1969).

On the northern fringe of South Kensington is the **Royal Albert Hall** ③① (tickets and tours: 020-7589 8212; www.royalalberthall.com). This

---

Hampton Court Palace

A short train ride from Waterloo Station takes you to **Hampton Court Palace** (tel: 020-8781 9500; www.hrp.org.uk; daily 10am–6pm; charge) just beyond the tidal reach of the Thames. It is famous as the lavish home of Henry VIII, who moved here with Anne Boleyn. Much later, in the 1690s, the sumptuous State Apartments (designed by Christopher Wren) were added for William and Mary, who also commissioned the famous Maze in the gardens. Today, the 1,000 rooms are filled with paintings, tapestries and furnishings from the past 450 years. ⓫

southeast corner is **Apsley House** (tel: 020-7499 5676; www.english-heritage.org.uk; Apr–Oct Wed–Sun 11am–5pm; charge), which was formerly the home of the Duke of Wellington, who defeated Napoleon at Waterloo in 1815. It contains furniture, silver, porcelain and paintings.

In the northeast corner of the park is **Speakers' Corner** ㉜, where orators and idiots passionately defend their beliefs. This tradition began when the Tyburn gallows stood here (1388–1783) and felons were allowed to make a final unexpurgated speech to the crowds before being hanged.

To the northwest of Kensington Gardens is **Notting Hill** ㉝, one of London's most highly sought-after residential districts. On the last Sunday and Monday of August the city's West Indian population stages Europe's largest street carnival here. The district's other famous attraction is the **Portobello Road Market**. On Saturdays the street becomes jammed as people browse through the antiques and bric-a-brac.

North London
The districts that make up the north of London each have their distinct

Henry VIII greets his fans at Hampton Court Palace

personalities. Regent's Park is graced with elegant Regency architecture; Camden Town is renowned for its lively nightlife of pubs, clubs, restaurants and music venues; and Hampstead is more like a country village transplanted into the midst of the metropolis.

Regent's Park

Regent's Park was first established as a royal hunting ground for Henry VIII, but took its current form in the early 19th century, when the Prince Regent (later George IV) commissioned John Nash to design a scheme for a processional thoroughfare and palace complex. The dream got only as far as the famed Regency terraces on the southern fringe of the park, which nevertheless represent Nash's architectural style at its best.

Many people come to the park to visit **London Zoo** (tel: 020-7722 3333; www.zsl.org; daily 10am–5-.30pm, winter until 4pm; charge), which is situated at the northern end. The zoo was founded in 1826 by Sir Stamford Raffles (who also founded Singapore). Among its attractions are the aviary designed by Lord Snowdon and the 1930s penguin pool.

St John's Wood

The district to the west of Regent's Park is called St John's Wood. At its heart is **Lord's Cricket Ground** (*see also p.57–8*), home of the Marylebone Cricket Club (MCC), the governing body of this quintessentially English sport. The **Cricket Museum** (tel: 020-7432 1033; www.lords.org; Mon–Fri

Vintage tableware on sale at Camden Lock Market

10am–5pm; charge) is filled with two centuries of memorabilia.

Camden

On the eastern side of Regent's Park is **Camden Town**, where weekend crowds flock to markets. Since 1972, **Camden Lock Market** has featured antiques, crafts, old clothes and talented buskers. A traditional canal boat runs trips from the West Yard area along Regent's Canal to Little Venice (tel: 020-7482 2660; www.londonwaterbus.com). Meanwhile, Camden High Street is full of bars, pubs and small-scale music venues.

ACCOMMODATION

The price of a hotel room in London is as high as any in Europe. However, cost does not always mean quality, so try to view a room before accepting it. In April to September, it is advisable to book before you arrive as hotels fill up fast. You can book online at www.visitlondon. com. The hotels listed below have been chosen either for their excellent positions or for providing welcoming English hospitality in characterful surroundings.

Westminster

Elizabeth Hotel
37 Eccleston Square
Tel: 020-7828 6812
www.elizabethhotel.com
This friendly hotel is situated in an elegant period square, two minutes' walk from Victoria station. There are 42 smart rooms, almost all with an ensuite bathroom. **££**

Goring Hotel
315 Beeston Place, Grosvenor Gardens
Tel: 020-7396 9000
www.goringhotel.co.uk
Famously, the Goring was where Kate Middleton stayed the night before her 2011 wedding to Prince William. The family-owned, delightfully traditional hotel near Buckingham Palace has a relaxed 'old-world' atmosphere. **£££££**

The West End

Hazlitt's
6 Frith Street
Tel: 020-7434 1771
www.hazlittshotel.com
Named after the great English literary critic, Hazlitt's occupies one of London's oldest houses (built in 1718), in the heart of Soho. The 23 rooms are all furnished with antiques. **£££–££££**

Lonsdale Hotel
9–10 Bedford Place
Tel: 020-7636 1812
www.lonsdalehotellondon.com
For a modest price, you get real character in the heart of Bloomsbury in this well-established 40-room bed and breakfast hotel (some rooms ensuite). **£–££**

St Martin's Lane
45 St Martin's Lane
Tel: 020-7300 5500
www.stmartinslane.com
Designed by Phillipe Starck, this is still the most fashionable hotel in London. It offers outlandish lighting, good if expensive food

Goring Hotel played host to Kate Middleton the night before she married Prince William

and 204 blindingly white bedrooms. Very well-placed for West End theatres and Trafalgar Square. **£££**

The Savoy
Strand
Tel: 020-7836 4343
www.fairmont.com/savoy
The Savoy is one of London's great institutions, with a reputation for comfort and personal service, and has recently reopened after a dramatic £100 million revamp. It's conveniently situated for theatreland and Covent Garden. **££££–£££££**

The City of London and the East End
The Tower Hotel
St Katharine's Way
Tel: 0871-376 9036
www.guoman.com/the-tower
This large (800+ rooms), modern hotel is located in the docklands near the City, and offers breathtaking views of Tower Bridge and the river. **£££**

The South Bank
County Hall Premier Inn
Belvedere Road
Tel: 0870-238 3300
www.premierinn.com
Occupying the old County Hall across the river from the Houses of Parliament, this hotel is an excellent choice for those on a tight budget. Advance booking is essential to procure one of the 314 rooms. **£–££**

Kensington and Chelsea
The Berkeley
Wilton Place, Knightsbridge
Tel: 020-7235 6000
www.the-berkeley.co.uk
Many people consider the Berkeley to be the best hotel in London. It's low-key, is seldom advertised, and has a comfortable country-house atmosphere. Facilities include a pool.
££££–£££££

Blakes Hotel
33 Roland Gardens

The Savoy is a London icon

Tel: 020-7370 6701
www.blakeshotels.com
This trendy and up-to-the-minute hotel is popular with theatrical and media folk. It's cosmopolitan, tolerant and laid-back in style. **£££–££££**

Cadogan Hotel
75 Sloane Street
Tel: 020-7235 7141
www.cadogan.com
This 19th-century institution is well-positioned between Chelsea and Knightsbridge. Actress Lily Langtry lived in what is now the bar, and Oscar Wilde was arrested in room 118. **£££–££££**

easyHotel
14 Lexham Gardens, Kensington
www.easyhotel.com
While this hotel is certainly a no-frills experience (some rooms don't even have a window), it is nevertheless ideal for budget travellers. This chain also has other branches in London. Internet bookings only. **£**

The Halkin
5 Halkin Street, Belgravia
Tel: 020-7333 1000
www.halkin.como.bz
The Halkin offers sleek design in a Georgian townhouse. It also has the only Michelin-starred Thai restaurant in Europe. **££££**

RESTAURANTS

London's restaurant scene offers variety as well as quality. For Michelin-starred restaurants go to Mayfair, for cheap Indian food head to the East End, and for everything inbetween try Soho. Booking ahead is sensible for Friday and Saturday nights, while lunchtimes offer good value for money as restaurants rely on more affordable set menus to bring in the customers.

Restaurant price categories

Prices are for a two-course dinner per person with a glass of house wine.

£ = under £20
££ = £20–30
£££ = £30–50
££££ = over £50

Westminster

Grumbles
35 Churton Street, Pimlico
Tel: 020-7834 0149
www.grumblesrestaurant.co.uk
This cosy neighbourhood bistro is conveniently located for Tate Britain. It offers homely cooking and good-value set-price menus at lunch and in the early evening. **££**

The West End

Benares
12a Berkeley Square House,
Berkeley Square
Tel: 020-7629 8886
www.benaresrestaurant.com
This is one of the few Indian restaurants in Europe to win a Michelin star. Dishes include Goan-style lobster Masala in coconut, clove and cinnamon sauce. **£££**

J. Sheekey
28–32 St Martin's Court
Tel: 020-7240 2565
www.j-sheekey.co.uk
Dishes here might include chargrilled squid with gorgonzola polenta, Cornish fish stew and New England baby lobster, followed by rhubarb pie, or the famed Scandinavian iced berries with white chocolate sauce. Booking is essential at this chic establishment. **££££**

Rules
35 Maiden Lane
Tel: 020-7836 5314
www.rules.co.uk
Established in 1798, this is Covent Garden's oldest restaurant, and the decor, notably the wonderful Art Nouveau stained-glass ceiling and the wood panelling, reflects its heritage. The robust food is very English, with beef, lamb and game from Rules' own estate in the Pennines. **££££**

Wagamama
4a Streatham Street
Tel: 020-7323 9223
www.wagamama.com
This canteen-style basement with communal tables and bench seating was the original of this Japanese chain. The menu features noodles, dumplings, soups and juices. **£**

The City of London and the East End

The Eagle
159 Farringdon Road
Tel: 020-7837 1353
This was the place that launched a thousand gastropubs. The food has a

Listings

The ornate interior of Rules

Mediterranean bias, and there's a good choice of European beers. **££**

St John
26 St John Street
Tel: 020-7251 0848
www.stjohnrestaurant.com
This restaurant close to Smithfield's meat market has a cult following. It offers simple but curious dishes such as Middlewhite belly and dandelion or pigeon and rabbit. **££££**

Tayyabs
83 Fieldgate Street
Tel: 020-7247 9543
www.tayyabs.co.uk
This Pakistani restaurant is chaotic and often has long queues, but it does offer good food and low prices. The Seekh kebabs are delicious; bring your own alcohol (no corkage). **££**

The South Bank
Masters Super Fish
191 Waterloo Rd
Tel: 020-7928 6924
Need a taxi? You'll find cabbies galore tucking into huge portions of fish and chips in this old-fashioned eatery. **£**

Tas
33 The Cut
Tel: 020-7928 2111
www.tasrestaurant.com
It's easy to go overboard on the meze at this Turkish restaurant, so save room for the equally tasty mains. Good for vegetarians. There is also a branch at 20–2 New Globe Walk – convenient for The Globe Theatre and Tate Modern. **£–££**

Chelsea
Bibendum
Michelin House, 81 Fulham Road
Tel: 020-7581 5817
www.bibendum.co.uk
Opened by Terence Conran in 1987, Bibendum continues to thrive. The Art-Deco building houses an oyster bar on the ground floor and a restaurant on the first floor. **££££**

Restaurant Gordon Ramsay
68 Royal Hospital Rd
Tel: 020-7352 4441
www.gordonramsay.com
This celebrity chef's creations – such as roasted sea scallops with octopus, black pudding tempura, cauliflower purée and parmesan velouté – are well worth his three Michelin stars. The lunchtime set menu, at £45 for 3 courses, is a bargain. **££££**

North London
The Horseshoe
28 Heath Street, Hampstead
Tel: 020-7431 7206
For real ales (the pub has its own microbrewery) and classic British food, this pub is a good option. Feast on lamb or beef, then tuck into trifle or fruit crumble and custard. **££**

The exterior of Restaurant Gordon Ramsay

NIGHTLIFE

If you're under 30 and believe the hype, London is one of the best places to party in the world. It certainly has built a solid reputation as one of the great international clubbing centres, with every kind of music and a vibrant gay scene. But not all nightlife is dance-till-dawn. Older hipsters will enjoy pubs, bars and jazz clubs.

Ronnie Scott's

The West End

Café de Paris
3–4 Coventry Street
Tel: 020-7734 7700
www.cafedeparis.com
This stylish old dancehall attracts an older crowd that likes to dress up smartly.

Madame Jo Jo's
8 Brewer Street
Tel: 020-7734 3040
www.madamejojos.com
This ultra-camp transvestite revue bar is popular with visiting businessmen and hen parties. The kitsch shows are always uplifting.

Ronnie Scott's
47 Frith Street
Tel: 020-7439 0747
www.ronniescotts.co.uk
Scott, who died in 1996, had eclectic taste, and this is still reflected in this legendary Soho venue, which has hosted some of the biggest names in jazz since 1959.

The East End

Cargo
83 Rivington Street
Tel: 020-7739 3440
www.cargo-london.com
This hip under-the-arches venue has long been a staple part of big nights out in Shoreditch. Entertainment includes live music, DJs and dancing until late (i.e. early).

Plastic People
147–9 Curtain Road
Tel: 020-7739 6471
www.plasticpeople.co.uk
This intimate basement DJ bar is a popular nightspot for the fashionable crowd in East London's Shoreditch.

North London

EGG
5–13 Vale Royal
Tel: 020-7609 8364
www.egglondon.net
A venue with three dance floors, EGG attracts big-name DJs, and is also noted for its gay nights.

Electric Ballroom
184 Camden High Street
Tel: 020-7485 9006
www.electricballroom.co.uk
This old dancehall attracts a mixed crowd with its retro 1970s, 80s and 90s nights. Upstairs you can get down to R&B and hip-hop.

Jazz Café
5 Parkway, Camden NW1
Tel: 0870-060 3777
www.thejazzcafe.co.uk
Intimate music venue in Camden Town that attracts some of the top names in jazz as well as soul, funk and other musical styles.

Listings

ENTERTAINMENT

An international city such as London is large and densely populated enough to support a bewildering variety of entertainment venues. To supplement the highlights below, you might also like to consult www.viewlondon.co.uk or the weekly magazine, *Time Out*, which is available from all good newsagents.

Concert halls

Barbican Arts Centre
Silk Street, City of London
Tel: 020-7638 8891
www.barbican.org.uk
This purpose-built arts complex contains a theatre, a cinema, an art gallery and a library as well an impressive concert hall, the usual venue for the London Symphony Orchestra.

Royal Albert Hall
Kensington Gore
Tel: 020-7589 8212
www.royalalberthall.com
This vast rotunda hosts large-scale concerts by ageing rock stars as well as the Promenade festival of classical concerts in summer.

Royal Festival Hall
Belvedere Road, South Bank
Tel: 0871-663 2500
www.southbankcentre.co.uk
As well as being the premier classical music venue, this complex offers free Friday lunchtime jazz and folk performances in the foyer.

Wigmore Hall
36 Wigmore Street
Tel: 020-7935 2141
www.wigmore-hall.org.uk
London's top venue for chamber recitals is this Edwardian hall, north of Oxford Street.

Sadler's Wells

Dance

Sadler's Wells
Rosebery Avenue
Tel: 0844-412 4300
www.sadlerswells.com
This modern venue near Islington presents innovative programmes of contemporary and classical dance.

Film

BFI Southbank
Belvedere Road, South Bank
Tel: 020-7928 3232
www.bfi.org.uk
The main branch of the British Film Institute presents a varied programme of arthouse and off-beat films on its three screens. There's also a Mediatheque where you can trawl selections from the film archives.

Prince Charles Cinema
7 Leicester Place
Tel: 020 7494 3654
www.princecharlescinema.com
Whereas the big multiplexes on nearby Leicester Square charge high prices for blockbuster films, this quirky little cinema round the corner offers a more interesting repertory programme at a more modest price.

Opera

London Coliseum
St Martin's Lane
Tel: 0871-911 0200
www.eno.org
This elegant Edwardian theatre is where the English National Opera stages performances in English; ticket prices are lower than at the Royal Opera.

Royal Opera House
Bow Street, Covent Garden
Tel: 020-7304 4000

www.roh.org.uk
Home to the Royal Ballet and the Royal Opera, this is a magnificent theatre with a worldwide reputation for lavish performances.

Theatre

National Theatre
South Bank
Tel: 020-7452 3000
www.nationaltheatre.org.uk
One of Britain's most famous modernist buildings contains three theatres which present a range of modern and classical drama.

The Old Vic
The Cut, near Waterloo Station
Tel: 0844-871 7628
www.oldvictheatre.com
This former music hall is now a repertory theatre with a strong reputation. Kevin Spacey is the artistic director.

Royal Court Theatre
Sloane Square, Chelsea
Tel: 020-7565 5000
www.royalcourttheatre.com

Royal Court Theatre

This stylish venue stages plays by contemporary playwrights. The bar-restaurant in the foyer is ideal for pre-theatre dinners.

Shakespeare's Globe
21 New Globe Walk, Bankside
Tel: 020-7902 1500
www.shakespeares-globe.org
A reconstruction of Shakespeare's original open-to-the-elements theatre, the Globe hosts summer seasons of his plays.

Listings

SPORTS AND ACTIVITIES

Even if your visit to London does not coincide with the 2012 Olympics, there is plenty on offer instead. You can attend a football match at Arsenal or Chelsea, watch cricket at Lord's, or see the tennis at Wimbledon. If you are feeling energetic enough to participate yourself, there are opportunities for horse riding, swimming and a host of other activities.

All England Lawn Tennis Club
Church Road, Wimbledon
Tel: 020-8946 2244
www.wimbledon.com
The Wimbledon tennis championship in June/July is one of Britain's best-loved sporting events.

Hampstead Heath Bathing Ponds
www.hampsteadheath.net
For hardier souls, these three pools (a men's, a women's and a mixed one) offer outdoor swimming throughout the year.

Hyde Park Stables
63 Bathurst Mews, Lancaster Gate
Tel: 020-7723 2813
www.hydeparkstables.com
Hyde Park is a great setting for horse riding; these stables offer it daily, year round.

Lord's Cricket Ground
St John's Wood
Tel: 020-7616 8500
www.lords.org
The hallowed turf of Lord's hosts many Test and domestic county cricket matches.

TOURS

A guided tour of London by bus is a good way to familiarise yourself with the city. Alternatively, a trip up the river on a sunny day lets you see the city from another angle and beat the congestion into the bargain. All tours that are registered with the London Tourist Board use qualified Blue Badge Guides.

Big Bus Company
Tel: 020-7233 9533
www.bigbustours.com
You can hop on and off these open-top buses anywhere along the two routes around Central London. Tickets include a free river cruise.

City Cruises
Tel: 020-7740 0400
www.citycruises.com
These sightseeing boat trips run from Westminster Pier to Greenwich daily. The company also runs lunch- and dinner-dance cruises.

Duck Tours are popular with children

Duck Tours
Tel: 020-7928 3132
www.londonducktours.co.uk
Starting at Chicheley Street near Waterloo, World War II amphibious vehicles drive past London landmarks before taking to the water.

Original London Walks
Tel: 020-7624 3987
www.walks.com
This company organises more than 200 walks, including Along the Thames Pub Walk, Historic City, Hidden London, and Ghost walks. Under 15s can join free with an adult.

The Original Tour
Tel: 020-8877 1722
www.theoriginaltour.com
Hop on and off these buses at over 90 different stops. You can buy tickets on the bus, and commentary is offered in many languages.

Theatreland Walking Tour
Tel: 020-7557 6700
www.londontheatre.co.uk
Book in advance for these two-hour theatrical-history walking tours every Sunday during the summer.

FESTIVALS AND EVENTS

No matter when you visit London there should be some special event or festival taking place, whether it's classical music at the Prom Concerts over the summer, the reggae at the Notting Hill Carnival at the end of August, the fireworks of Guy Fawkes Night on 5 November, or carol services in the run up to Christmas.

January/February
Chinese New Year
Around end of January or beginning of February, colourful street celebrations centre around Gerrard Street in Chinatown, Soho.

March/April
Oxford and Cambridge Boat Race
www.theboatrace.org
You can watch this famous rowing event between Oxford and Cambridge

universities along the river from Putney to Chiswick Bridge on the last Saturday of March or first Saturday of April. There are also large screens at Bishops Park, Fulham and Furnival Gardens, Hammersmith.

April
London Marathon
www.virginlondonmarathon.com
One of the world's biggest runs, the marathon attracts thousands of participants, and thousands more to spectate along the route from Blackheath to Buckingham Palace. It takes place on a Sunday in late April.

May
Chelsea Flower Show
The Royal Hospital, Chelsea
www.rhs.org.uk
The Queen, as patron of the Royal Horticultural Society, usually opens this week-long show in late May on the first Monday.

June
Royal Academy Summer Exhibition
Burlington House, Piccadilly
www.royalacademy.org.uk
Large exhibition of work by professional and amateur artists, with almost everything up for sale. It lasts until August.

July
Henry Wood Promenade Concerts
Royal Albert Hall, South Kensington
www.bbc.co.uk/proms
A series of around 100 classical concerts begins in July and culminates in early September with the rumbustious Last Night, which features patriotic singing and flag-waving.

August
Notting Hill Carnival
Ladbroke Grove
www.thenottinghillcarnival.com
Over the bank holiday weekend at the end of the month, this colourful West Indian street carnival features steel bands, reggae and stalls selling food and drink.

September
London Open House Weekend
www.londonopenhouse.org
Around the middle of the month, historic and architecturally interesting buildings all over London open their doors to a curious public, free of charge.

November
London to Brighton Veteran Car Run
www.lbvcr.com
On the first Sunday of the month, hundreds of immaculately preserved cars and their proud owners start out from Hyde Park and make their way sedately to Brighton.

December
New Year's Eve
Trafalgar Square/Embankment
Vast crowds gather in Trafalgar Square, and a fireworks display is launched at midnight from around the London Eye on the banks of the Thames.

The Chelsea Flower Show is a riot of colour, held every May

The southeast

The southeast of England is often cited as the most affluent part of the country, and a cursory glance at its history suggests that this has long been the case. It is a region fringed with busy ports, dotted with grand castles and stately homes, and carpeted with rich farmland. This prosperous heritage has helped furnish an attractive coastline with a good selection of activities to offer visitors.

Brighton

Population: 160,000		696 955; www.bsuh.nhs.uk
Local dialling code: 01273		**Media:** *The Argus*
Tourist office: 4-5 Pavilion Buildings; tel: 01273-290 337; www.visit brighton.com		**Train station:** Queens Road; tel: 0845-127 2920; www.national rail.co.uk
Main police station: John Street; tel: 0845-607 0999		**Coach station:** 11–12 Pool Valley; tel: 01273-202 020; www.buses.co.uk
Main post office: 2–3 Churchill Square		**Car hire companies:** Thrifty; tel: 01273-738 227; www.thrifty.co.uk
Main hospital: Royal Sussex County Hospital, Eastern Road; tel: 01273-		**Taxi companies:** tel: 01273-204 060; www.brightontaxis.com

The southeast is the most populous region of Britain after London, with major conurbations around Brighton, Portsmouth and Southampton on the south coast, and around Reading in the Thames Valley. It is also the most prosperous region after London, with low unemployment rates and high per capita income. Indeed, the region is often seen as operating within London's sphere of influence, and many of its residents commute to London for work. As a result, visitors find that transport links are good, and most places can easily be managed on day trips from the capital.

The Thames Valley

The Thames is a river of plenty and has made its valley into fertile farmland. In the Middle Ages the river was so thick with salmon even the poor ate it as a staple. Great monasteries flourished here, and kings and queens have made it their home.

Windsor

England's most famous castle lies next to the Thames at **Windsor ❶**,

50 minutes by train from London's Waterloo. Since the 12th century, **Windsor Castle** (tel: 020-7766 7304; www.royalcollection.org.uk; daily Mar–Oct 9.45am–5.15pm, winter until 4.15pm; charge) has been the residence of monarchs. William the Conqueror first established a fortification here, and nearly every sovereign since has made their own addition. To the south of the castle is the Great Park, comprising some 4,800 acres (1,920 hectares) of lush greenery.

By way of contrast, Windsor is also the location of **Legoland** (tel: 08705-040 404; www.legoland.co.uk; daily Apr–Oct, variable hours; charge), located 2 miles (3km) from the town centre on the B3022. This theme park's 150 acres (60 hectares) accommodates rides, shows and workshops.

Enjoying the thrill of the rides at Legoland

Across the river from Windsor is **Eton College** (tel: 01753-671 000; www.etoncollege.com; Apr–Sept during school holidays: daily 10.30am–4.30pm, during term time: Wed, Fri–Sun 1.30–4.30pm; charge), that most famous of English public schools, founded in 1440 by the 18-year-old Henry VI. To the visitor, Eton is a cluster of red-brick Tudor buildings with little towers and hulking chimneys. The chapel has 15th-century wall paintings depicting the miracles of the Virgin. The cloisters dating from the 1440s are stunning.

Around Maidenhead

Upriver from Eton lies **Maidenhead** ❷, noteworthy for its Railway Bridge designed by Brunel. Its 128ft (38m) arches are the largest brick spans ever constructed. From Maidenhead the A4130 leads to Henley, but there are several picturesque villages and towns clustered around the river nearby.

Bray, nestled in a bend in the Thames just south of Maidenhead, has a lovely church that dates from 1293, as well as two of Britain's best restaurants (*see p.115*). Upstream is Cliveden

Visitors following the resplendent pathway to Winsdor Castle

Bucks and Herts

North of the Thames Valley, the counties of Buckinghamshire and Hertfordshire wrap themselves around Greater London. As the prime commuter belt, these counties may perhaps be lacking a distinctive regional identity of their own, but they are not without important visitor attractions. Buckinghamshire, for example, has the French-style

Waddesdon Manor (tel: 01296-653 226; www.waddesdon.org.uk; Apr–Oct Wed–Fri noon–4pm, Sat–Sun 11am–4pm; charge) owned by the Rothschild family. Hertfordshire has the historic town of **St Albans**, with its **cathedral** (tel: 01727-860 780; www.stalbanscathedral. org; daily 8.30am–5.45pm; donations) and Roman remains.

Reach, the setting for **Cliveden**, once the home of a Prince of Wales, several dukes and the Astor family, but now run as a luxury hotel.

Another picturesque riverside village is **Cookham**, best known as the home of the artist Stanley Spencer (1891–1959). The **Stanley Spencer Gallery** (tel: 01628-471 885; www. stanleyspencer.org.uk; Apr–Oct daily 10.30am–5.30pm, Nov–mid-Jan Thur–Sun 11am–4.30pm; charge) is housed in the King's Hall on the High Street. A copy of his painting of the Last Supper is in the nearby **Holy Trinity Church**.

Henley-on-Thames

The small market town of **Henley-on-Thames** ❸ is renowned for the four-day Royal Regatta, usually held in the first week of July, and attracting rowers from all over the globe (*see p.36*). Less celebrated regattas are held at weekends throughout the summer.

The town's **River & Rowing Museum** (tel: 01491-415 600; www. rrm.co.uk; daily May–Aug 10am–5.30pm, Sept–Apr until 5pm; charge) casts its net wider by offering visitors a re-creation of The Wind in the Willows, Kenneth Grahame's much-loved children's classic, published in 1908.

The luxurious Cliveden hotel, once the home of dukes and a Prince of Wales

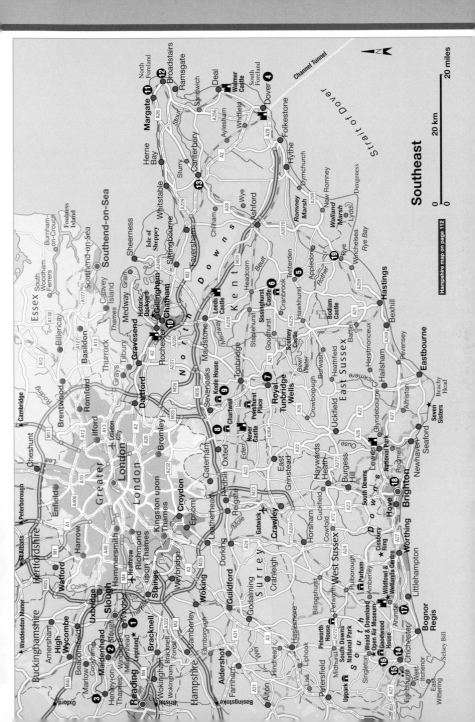

Southeast

Hampshire map on page 112

0   20 miles
0   20 km

N

Kent

The county of Kent lies to the south of the Thames estuary, between London and the Channel. Any part of it can be seen on a day trip from the capital, and the historic centres of Canterbury, Dover and Chatham are well worth a visit.

Dover and the Weald

At **Dover** ❹, the Kent coast is 21 miles (34km) from France. As the nearest point to the Continent, this is the way invaders came: Romans, Angles, Saxons and Britain's last conquerors, the Normans. On Dover's cliffs the Romans built a lighthouse and the Normans a **castle** (tel: 01314-211 067; www. english-heritage.org.uk; daily Apr–Sept 10am–6pm, Oct until 5pm; charge).

The counties of Kent and Sussex have a common geology, in which the strata run east to west. The chalky **South Downs**, in Sussex, have a walking trail along their summit, and reach the sea at the spectacular cliffs of Beachy Head near Eastbourne; Kent's **North Downs** end at the white cliffs of Dover.

In between the North and South Downs is the **Weald**, an excellent area for fruit growing, particularly apples, and grapes for white English wines. Hops grown for beer were once picked by London's East Enders on working holidays, but today, barely 50 hop farms remain.

Heading west from Dover towards the High Weald, there is the white weatherboard town of **Tenterden** ❺, home to the **Kent and Sussex Steam Railway** (tel: 01580-765 155; www.kesr.org.uk; see website for timetable; charge). A few miles further west is **Sissinghurst Castle** ❻ (tel: 01580-710 701; www.national trust.org.uk; mid-Mar–Oct Fri–Tue 10.30am–5pm; charge), a 16th-century manor house with spectacular

The brightly coloured gardens at Sissinghurst Castle

One of many picturesque streets in Tunbridge Wells

northwest is **Chartwell** ❽ (tel: 01732-868 381; www.nationaltrust.org.uk; mid-Mar–Oct Wed–Sun 11am–5pm, July–late Aug Tue–Sun same times; charge), Winston Churchill's home from 1924 until his death in 1965. Visitors can see the wartime leader's studio with many of his paintings, as well as the study where he wrote his books.

Sevenoaks is the town 5 miles (8km) to the east on the far side of the A21, and on its outskirts is **Knole** ❾ (tel: 01732-450 608; www.nationaltrust.org. uk; mid-Mar–Oct Wed–Sun noon–4pm; charge), one of the largest private houses in the country. It was the Archbishop of Canterbury's residence until confiscated by Henry VIII, and Elizabeth I gave it to Thomas Sackville who greatly extended it. It has 365 rooms, 52 stairways and seven courtyards.

gardens created by Vita Sackville-West, poet, novelist and gardener, and her politician husband Harold Nicolson from the 1930s onwards.

Tunbridge Wells to Sevenoaks
Continuing westwards is **Royal Tunbridge Wells** ❼, situated half way down the A21 between London and Hastings. The town achieved fame and fortune when Dudley, Lord North, a notorious hypochondriac, discovered the health-giving properties of the local springs in 1606. Court and fashion followed, and the waters, rich in iron salts, are still taken today at the **Pantiles**, a terraced walk with shops behind a colonnade.

Some 18 miles (29km) to the

The north Kent coast
Now heading east, there is the county town of Maidstone on the River Medway, which flows into the Thames estuary between Rochester and Chatham 10 miles (16km) to the north. A Norman castle stands above the river at **Rochester** (tel: 01634-402 276; www. english-heritage.org.uk; Apr–Sept daily 10am–6pm, Oct until 4pm; charge). Nearby **Chatham** ❿ grew around the Royal Navy dockyard established by Henry VIII. The **Historic Dockyard** (tel: 01634-823 800; www.thedockyard. co.uk; daily mid-Feb–Mar and Nov 10am–4pm, Apr–Oct 10am–6pm; charge) is now a museum, which charts 400 years of maritime history.

★ REGENCY STYLE

From 1811, King George III was too ill to rule, and so his son, also called George, ruled as his proxy as the Prince Regent until he became king himself in 1820 on his father's death. The Regency period came to be associated with a distinctive style of architecture and design, which bridged the transition from Georgian to Victorian.

One of the characteristics of the Regency style was opulence. The Prince Regent himself lived a thoroughly decadent life and much of the aristocracy followed suit – reckless behaviour considering that the French Revolution was still within living memory. As well as racking up large debts, numerous mistresses and various illegitimate children, the Prince Regent also grossly overate and drank, making him not only obese, but also chronically ill. His profligacy did, however, leave at least one positive legacy, as many of the places he frequented were rebuilt in grand style, with fine architecture and extravagant interior decoration.

Many of the finest Regency buildings can be found in London and the south of England – and the southeast region in particular boasts some of the most extraordinary. **Brighton Pavilion** became the Prince Regent's showpiece residence, with Indo-Saracenic domes and minarets on the outside and chinoiserie decoration inside. The architect of this enchanting mish-mash was John Nash, who became instrumental in bringing his patron's extravagant schemes to fruition. His Royal commissions included Regent's Park, Regent Street and Buckingham Palace. The style he did so much to develop combined a neoclassical grammar with

The majestic exterior of the Brighton Pavilion

motifs such as white-painted stucco façades, porches with columns, bow windows and wrought-iron balconies. Houses are typically arranged in terraces, crescents and circuses.

Brighton and Hove have some of the most spectacular Regency townscapes. Kemp Town in Brighton was designed by Amon Henry Wilds and Charles Busby, the latter also designing the Brunswick estate in Hove. Soon after they were completed, in the 1820s, the grand houses on these smart streets and crescents were occupied by aristocrats and society figures.

Another town in the southeast to bear the elegant imprint of Regency style is **Tunbridge Wells**. It had first achieved fashionability in the Georgian era under society dandy and party planner, 'Beau' Nash. The 1820s and '30s brought renewed vigour to the town's social scene and new impetus for building projects. Among the most prominent were Calverley Park Crescent and Holy Trinity Church, both designed by Decimus Burton, who had already achieved renown as the architect of London Zoo and the Athenaeum gentlemen's club on Pall Mall.

One of the finest Regency country houses in the southeast is **Wotton House** near Aylesbury in Buckinghamshire. Its designer was John Soane, whose other works include the Bank of England, and his own London house (now a museum – see p.78). Wotton House is not open to the public, though its parkland, landscaped by 'Capability' Brown, is (tel: 01844-238 363; Apr–early Sept Wed 2–5pm; charge).

Regency houses are often arranged in elegant terraces

A delicious spread for afternoon tea in Royal Tunbridge Wells

Further east lies **Margate** ⓫, which the railway opened up to London's East Enders as one of the capital's most popular seaside resorts, and just beyond – close to Britain's most easterly spot – is **Broadstairs** ⓬, a more upmarket resort with a sheltered sandy bay. The latter is famous for its associations with Charles Dickens, who holidayed there in the 1850s and 1860s *(see p.40)*.

Canterbury

A little inland is **Canterbury** ⓭, Britain's most famous religious centre. The Conqueror's Castle, the cathedral and its Thomas Becket Shrine were a magnet for pilgrims for centuries. Despite German aerial bomb attacks in 1942, much of Canterbury's medieval character remains, and there are a number of good pubs in its narrow streets.

The town's main attraction is, of course, its medieval **cathedral** (tel: 01227-762 862; www.canterbury-cathedral.org; summer Mon–Sat 9am–5.30pm, winter until 5pm, Sun 12.30–2.30pm; charge). The first church on the site was established in AD597 by St Augustine, after Pope Gregory the Great had sent him to convert the heathen English.

Elsewhere in the city are the remains of the original Roman city walls, and, for the young at heart, the **Rupert Bear Museum** (tel: 01227-475 202; www.canterbury.gov.uk; daily 10am–5pm; charge).

Sussex

Sussex – divided into the counties of East and West Sussex – is now generally associated with coastal resorts and

Chichester is the site of a lovely cathedral

rolling countryside. Historically, however, it is notable as the landing place of William the Conqueror in 1066 and scene of the Battle of Hastings.

Chichester

The county town of Sussex is **Chichester** ⓮, a rural market town with a fine **cathedral** (tel: 01243-812 482; www.chichestercathedral.org.uk; daily summer 7.15am–7pm, winter until 6pm; donations). Little of Chichester's Roman walls remain, but a mile or so to the west, at **Fishbourne** ⓯ (tel: 01243-785 859; www.sussexpast.co.uk; daily Mar–Oct 10am–5pm, Feb and Nov–mid-Dec 10am–4pm; charge), is Britain's largest Roman palace, excavated in 1960. Its mosaics are miraculously well preserved and its scale formidable.

On the South Downs behind Chichester is **Goodwood** ⑯, site of a racecourse and stately home *(see p.59)*. At the summit is an Iron-Age hill fort, giving wonderful views before dropping down to Singleton and the **Weald and Downland Open Air Museum** (tel: 01243-811 348; www. wealddown.co.uk; daily 10.30am–6pm, winter until 4pm; charge). The museum comprises buildings from the 13th to 19th centuries which have been conserved and rebuilt.

To the east, the River Arun emerges from the South Downs around the town of **Arundel** ⑰. The townscape is dominated by **Arundel Castle** (tel: 01903-882 173; www. arundelcastle.org; Apr–Oct Tue–Sun 10am–5pm; charge), the lavish home of the Dukes of Norfolk.

Brighton

Further east up the coast is the celebrated resort of **Brighton** ⑱. It has a raffish air, and has long attracted alternative lifestylers with its bars, restaurants and vintage shops. Much of the pleasure of visiting lies in walking its streets, particularly the warren of alleys known as The Lanes. In 1785 George IV (then Prince of Wales) stayed in a villa on the Old Steine, later redesigned by John Nash as the **Royal Pavilion** (tel: 03000-290 900; www. brighton-hove-rpml.org.uk; daily Apr–Sept 9.30am–5.45pm, Oct–Mar 10am–5.15pm; charge). Indian in style outside and Oriental within, the Pavilion is a decorative wonder *(see pp.108–9)*.

Nearby is **Brighton Pier**, with its endearing amusement arcades, fish and chip shops and fun fair (daily; rides until 10pm, Sat until 11pm).

The East Sussex coast

Further along the coast, the chalk cliffs rise up in a formation known as the 'Seven Sisters' before reaching their peak (530ft/160m) at **Beachy Head**.

The southeast

Brits and tourists flock to Brighton and its historic pier when the sun shines

On the levels to the east is Pevensey, the landing place of William, Duke of Normandy, the last man to invade Britain. He defeated King Harold at Senlac Field, just inland from Hastings. William marked his victory by building the high altar of the abbey church at **Battle** (tel: 01424-775 705; www.english-heritage.org.uk; daily Apr–Sept 10am–6pm, Oct until 4pm; charge).

To the east is the small town of **Rye** 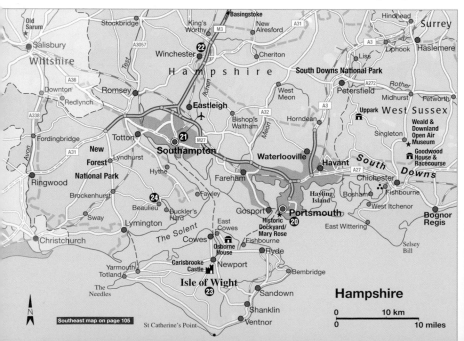, with its walls, gates and fine buildings. A colony of artists here exhibits its work in local studios and galleries. From Rye the land lies flat across Romney Marsh, a low-lying wetland area that is home to a special breed of sheep and wading birds.

Hampshire

Hampshire has always had a close relationship with the sea, with several major ports along its shores as well as seaside resorts and the Isle of Wight off its coast. Inland, there is beautiful countryside and the county town of **Winchester**.

Hampshire's ports

Historically, **Portsmouth** ❷⓪ – or 'Pompey' as it's known – was Britain's most important naval base. The **Royal Navy Museum** is here, at the **Historic Dockyard** (tel: 023-9283 9766; www.historicdockyard.co.uk; daily Apr–Oct 10am–6pm, Nov–Mar 10am–5.30pm; charge), but most visitors head for Nelson's flagship **HMS Victory**, on which he died at the Battle of Trafalgar in 1805 and the hulk of *Mary Rose* (set to reopen in 2012; tel: 02392-728060; www.historicdockyard.co.uk), Henry VIII's 'favourite warship', dredged up in

Waves lapping at Beachy Head cliffs

The Isle of Wight

Ferries cross to the **Isle of Wight ㉓** from Lymington to the west of South-ampton, as well as from Portsmouth to the east. At the northern tip of this 147-sq-mile (380-sq-km) island is **Cowes**, at the mouth of the Medina River, where Cowes Week – the yachtsman's Ascot *(see p.33)* – takes place in August. On the far side of the Medina is **Osborne House** *(see p.25)*, Queen Victoria's favourite residence.

To the south is **Newport**, the island's capital, and close by is **Carisbrooke Castle** (tel: 01983-522 107; www. english-heritage.org.uk; daily Apr–Sept 10am–5pm, Oct until 4pm; charge), built by Elizabeth I as a defence against the Spanish Armada and also remembered as the prison where Charles I was held before being tried and executed.

Beaulieu

Back on the mainland, the small town of **Beaulieu ㉔** (pronounced Bew-lee) is home to Britain's best-known motor museum at **Palace House** (tel: 01590-612 345; www.beaulieu.co.uk; daily June–Sept 10am–6pm, Oct–May until 5pm; charge).

The southeast

1982. Soaring above the harbour, the **Spinnaker Tower** (tel: 023-9285 7520; www.spinnakertower.co.uk; daily 10am–6pm; charge) offers great views and exhibitions on the area's history.

To the west is the port of **South-ampton ㉑**, from where the army that won the battle of Agincourt embarked, the *Mayflower* sailed for America, and many ocean liners have followed since.

An easy drive north of Southamp-ton is **Winchester ㉒**, once England's capital city. Beneath the medieval and modern city is a Roman town, and a Norman cathedral replaced its Saxon predecessor (tel: 01962-857 200; www. winchester-cathedral.org.uk; Mon–Sat 9.30am–5pm, Sun 12.30–3pm; charge). The palace, cloisters, colleges and mill are all breathtaking.

> ### The New Forest
>
> Behind Hampshire's coast is the 100-sq-mile (260-sq-km) woodland of the **New Forest National Park**. Despite its name, there's little 'new' about this area: this was forest even in the days of William the Conqueror. When driving through the National Park, remember that wild ponies have priority.

ACCOMMODATION

The southeast of England is rich in stately homes, and while there are some you can only visit, there are others you can actually stay in. If, however, your budget doesn't stretch to such grandeur, try instead one of the region's many excellent historic coaching inns, for cosiness and informality.

Accommodation price categories

Price categories are for a standard double room including breakfast and VAT (value added tax) during high season:

£ = under £80
££ = £80–150
£££ = £150–250
££££ = £250–350
£££££ = over £350

Thames Valley

Cliveden
Taplow, Berkshire
Tel: 01628-668 561
www.clivedenhouse.co.uk
One of the most beautiful and luxurious hotels in Britain is surrounded by acres of National Trust parkland. **££££**

Hotel du Vin
New Street, Henley-on-Thames
Tel: 01491-848 400
www.hotelduvin.com
Occupying an old brewery close to the river, this luxury boutique hotel has 43 smart rooms and a recommended bistro. **££–£££**

Kent

Falstaff
8–10 St Dunstan's Street, Canterbury
Tel: 01227-462 138
www.thefalstaffincanterbury.com
This historic coaching inn is situated within easy reach of the cathedral and shops. **££**

Hotel du Vin and Bistro
Crescent Road, Tunbridge Wells
Tel: 01892-526 455

The dining room at Cliveden

www.hotelduvin.com
A central location, individually decorated rooms, great breakfasts and a superb bistro are among the many reasons to stay here. **££**

Sussex

Amberley Castle
Near Arundel
Tel: 01798-831 992
www.amberleycastle.co.uk
This 12th-century castle has been opulently revamped with antique furniture and Jacuzzis in every bathroom. **££££**

Hotel du Vin
Ship Street, Brighton
Tel: 01273-718 588
www.hotelduvin.com
A plum location near the sea front combines with the character of a historic building to make this a top choice for Brighton. Suites are ideal for romantic getaways. **££–£££**

Hotel Pelirocco
10 Regency Square, Brighton
Tel: 01273-327 055
www.hotelpelirocco.co.uk
All rooms are playfully designed, with their own playstations, in this chic hotel in the best-preserved Regency square in town. **££**

Hampshire

Wykeham Arms
75 Kingsgate Street, Winchester
Tel: 01962-853 834
www.fullershotels.com
This 18th-century coaching inn near the cathedral combines old-world charm with modern comforts. **££**

RESTAURANTS

Whether it's Michelin-starred or gourmet vegetarian cooking, Italian or Indian cuisine, or just freshly caught seafood tipped out on to a plate, the southeast region offers tantalising choices for all tastes and budgets.

Thames Valley
The Fat Duck
1 High Street, Bray
Tel: 01628-580 333
www.thefatduck.co.uk
Heston Blumenthal creates adventurous dishes such as snail porridge and nitro-scrambled egg-and-bacon ice cream. His quest for new tastes earned him three Michelin stars. There's a sample menu. **££££**

The Waterside Inn
Ferry Road, Bray
Tel: 01628-620 691
www.waterside-inn.co.uk
In an idyllic spot overlooking the Thames, this is one of England's most exceptional restaurants. Three Michelin stars. **£££**

Kent
The Goods Shed
Station Road West, Canterbury
Tel: 01227-459 153
www.thegoodsshed.co.uk
A disused railway building now serves as a farmers' market and restaurant, with fresh, seasonal (often organic) food. **££–£££**

Osteria Posillipo
14 Albion Street, Broadstairs
Tel: 01843-601 133
www.posillipo.co.uk
This family-friendly Italian restaurant enjoys a great location, with a terrace overlooking the seafront. The large menu includes rustic pasta dishes, pizzas and seafood. **££**

Thackeray's House
85 London Road, Tunbridge Wells
Tel: 01892-511 921
www.thackerays-restaurant.co.uk

A sign outside The Fat Duck

Occupying the former home of the 19th-century novelist, this restaurant is critically acclaimed for its modern French cuisine. **£££**

Sussex
Landgate Bistro
5–6 Landgate, Rye
Tel: 01797-222 829
www.landgatebistro.co.uk
Housed in two connected Georgian cottages, the Landgate Bistro offers local fish, Romney Marsh lamb and homemade puddings. **£–££**

Terre à Terre
71 East Street, Brighton
Tel: 01273-729 051
www.terreaterre.co.uk
Innovative vegetarian cooking and organic wine make this restaurant stand out. **££**

Hampshire
Bombay Bay
Southsea Marina, Fort Cumberland Road, Portsmouth
Tel: 023-9281 6066
www.bombaybay.co.uk
Offers a light, modern Indian menu and spectacular views of the marina . **£–££**

Listings

NIGHTLIFE AND ENTERTAINMENT

The biggest centre for nightlife in the southeast is undoubtedly Brighton, with a youthful population and a vibrant gay scene. For more sedentary entertainment, there are many towns with good theatres, arts cinemas and concert venues.

Nightclubs

Concorde 2
Madeira Shelter Hall, Madeira Drive, Brighton
Tel: 01273-673 311
www.concorde2.co.uk
What is probably Brighton's most famous club offers top DJs and live-music acts.

Audio Brighton
10 Marine Parade, Brighton
Tel: 01273-606 906
www.audiobrighton.com
Crowds flock to this venue near the seafront for big club nights featuring the latest music.

Film

Trinity Theatre
Church Road, Tunbridge Wells
Tel: 01892-678 678
www.trinitytheatre.net
This arts venue offers a selection of art-house films, theatre, music and comedy.

Music

Brighton Dome
29 New Road, Brighton
Tel: 01273-709 709
www.brightondome.org
The former stable block for the Royal Pavilion features concert hall and theatre venues.

Theatre

Komedia Theatre
44–7 Gardner Street, Brighton
Tel: 0845-293 8480
www.komedia.co.uk
An old billiards hall has a new life as a comedy and theatre venue, attracting big-name acts.

Marlowe Theatre
The Friars, Canterbury
Tel: 01227-787 787
www.marlowetheatre.com
This brand-new theatre with excellent facilities has an impressive programme.

SPORTS AND ACTIVITIES

Sailing is a major leisure activity around the south coast of Britain, and there are plenty of opportunities to ply the waters and test your knowledge of the tides. For landlubbers, the New Forest offers walking and horse riding amidst glorious scenery.

Burley Villa School of Riding
Bashley Common Road, New Milton
Tel: 01425-610 278
www.burleyvilla.co.uk
For pony trekking in the New Forest, or brushing up your equestrian skills with a few lessons, this is the place to come.

Elite Sailing
Chatham Maritime Marina, Chatham
Tel: 01634-890 512
www.elitesailing.co.uk

This sailing school on the north Kent coast offers courses and sailing weekends at very reasonable prices.

First Class Sailing
Shamrock Quay,
Southampton
Tel: 02380-011 077
www.firstclasssailing.com
Join a crew and sail the Solent for the chance to see the Needles off the west coast of the Isle of Wight.

TOURS

Whether on foot or by boat, there is no shortage of guided tours around the historic and picturesque sights of the southeast. In addition to the tours below, consider also downloading commentaries; see www.kent-tours.co.uk and www.tourist-tracks.com.

Canterbury Tourist Guides
12-13 Sun Street,
The Buttermarket
Tel: 01227-459 779
www.canterbury-walks.co.uk
Experienced guides offer tours of the cathedral, museums and historic city.

Portsmouth Harbour Tours
Portsmouth Historic Dockyard
Tel: 02392-728 060
www.historicdockyard.co.uk

These 45-minute boat tours with commentary offer a fascinating survey of the basis of Britain's naval power.

Winchester Tourist Guides
Winchester Guildhall,
High Street
Tel: 01962-840 500
www.winchestertouristguides.com
Tickets for reasonably priced walking tours of the city can be purchased from the local Tourist Information Centre.

FESTIVALS AND EVENTS

Summer is a particularly busy time on the arts scene in the southeast, as festivals in many of the major cultural centres kick off. For sporting fans, the major dates for the calendar are Cowes Week and Henley Royal Regatta.

Listings

May
Brighton Festival
Various venues
www.brightonfestival.org
One of Britain's biggest arts festivals covering a full range of media and events for children.

June
Dickens Festival
Broadstairs, Kent
www.broadstairsdickensfestival.co.uk
The annual Charles Dickens jamboree takes place in various locations in Broadstairs.

July
Henley Royal Regatta
Henley-on-Thames
www.hrr.co.uk
Five days of rowing races on the Thames draw a crowd of well-dressed champagne quaffers.

Henley Royal Regatta is an exclusive event

August
Cowes Week
Cowes, Isle of Wight
www.cowes.co.uk
Over a thousand yachts compete in dozens of races each day on the Solent.

October
Canterbury Festival
Kent, various venues
www.canterburyfestival.co.uk
Kent's two-week international arts festival with theatre, music, art, film and comedy.

The southwest

The mystique of the West Country transcends its reputation as Britain's most popular holiday destination. Situated to the south of the Bristol Channel and on the edge of the Atlantic, the region comprises Wiltshire, Dorset, Somerset, Devon and Cornwall, rural counties tucked away with hidden fishing hamlets and Britain's warmest winter weather.

Bristol

Population: 430,000

Local dialling code: 0117

Tourist office: 1 Canons Road; tel: 0333-321 0101; www.visit bristol.com

Main police station: Nelson Street; tel: 0845-456 7000

Main post office: 12 Baldwin Street

Main hospital: Bristol Royal Infirmary, Marlborough Street; tel: 0117-923 0000; www.uh bristol.nhs.uk

Media: *Bristol Evening Post*

Train station: Temple Meads; tel: 0870-580 8080; www.national rail.co.uk

Bus station: Marlborough Street; tel: 0845-606 4446; www.firstgroup. com

Taxi companies: tel: 0117-327 0029; www.taxibristol.co.uk

The southwest of England is steeped in legend. This is the land of King Arthur, Camelot and the Holy Grail; the land of Jack the Giant Killer and the myth of an ancient Druid who gave weary travellers sips of water from a golden cup. History here takes on a romantic quality, with fact obscured by time and fiction embellished with tales of piracy, smuggling and shipwrecks.

Hardy country

Few literary works bear the impress of place as strongly as the novels of Thomas Hardy (1840–1928). Set in 'Wessex', Hardy's stories range across the modern counties of Dorset, Wiltshire and Somerset, venturing at times into Hampshire to the east and Devon and Cornwall to the west.

Salisbury and Stonehenge

The town of **Salisbury** ❶ featured as 'Melchester' in the Hardy novels and retains its old-England feel even today. The **cathedral** (tel: 01722-555 120; www.salisburycathedral.org.uk; Mon–Sat 9am–5pm, Sun noon–4pm; charge) has a spectacular spire, yet foundations only a few feet deep. The cathedral close offers a survey of English architectural styles through the ages.

A few miles north, on Salisbury Plain, is **Stonehenge** ❷ (tel: 0870-333 1181; www.english-heritage.org.uk; daily, Jun–Aug 9am–7pm, mid-Mar–May and Sept–mid-Oct 9.30am–6pm, mid-Oct–mid-Mar 9.30am–4pm; charge), a circle of standing stones believed to date from 2,400BC.

Shaftesbury to Sherborne

Heading west from Salisbury, the road climbs to the hill town of **Shaftesbury**. Hardy renamed it 'Shaston' in his 1895 novel *Jude the Obscure*. You can put the clock back centuries by climbing in the footsteps of pilgrims up the cobbled **Gold Hill** to St Edward the Martyr's resting place.

Northwest of Shaftesbury in the village of Stourton is **Stourhead** (tel: 01747-841 152; www.nationaltrust.

A view of charming Lyme Regis from the harbour

org.uk; garden daily 9am–6pm; house Mar–early Nov Fri–Tue 11am–5pm; charge), a country house with magnificent gardens around the lake. To the west of Shaftesbury on the A30 is **Sherborne**, a medieval market town that is burial place of two Saxon kings.

The Jurassic Coast

Heading down to the coast, and starting near the border with Devon, there is the old fishing town of **Lyme Regis** ❸. This was once a fashionable resort, and Jane Austen featured the town in her novel, *Persuasion*. Her house, Bay Cottage (now a café), is near the harbour end of the Parade.

Eastwards from Lyme Regis is the so-called **Jurassic Coast**, rich in fossils. An ichthyosaurus was discovered here in 1811. Further along is **Bridport** ❹ ('Port Bredy' to Hardy), with its extraordinary harbour, West Bay, separated from the town by a long and narrow channel flanked by two piers only feet apart. It's a needle-threading operation for small craft to enter the little basin.

Salisbury cathedral's interior is an architectural triumph

The southwest

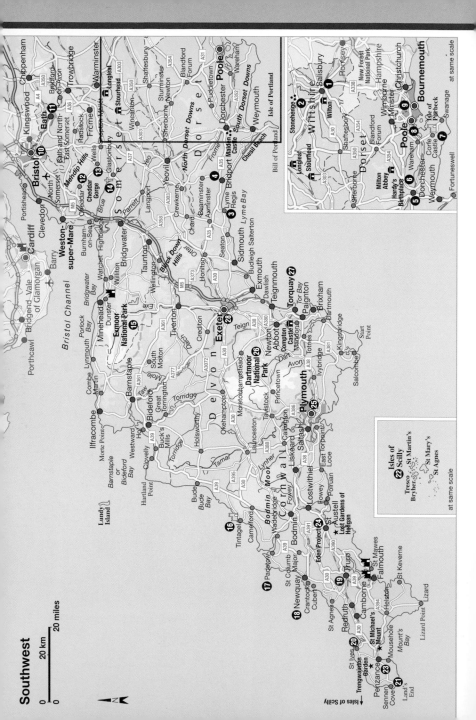

Southwest

0 | 20 km
0 | 20 miles

N

Isles of Scilly
22
Tresco
Bryher
St Martin's
St Agnes
St Mary's

at same scale

Wiltshire
Salisbury
Romsey
1
Stonehenge
2
Wilton
New Forest National Park
Christchurch
Bournemouth
9
Wimborne Minster
Ringwood
Hampshire
Longleat
Stourhead
Shaftesbury
Blandford Forum
Poole
8
Isle of Purbeck
7
Wareham
Swanage
Sherborne
Milton Abbey
Hardy's Birthplace
5
Dorchester
6
Weymouth
Corfe Castle
Fortuneswell
Dorset

at same scale

Warminster
Chippenham
Kingswood
Bath
11
Bradford-on-Avon
Trowbridge
Melksham
Radstock
Frome
Longleat
Stourhead
Shaftesbury
Blandford Forum
Sturminster Newton
Poole
Poole
Dorset
Puddletown
Dorchester
Wareham
Isle of Portland
Weymouth
Chesil Beach
Bill of Portland
South Dorset Downs
North Dorset Downs
Wincanton
Cerne
Yeovil
Crewkerne
Beaminster
Bridport
Maiden Castle
4
Axminster
Lyme Regis
3
Chard
Lyme Bay
Seaton
Sidmouth
Budleigh Salterton
Exmouth
Dawlish
Teignmouth

Porthcawl
Bridgend
Vale of Glamorgan
Cardiff
Barry
Penarth
Portishead
Clevedon
Weston-super-Mare
Burnham-on-Sea
Highbridge
Bridgwater
Bristol
10
North Somerset
Bath and North East Somerset
Cheddar Gorge
12
Mendip Hills
Wells
Glastonbury
13
Somerset
Langport
Bridgwater
Taunton
Wellington
Black Down Hills
Honiton
Otter
Exe
Bristol Channel
Portishead
Minehead
Watchet
Williton
Dunster
Exmoor National Park
14
Porlock
Porlock Bay
Combe Martin
Ilfracombe
Morte Point
Lynmouth
Lundy Island
Hartland Point
Clovelly
Buck's Mills
Westward Ho!
Bideford
Barnstaple
Barnstaple or Bideford Bay
Great Torrington
South Molton
Crediton
Tiverton
Exeter
28
Newton Abbot
Torquay
27
Tor Bay
Paignton
Brixham
Dartmouth
Start Point
Kingsbridge
Salcombe
Dartmoor National Park
26
Moretonhampstead
Princetown
Tavistock
Compton Castle
Maldon
Totnes
Ivybridge
Plymouth
25
Saltash
Calington
Liskeard
Callington
East Looe
Looe
West Looe
Polperro
Fowey
Lostwithiel
Bodmin
Bodmin Moor
Camelford
Wadebridge
Padstow
17
Tintagel
16
Bude
Bude Bay
Holsworthy
Okehampton
Launceston
Cornwall
St Austell
Eden Project
24
Lost Gardens of Heligan
Truro
19
St Austell
Mevagissey
Falmouth
St Mawes
St Keverne
Helston
Lizard Point
Lizard
Camborne
Redruth
St Agnes
Newquay
18
Crantock
Cubert
St Columb Major
St Ives
20
Camborne
St Michael's Mount
Mousehole
Mount's Bay
Penzance
Trengwainton Garden
23
Sennen Cove
Land's End
21
Isles of Scilly →

Italic place labels and feature names as shown on map

Further east, **Chesil Beach** curves
out to where it becomes the slender
link that makes the **Isle of Portland**
only a courtesy title. It is in fact,
only a peninsula. The lighthouse on
the island's south tip overlooks the
broken water of the treacherous Portland Race.

Thomas Hardy's heartlands

The green of the high hills inland of
Weymouth comes as a welcome relief.
Dorchester ❺, the county town of
Dorset, is best approached from the

Iron-Age hillfort of **Maiden Castle**,
just southwest of the town. Thomas
Hardy referred to the town as 'Casterbridge' in his novels, and his statue
stands at the top of the High Street.
The courtroom in the **Shire Hall**
remains remarkably unchanged since
1834 when the Tolpuddle Martyrs
were convicted for trying to gain
better working conditions.

There is a collection devoted
to Hardy in the **Dorset County
Museum** (tel: 01305-262 735; www.
dorsetcountymuseum.org; Apr–Oct
Mon–Sat 10am–5pm, Nov–Mar until
4pm; charge) on High West Street. A
small cottage in Higher Bockhampton
was **Hardy's Birthplace ❻**, just north
of Dorchester in 1840 (tel: 01305-
262 366; www.nationaltrust.org.uk;
mid-Mar–Oct Wed–Sun 11am–5pm;
charge). He died in 1928 in the
grand house he designed himself,
Max Gate (tel: 01297-489 481; www.

The southwest

Weymouth harbour

The Corfe Castle ruins surrounded by green fields

The southwest

nationaltrust.org.uk; Apr–Oct Wed–Sun 11am–5pm; charge), on Wareham Road in Dorchester (see p.43).

The coastline to Bournemouth

The 30-mile (48km) coast from Weymouth east to Swanage, below Poole Harbour, is strictly for walking, but is approachable by car at West Lulworth, Kimmeridge and Worth Matravers. Towards the east, the chalk hills around the Isle of Purbeck break at the picturesque ruin of **Corfe Castle** ❼ (tel: 01929-481 294; www. nationaltrust.org.uk; daily Mar and Oct 10am–5pm, Apr–Sept 10am–6pm, Nov–Feb 10am–4pm, charge).

Just to the north is **Poole** ❽, with its quay overlooking yachts, shipyards and chandler's stores, and the creeks, mud flats and islands of Poole Harbour beyond. Curving steps meet under the portico of the Custom House with its coat of arms representing an authority the Dorset smuggler never acknowledged.

Beyond Poole are the hotels and elegant terraces of **Bournemouth** ❾, a sedate resort built at the end of the 19th century, while just to the east is **Christchurch** on the mouth of the Avon. Its priory has a turret with an interlaced pattern of Norman arches that recalls Pisa's leaning tower.

Bristol, Bath and environs

To the north of Hardy Country are the cities of Bristol and Bath, situated on the River Avon, which flows north into the Severn Estuary. In the Somerset countryside beyond are the ancient religious centres of Wells and Glastonbury.

Bristol

John Cabot set off for Newfoundland from the port of **Bristol** ❿ in 1497; later on it was a gateway to the Empire. The **British Empire and Commonwealth Museum** (tel: 0117-925 4980; www.empire museum.co.uk; daily 10am–5pm; charge) occupying Old Bristol

Station, charts Britain's colonial expansion from 1500 until 1914.

Other attractions have flowered around the redeveloped docks, including contemporary arts venue, the **Arnolfini Gallery** (tel: 0117-917 2300; www.arnolfini.org.uk; Tue–Sun 11am–6pm; free), and **At-Bristol** (tel: 0845-345 1235; www.at-bristol.org.uk; Mon–Fri 10am–5pm, Sat–Sun 10am–6pm; charge), a complex of interactive science museums geared to children. Also here is the **SS *Great Britain***, designed by Isambard Kingdom Brunel (1806–59), which can be visited in its original dock (tel: 0117-926 0680; www.ssgreatbritain.org; daily 10am–5.30pm, Nov–Mar until 4.30pm; charge).

Bath

The celebrated spa town of **Bath ⓫** lies 13 miles (21km) southeast of

Visitors perusing the work on display at the Arnolfini gallery in Bristol

Bristol. The steamy core of it all is the **Roman Baths** (tel: 01225-477 785; www.romanbaths.co.uk; daily Mar–June and Sept–Oct 9am–5pm, July–Aug until 9pm, Nov–Feb 9.30am–4.30pm; charge), at basement level to the modern city, and its adjoining **Pump Room**, which became the hub of fashionable society in the 18th century.

The city owes its good looks to Bath stone and the genius of two men, the elder and younger John Wood, who in the 18th century gave its streets, squares and crescents an impressive harmony. Bath's architectural heritage has been wonderfully preserved, with architectural masterpieces including Robert Adam's **Pulteney Bridge**, and, in the Upper Town, the **Royal Crescent**, **The Circus**, the **Assembly Rooms** (tel: 01225-477 789; www.nationaltrust.org.uk; daily 10.30am–6pm, Nov–Feb until 5pm; charge) and **Queen Square**.

The Mendips

To the south of Bristol are the Mendip Hills. Across the crest of the hills runs the West Mendip Way, a popular hiking trail that twists from Wells, 20 miles (32km) southwest of Bath, to the Bristol Channel and offers superb countryside vistas.

Cheddar Gorge ⓬ cuts through the Mendips to the northwest of Wells. In Cheddar village itself you can visit vast caverns carved by a river that now runs underground (tel: 01934-742 343; www.cheddarcaves.co.uk; daily 10.30am–5pm, July–Aug until 5.30pm; charge).

At the southern tip of the Mendips is the city of **Wells ⓭**, centred

The southwest

around its **cathedral** (tel: 01749-674 483; www.wellscathedral.org.uk; daily 7am–7pm, Oct–Mar until 6pm; charge), a massive Gothic shrine that took four centuries to build. Unlike other English cathedrals, the two main towers were built outside the church proper, thus extending the western façade into a massive gallery for 400 individual statues. Outside the cathedral, the **Vicar's Close** comprises the only complete medieval street remaining in Britain, and to the south is the magnificent **Bishop's Palace** (tel: 01749-678 691; www.bishopspalacewells.co.uk; daily Apr–Oct 10.30am–6pm; charge).

Glastonbury

It's a pity that the abbey at **Glastonbury** ⑭, 6 miles (10km) southwest, has not been preserved in the same way, for it was once the richest in England. Little remains but a few ruined pillars and walls – the result of Henry VIII's dissolution of the monasteries.

The origins of the abbey are shrouded in myth. One legend centres on Joseph of Arimathea, the man who gave his tomb to Christ. Having sailed to Britain to convert the heathens in AD60, he was leaning on his staff on Wearyall Hill, when it rooted and flowered, an omen that he should settle and found the abbey. Joseph brought with him the chalice from the Last Supper, the Holy Grail. In the 6th century King Arthur came to Glastonbury in search of the Holy Grail; tradition says he and Guinevere are buried under the abbey floor.

The Glastonbury abbey ruin, though delightful, is a shadow of its former grandeur

A short walk to the steep, conical hill called **Glastonbury Tor**, which rises up from the flat Somerset plain, is worthwhile for the view from the top, surmounted by the remains of the 15th-century St Michael's Church.

Devon and Cornwall

Historically, the extreme southwest of Britain has been cut off from the mainstream of British culture both by geography and choice. The peninsula was settled by hard-working Celts from Brittany who scraped a living off the essentials of the land. They dug tin and copper, grazed their sheep and cattle on windswept moors, and braved treacherous currents to take fish from the sea.

The north coast

The boundary between Somerset and Devon falls within the 265 sq miles (690 sq km) of **Exmoor National Park ⓯**. The landscape ranges from windswept ridges covered with bracken and heather to forested ravines carved out by white water streams.

To the west along the Devon coast, **Westward Ho!** is a popular seaside resort named after the novel by Charles Kingsley (1819–75). It has 3 miles (5km) of sandy beaches. Next along is the village of **Clovelly**, where cars are banned and donkeys carry visitors' luggage. The steep cobbled street descends to the sea in a series of steps.

Passing into Cornwall, the rolling waves at **Bude** have long attracted surfers, while Summerleaze Beach, a sheltered, sandy expanse north of the River Neet, is better for swimmers.

Further west is **Tintagel Castle ⓰** (tel: 01840-770 328; www.english-heritage.org.uk; daily Apr–Sept 10am–6pm, Oct until 5pm; charge), where tradition claims Arthur was born or washed ashore, and built a castle for Guinevere and the Knights of the Round Table. All that remains are the ruins of a 6th-century Celtic monastery and a 12th-century bastion, most of it washed away by the sea.

Next along the north Cornwall coastline is the old fishing port of **Padstow ⓱**, named after St Petroc, a Celtic missionary who landed here in the 6th century to convert the heathen Cornish. Clustered around the harbour are the historic Abbey House, St Petroc Church and Raleigh Cottage, where Sir Walter collected port dues as the Royal Warden of Cornwall.

The next major coastal town is **Newquay ⓲**, Cornwall's Malibu – where surfers cruise the waves. It is also the setting for **Newquay Zoo** (tel: 01637-873 342; www.

Enjoying the view at Padstow Harbour

⭐ LIGHTHOUSES

The southwest of Britain is fringed with ports that serve the Atlantic's shipping routes and fishing grounds. These same ports face the full force of the ocean's storms, and the rocky coast around is littered with shipwrecks. It's no wonder then, that Devon and Cornwall have a large share of the country's lighthouses, many of which represent spectacular feats of engineering.

Eddystone Lighthouse, 13 miles (21km) southwest of Plymouth, is probably the most famous lighthouse in Britain. It is the fourth structure to have been built on the treacherous Eddystone Rocks. The first was completed in 1698, but was swept away (with its builder) during a storm in 1703. The second lighthouse suffered a catastrophic fire. The third lighthouse had to be dismantled after erosion caused it to shake every time a wave hit. It was rebuilt on Plymouth Hoe as a memorial to its designer, John Smeaton. The current lighthouse came into service in 1882, and is still in operation. It is 161ft (49m) high, and now has a helipad on top. The light has a range of 22 nautical miles (41km).

Another famous lighthouse – and one you can actually visit – is at Britain's most southerly point, Lizard in Cornwall. Built in 1752, it is 62ft (19m) tall and its light can be seen up to 26 nautical miles (48km) away.

A view of Housel Bay and the Lizard lighthouse

Within the engine room is the **Lizard Lighthouse Heritage Centre** (tel: 01326-290 202; www.trinityhouse. co.uk; check website for opening times; charge). Visitors can climb the lighthouse tower, sound the foghorn, track ships in the local area and listen to lighthouse keepers' stories.

The lighthouse at **Start Point** near Dartmouth is a picturesque sight, perched at the end of a peninsular that juts out into the sea for almost a mile. Guided tours lasting 45 minutes are offered to visitors most days, subject to weather conditions (tel: 01803-771 802; www.trinityhouse. co.uk; check website for opening times; charge).

At Gwythian, near St Ives, is the white octagonal **Godrevy Lighthouse** – said to have been the inspiration for Virginia Woolf's novel, *To the Lighthouse*. Although it is not open to the public, you can walk along the rugged cliff tops to see it. Down below are popular surfing beaches, and the local colony of seals often lolls around on the sand at Mutton Cove.

In the face of automation, the last lighthouse keepers departed in the 1990s. Many of their old cottages have now been renovated and are rented out to holiday-makers. Cottages are available at Anvil Point in Dorset, Bull Point and Start Point in Devon, and at Lizard, Pendeen and St Anthony in Cornwall. Holiday bookings are handled by Rural Retreats (www. ruralretreats.co.uk) and Cornish Cottages (www.cornishcottagesonline. com – for Lizard only).

Start Point Lighthouse has a cottage available to rent

The first Eddystone Lighthouse was built in 1698 but destroyed five years later

The harbour office in Mousehole

newquayzoo.org.uk; daily Apr–Sept 9.30am–6pm, Oct–Mar 10am–5pm; charge) in Trenance Gardens.

Tin smelting capital

The corridor between the nearby towns of Redruth and Camborne, southwest and inland, was the centre of Cornish tin mining for more than 200 years. **The Cornwall Industrial Discovery Centre** (tel: 01209-210 900; www. chycor.co.uk; Apr–Oct Sun–Fri 11am–5pm; charge) at Pool, just outside Camborne, charts the industry's history.

Truro ⑲, to the east, is the cathedral city of Cornwall and the unofficial capital. In the 18th century it was both a centre for tin smelting and a society haunt that rivalled Bath. The town's **Royal Cornwall Museum** (tel: 01872-272 205; www.royal cornwallmuseum.org.uk; Mon–Sat 10am–5pm; charge) has displays of antiquities and local history.

One of the last ports of call in north Cornwall is **St Ives** ⑳ (see box).

Land's End

Penwith is the name given to the windswept piece of land that juts out into the Atlantic at the end of Cornwall. At the southwestern extremity is **Land's End** ㉑. Land's End Centre (tel: 0871-720 0044; www.landsend-landmark. co.uk; daily 10am–dusk; charge) offers a discovery trail and exhibitions.

Offshore, to the west of Land's End, are the **Isles of Scilly** ㉒ (pronounced silly), which can be reached by ferry or helicopter from Penzance. Tresco, one of the five inhabited islands, has the **Abbey Gardens** (tel: 01720-424 108; www.tresco.co.uk; daily 10am–4pm; charge), while St Mary's is home to the **Isles of Scilly Museum** (tel: 01720-422 337; www.iosmuseum.org; Easter–Sept Mon–Fri 10am–4.30pm,

---

St Ives

The fishing village of **St Ives** has been popular with artists since the end of the 19th century. Among them was the sculptor Barbara Hepworth (1903–75) whose home is now the Barbara Hepworth Museum. The works of other artists from St Ives' heyday – including Ben Nicholson, Peter Lanyon and Naum Gabo – form the permanent exhibition at **Tate St Ives** (both museums: tel: 01736-796 226; www.tate.org.uk; Mar–Oct daily 10am–5.20pm, Nov–Feb Tue–Sun 10am–4.20pm; charge), which occupies a stunning building by Porthmeor Beach.

Sat 10am–noon, Oct–Easter Mon–Sat 10am–noon; charge).

Back on the mainland, two picturesque villages sit on the south shore of Penwith. **Mousehole** (pronounced mowzel), named after an old smugglers' cave, is as tiny as the name suggests, a cluster of granite cottages and half-timbered pubs. Nearby **Newlyn** has the **Newlyn Gallery** (tel: 01736-363 715; www.newlynartgallery.co.uk; Mon–Sat 10am–5pm; donation), featuring work by regional artists.

Penzance

Penzance ❷❸ has long been the premier town of western Cornwall thanks to its commanding site on Mount's Bay. Within the town lies the Barbican, an 18th-century fish market transformed into a lively arts and crafts centre, and many historic buildings, including the **Penlee House Gallery and Museum** (tel: 01736-363 625; www.penleehouse.org.uk; Mon–Sat Easter–Sept 10am–5pm, Oct–Easter 10.30am–4.30pm; charge), with works by artists of the Newlyn School.

Sitting in Mount's Bay is **St Michael's Mount** (tel: 01736-710 507; www.stmichaelsmount.co.uk; Apr–Oct Sun–Fri 10.30am–5pm; charge). At low tide there is a causeway to the island; at other times visitors go by ferry. According to legend, a fisherman saw St Michael standing on the granite outcrop, so a priory was founded here in 1140. It became a grand private house in the 17th century.

To the east, beyond the treacherous Lizard Point lies the port of **Falmouth**. **Pendennis Castle** (tel: 01326-316 594; www.english-heritage.org.uk; Apr–Jun 10am–5pm, Jul–Aug until 6pm, Oct until 4pm; charge) guarded the town for three centuries against Spanish and French raids; you can learn more at the **National Maritime Museum** (tel: 01326-313 388; www.nmmc.co.uk; daily 10am–5pm; charge) on the town's redeveloped Discovery Quay.

Further up the south coast, near St Austell, is the **Eden Project** ❷❹ *(see box p.130)*.

The southwest

Fun and games in Mount Bay, with St Michael's Mount as the backdrop

Greenhouses and bees, all part of the Eden Project experience

Plymouth to Exeter

Plymouth ㉕, on the Devon-Cornwall border, is the city from where Drake, Raleigh and the Pilgrim Fathers embarked on their various adventures. On the Hoe – the open space atop the low limestone cliffs above the harbour – is **Smeaton's Tower**, a red-and-white striped lighthouse that offers excellent views. Nearby is the 17th-century **Royal Citadel** (tel: 01752-255 629; www.english-heritage. org.uk; May–Sept Tue and Thur, tours at 2.30pm; charge), and down by the port is the cobblestoned quarter known as the Barbican, with its pubs, cafés and art galleries. On the other side of the harbour is the **National Marine Aquarium** (tel: 01752-220 084; www.national-aquarium.co.uk; daily Apr–Oct 10am–6pm, Nov–Mar until 5pm; charge), with sharks, turtles and squids.

Directly inland from Plymouth is **Dartmoor National Park ㉖**, 365 sq miles (915 sq km) of wild forest and moorland, while to the east is the port of **Dartmouth**, home to Britannia Royal Naval College, which has trained the likes of Prince Charles to be naval officers. Just up the coast lies Torbay, a conurbation of **Torquay ㉗**, Paignton and Brixham which is known as the English Riviera because of its mild climate and long beaches.

To the north of Torquay is **Exeter ㉘**, a lively university and cathedral city. The skyline is dominated by the **cathedral** (tel: 01392-285 983; www. exeter-cathedral.org.uk; Mon–Sat 9am–4.45pm; charge), which was built between the 11th and 14th centuries. It is notable for its vaulted ceiling, carved to resemble the radiating branches of a palm tree.

The Eden Project

Cornwall's biggest attraction is the **Eden Project** (tel: 01726-811 911; www.edenproject.com; Apr–Oct daily 9.30am–6pm, Nov–Mar until 3pm; charge). It comprises several huge futuristic-looking greenhouses called 'biomes' – a humid tropical one and a warm temperate zone – plus a large outdoor landscaped area, all mimicking the planet's various climates.

ACCOMMODATION

Visitors to the southwest of England are well catered for with hotels and guesthouses. In high season many of the best are heavily booked up, but because these are sunnier climes, it may be worth planning your visit for spring or autumn, when the crowds have dispersed and the prices are lower.

Accommodation price categories

Price categories are for a standard double room including breakfast and VAT (value added tax) during high season:

£ = under £80
££ = £80–150
£££ = £150–250
££££ = £250–350
£££££ = over £350

Chic decor at Ston Easton Park

Hardy Country
Summer Lodge
Summer Lane, Evershot
Tel: 01935-482 000
www.summerlodgehotel.co.uk
This Georgian dower house set in mature gardens is luxuriously furnished and noted for its high standards of service. **££**

White Hart
1 St John Street, Salisbury
Tel: 01722-327 476
www.mercure.com
This elegant Georgian establishment – thought by many to be the best hotel in town – combines old-world comforts with modern conveniences. **££**

Bath and environs
Bloomfield House
146 Bloomfield Road, Bath
Tel: 01225-420 105
www.ecobloomfield.com
For a B&B with a difference, try this gorgeous Georgian family house, offering 4-poster beds and even impressive eco credentials. **££**

The Queensberry Hotel
Russel Street, Bath
Tel: 01225-447 928
www.thequeensberry.co.uk
This smart boutique hotel occupying three Georgian houses knocked together offers comfort, character and the esteemed Olive Tree restaurant. **££–£££**

Royal Crescent Hotel
16 Royal Crescent, Bath
Tel: 01225-823 333
www.royalcrescent.co.uk
The ultimate address in Bath has antique furnishings, individually decorated rooms, a renowned restaurant and secluded garden. **££££**

Ston Easton Park
Ston Easton, nr Bath
Tel: 01761-241 631
www.stoneaston.co.uk
Sample aristocratic life at this Palladian mansion in the Mendip Hills, with Humphrey Repton gardens, Chippendale 4-posters and an old-fashioned kitchen garden to supply the dinner table. **££££**

Devon and Cornwall
Abbey Hotel
Abbey Street, Penzance
Tel: 01736-366 906
www.theabbeyonline.co.uk
Owned by Jean Shrimpton, supermodel of the 1960s, this delightful blue-stuccoed hotel is renowned for its warmth of atmosphere. It also offers period features, views over the harbour and a Michelin-starred restaurant. **££**

Burgh Island Hotel
Bigbury-on-Sea, Devon
Tel: 01548-810 514
www.burghisland.com
This Art-Deco hotel is closely associated with Agatha Christie, who wrote two of her books here. The hotel is on an island, so access is by sea tractor. **££££**

Gidleigh Park
Chagford, Devon
Tel: 01647-432 367
www.gidleigh.com
Quintessentially English, this neo-Elizabethan mansion situated within Dartmoor National Park has a two-Michelin starred restaurant, log fires and impeccable service. **££££**

Island Hotel
Tresco, Isles of Scilly
Tel: 01720-422 883
ww.tresco.co.uk
This fine hotel has a great location in sub-tropical gardens, a private beach, a pool – even its own sailing school. The restaurant is renowned for its modern British cuisine. **£££**

The Lugger Hotel
Portloe, Truro
Tel: 01872-501 322
www.luggerhotel.com
A stay at the Lugger involves a perfect setting in a tiny Cornish fishing village, luxurious rooms with seaviews, and a wonderful restaurant serving local seafood with panache. **££**

Michael House
Trelake Lane, Treknow, Tintagel
Tel: 01840-770 592
www.michael-house.co.uk
Among the benefits of this vegetarian and vegan guest-house are its wonderful location, seaviews and reasonable tarriffs. **£**

Old Quay House
28 Fore Street, Fowey
Tel: 01726-833 302
www.theoldquayhouse.com
Right on the quayside, a traditional exterior conceals sleek modern decor. The views are stupendous and the Q Restaurant is highly recommended. **££–£££**

RESTAURANTS

Many visitors head straight for Rick Stein's renowned restaurants in Padstow, but it is also worth seeking out less famous places in the other fishing towns around the coast; prices aren't as steep, but the seafood is just as fresh.

Restaurant price categories
Prices are for a two-course dinner per person with a glass of house wine.

£ = under £20
££ = £20–30
£££ = £30–50
££££ = over £50

Hardy Country
The Haunch of Venison
1 Minster Street, Salisbury
Tel: 01722-411 313
www.haunchofvenison.uk.com
Reputedly the oldest hostelry in Salisbury, this fine institution serves hearty portions of comforting British classics. **££**

No 6 French Restaurant
6 North Square, Dorchester
Tel: 01305-267 679

www.no6-restaurant.co.uk
A stylish French bistro that makes good use of local produce. There is outdoor dining during the warmer months of the year. **££**

Perrys Restaurant
4 Trinity Road, Weymouth
Tel: 01305-785 799
www.perrysrestaurant.co.uk
This smart restaurant overlooking the harbour offers well-executed dishes with no gimmicks. The weekday set lunch menu is a bargain. **££**

Bristol, Bath and environs

The Circus
34 Brock Street, Bath
Tel: 01225-466 020
www.thecircuscafeandrestaurant.co.uk
This chic family-run café-restaurant serves
rustic, British food that is presented with style
and panache. **££**

Culinaria
1 Chandos Road, Bristol
Tel: 0117-973 7999
www.culinariabristol.co.uk
This bistro places the emphasis on top-
quality, seasonal ingredients. The set lunch
menus are stupendous. **££**

The Moody Goose
The Old Priory Hotel, Church Square,
Midsomer Norton
Tel: 01761-416 784
www.moodygoose.co.uk
Occupying a 12th-century priory near Bath,
this restaurant offers exquisite modern
British cuisine prepared with locally-
sourced poultry, meat and game. **£££**

Devon and Cornwall

Barbican Kitchen
Black Friars Distillery, 60 Southside Street,
Plymouth
Tel: 01752-604 448
www.barbicankitchen.com
This brasserie run by the Tanner brothers
serves Devon red beef burgers and smoked
Dartmouth haddock. Ideal for lunch. **£–££**

St Petroc's Bistro
4 New Street, Padstow
Tel: 01841-532 700
www.rickstein.com
A less expensive place to try the cutting
edge of Rick Stein's fish cooking (see
below), but you still need to book. **£££**

The Seafood Restaurant
Riverside, Padstow
Tel: 01841-532 700
www.rickstein.com
Run by Rick Stein, this is one of the best
seafood restaurants in Britain, offering simple
dishes using only the freshest ingredients.
Booking essential. **££££**

Listings

NIGHTLIFE AND ENTERTAINMENT

The region's towns and cities form the main centres for both nightlife and cultural
fare, though there are smaller venues such as the extraordinary Minack theatre in
more remote areas. For clubbing, towns such as Bristol and Bournemouth have
the most action, and websites such as www.venue.co.uk and www.skiddle.com are
worth consulting.

Nightclubs
Goldfingers
48 Catherine Street, Salisbury
Tel: 01722-329 223
www.goldfingersnightclub.com
This well-established venue has Fridays and
Saturdays as its clubnights (which are often
themed and involve fancy dress).

Lava Ignite
Firvale Road, Bournemouth
Tel: 01202-311 178
www.lavaignite.com

Drinks at the Lighthouse, Poole

Large commercial club with four rooms and the latest sound systems.

Music
Colston Hall
Colston Street, Bristol
Tel: 0117-922 3686
www.colstonhall.org
This historic concert hall hosts major names from the world of classical music as well as ageing rockstars topping up their pensions.

Lighthouse
Kingland Road, Poole
Tel: 0844-406 8666
www.lighthousepoole.co.uk
As well as presenting theatre, dance and big-name comedy acts, this is the home venue for the Bournemouth Symphony Orchestra.

Film
Watershed
1 Canon's Road, Harbourside, Bristol

Tel: 0117-927 5100
www.watershed.co.uk
This film and digital media centre presents a wide range of repertory and cutting edge cinema.

Theatre
Bristol Old Vic
King Street, Bristol
Tel: 0117-987 7877
www.bristololdvic.org.uk
This historic venue presents classic drama by one of the country's most prestigious theatre companies.

Minack Theatre
Porthcurno, Penzance
Tel: 01736-810 181
www.minack.com
This open-air theatre is carved into the cliffs overlooking the sea. The summer season (June–September) offers everything from Shakespeare to musicals and children's shows.

SPORTS AND ACTIVITIES

Spectacular scenery, a long coastline and benevolent weather make outdoor activities a major attraction to visitors to the southwest. You can try your hand at sailing a vintage yacht, trek across Dartmoor on horseback, kayak up Exeter Ship Canal or bowl along country lanes on a tandem.

Classic Sailing
Parton Vrane, Portscatho, Cornwall
Tel: 01872-580 022
www.classic-sailing.co.uk
No experience is needed to embark on a weekend expedition on a tall ship, or help crew a Bristol pilot cutter or a sailing trawler on a longer voyage. Fully qualified skippers provide instruction, and you can also gain Royal Yacht Association qualifications.

Saddles and Paddles
No. 4 Kings Wharf, The Quay, Exeter
Tel: 01392-424 241
www.saddlepaddle.co.uk

This company has various bikes for hire including mountain bikes, tandems and bikes with trailers or tag-alongs for children. Alternatively, you can rent a single or double kayak and go for a paddle up the old ship canal.

Skaigh Stables
Belstone, Okehampton, Devon
Tel: 01837-840 429
www.skaighstables.co.uk
Enjoy the rugged scenery of Dartmoor on horseback by signing up for a morning or afternoon ride, a day-long pub ride or you can organise your own tailor-made itinerary.

TOURS

Steam railways, river cruises and themed walking tours are just a few of the ways to discover the townscapes, countryside and coastlines of this region – and along the way there are plenty of opportunities to learn about local history and culture or discover hidden gems.

Bristol Packet Boat Trips
Wapping Wharf, Gas Ferry Road, Bristol
Tel: 0117-926 8157
www.bristolpacket.co.uk
Enjoy a tour of Bristol docks in an old Bristol Packet, or up the Bristol Channel in a more modern cruiser.

Dartmouth Steam Railway and River Boat Company
5 Lower Street, Dartmouth
Tel: 01803-555 872
www.dartmouthrailriver.co.uk

This company organises steam railway trips along the English Riviera Geopark coast line, river and harbour cruises, and a wide range of other day trips and evening events.

Jane Austen Walking Tour
Jane Austen Centre, 40 Gay Street, Queen Square, Bath
Tel: 01225-443 000
www.janeausten.co.uk
These 90-minute morning tours take visitors round the city of Bath as Jane Austen knew it.

FESTIVALS AND EVENTS

While the major towns and cities host specialist arts festivals – from film to classical music – the smaller, more remote towns and villages of the region take advantage of the great outdoors to put on the family-orientated events that are an essential part of English summers.

The Dartmouth Royal Regatta

May/June
Bath International Music Festival
www.bathmusicfest.org.uk
Prestigious festival of chamber and orchestral music, opera, and some jazz, from mid-May to early June.

August
Dartmouth Royal Regatta
www.dartmouthregatta.co.uk
The last weekend of the month offers rowing and sailing events, aerial performances by the Red Arrows and fireworks.

September
Salisbury Food and Drink Festival
www.salisburyfestival.co.uk
Foodie events in mid-September showcasing regional produce.

November
Encounters
Watershed, 1 Canon's Road, Bristol
www.encounters-festival.org.uk
The region's top film festival, around the middle of the month, has its emphasis on contemporary world cinema.

East Anglia

East Anglia hasn't changed much for centuries. Undisturbed by both the sooty touch of the Industrial Revolution and the bombs of World War II, many villages and towns remain unspoilt. The region's landscapes also retain their distinctive characteristics – from the wilds of north Norfolk to the rolling green tranquillity of Suffolk and the black flatlands of the Cambridgeshire fens.

Cambridge

Population: 130,000

Local dialling code: 01223

Tourist office: Cambridge Tourist Information Centre, Peas Hill; tel: 0871-226 8006; www.visit cambridge.org

Main police station: Parkside Police Station, Parkside; tel: 0345-456 4564

Main post office: 57–8 St Andrew's Street

Main hospital: Addenbrookes Hospital, Hills Road; tel: 01223-

245 151; www.cuh.org.uk

Media: *Cambridge Evening News*

Train station: Station Road; tel: 0845-600 7245; www.national rail.co.uk

Bus station: Drummer Street; tel: 0871-200 2233; www.stage coachbus.com

Car hire companies: Europcar; tel: 01223-365 438; www.europ car.co.uk

Taxi companies: tel: 01223-929 026; www.taxicambridge.co.uk

East Anglia, comprising the four counties of Cambridgeshire, Norfolk, Suffolk and Essex, bulges into the North Sea between the Thames estuary and the Wash. Interestingly, the region has the least annual rainfall in all of Britain. You may not have guessed this, however, since it is also a region of fens and rivers, of lakes, called meres or broads, and bird-filled coastal marshes. Few places rise higher than 300ft (90m) above sea level, yet the region has its own particular

beauty – an expansive landscape of farmland and big skies, as evoked by painter John Constable and composer Benjamin Britten.

Cambridgeshire

Cambridge ❶, which takes its name from the River Cam, was founded in the 12th century by a number of religious orders – though settlements had existed before. In 1209, a handful of scholars fled Oxford after a disagreement with the town authorities and settled in Cambridge; the first college, Peterhouse, was subseqently founded by the Bishop of Ely in 1284. Over the coming centuries other colleges would be founded by the church, gentry and a succession of monarchs.

The university town

At the heart of the university on King's Parade is **King's College**  (tel: 01223-331 212; www.kings.cam. ac.uk; termtime: Mon–Sat 9.30am– 3.30pm, Sun 1.15–2.30pm; out of term: Mon–Sat 9.30am–4.30pm, Sun 10am–5pm; charge), founded in 1441 by Henry VI. It is a worthwhile experience to stand in the ancient pews of its chapel – considered the glory of Cambridge – in order to listen to the voices of the famous choir float up to the magnificent fan-vaulted ceiling.

The Great Court at Trinity College is the largest university court in the world

Punting under Cambridge's iconic Bridge of Sighs

Next door is the **Senate House** (closed to the public), the university parliament, built by James Gibbs between 1722 and 1730, and now used for degree ceremonies. Next door to this, on the corner of Trinity Street, is **Gonville and Caius College**. Opposite, from the top of Great St Mary's Church, visitors enjoy spectacular views.

The beauty of Cambridge is its compactness; a few steps in any direction brings you a different encounter with history. In the gardens of **Christ's College** there is a tree said to have shaded the poet John Milton (1608–74) as he worked. The Great Court at **Trinity College** 🅑, is the largest university court in the world, but look closely at the figure of its founder, Henry VIII, above the gateway: instead of a sceptre he holds a chair leg. Further north is **St John's**, with its magnificent three-storey gatehouse. Behind it is the **Bridge of Sighs** 🅒, loosely modelled on its more famous namesake in Venice.

The best way to see many colleges is to hire a punt – either self-hire or

East Anglia

Imperial War Museum

Just to the south of Cambridge is the small village of Duxford and the location of Europe's biggest air museum, the **Imperial War Museum** (tel: 01223-837 000; www.duxford.iwm.org.uk; daily 10am–6pm in summer, until 4pm in winter; charge). As well as warplanes such as the Spitfire and Lancaster, it has a Concorde, naval helicopters and numerous tanks.

chauffered, gondolier-style – from the boatyard at the end of **Mill Lane** (see p.34–5). Drifting along the 'Backs' affords fine views of King's College Chapel, the Wren Library at Trinity and a succession of picturesque bridges.

Walking back in the other direction, Kings Parade eventually becomes

Trumpington Street, and the **Fitzwilliam Museum** **D** (tel: 01223-332 900; www.fitzmuseum.cam.ac.uk; Tue–Sat 10am–5pm, Sun noon–5pm; free) comes into view. It contains an extraordinary collection of art and antiquities. Beyond the Fitzwilliam the **Botanic Gardens** **E** (tel: 01223-336 265; www.botanic.cam.ac.uk; daily, Apr–Sept 10am–6pm, Feb, Mar, Oct until 5pm, Nov–Jan until 4pm; charge) make a haven for tired visitors.

The Fens

To the north of Cambridge are the Fens, an area of 2,000-sq-miles (5,200-sq-km) of marshland that was drained in the 17th century to provide rich arable land. A short drive north of Cambridge offers the chance to compare the old fens with the new. **Wicken Fen** (signposted off the A10) has been

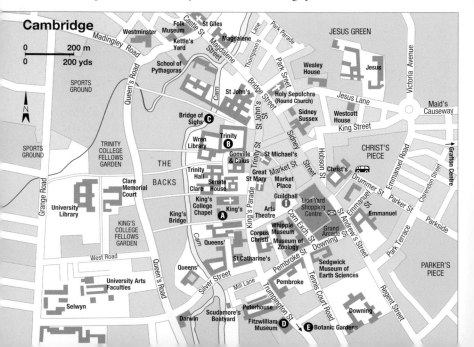

Beautiful stained glass windows at Ely Cathedral

Georgian streets (South Brink and North Brink) and the elegant **Peckover House** (tel: 01945-583 463; www.nationaltrust.org.uk; mid-Mar–Oct Sat–Wed 1–5pm, Apr Thur and Fri also; charge) illustrate the prosperity fen drainage brought.

Norfolk

In the 11th century, when the area was surveyed by the compilers of the Domesday Book, the counties of East Anglia were some of the richest and most highly populated in the country. Later, the region became a sanctuary from the power struggles that wracked the rest of the kingdom, and it was to Norfolk that many religious orders fled for peace. They left a legacy of over 600 churches, cathedrals and abbeys.

Norwich

Norwich ❹ was once the third-richest town in England, and was once said to have a church for every week of the year and a pub for every day. Within the old city walls 32 medieval churches still stand, and towering above them is the **Cathedral** (tel: 01603-218 300; www.cathedral.org.uk; daily 7.30am–6.30pm; charge), with its fine Cloisters Cathedral Close.

Norwich Castle, built by the Normans as a royal palace on Castle Meadow, is now home to the city's **Museum and Art Gallery** (tel: 01603-493 625; www.museums.norfolk.gov.uk; July–Sept Mon–Sat 10am–5pm, Sun 1–5pm, Oct–June Mon–Sat 10am–4.30pm, Sun 1–4.30pm; charge). It showcases the work of the Norwich School of Artists and Lowestoft Porcelain.

maintained as an undrained nature reserve. Its reed banks contrast with the black soil and drainage ditches of the surrounding fields.

A little further north still, and the low-lying expanse of the Fens is broken by the **Isle of Ely**. This knoll of solid land is dominated by **Ely ❷**. Its cathedral (tel: 01353-667 735; www.elycathedral.org; daily 7am–6.30pm, winter until 5.30pm on Sun; charge) is a spectacular Norman edifice, completed in 1351.

Beyond Ely, driving towards the Wash, is the market town of **Wisbech ❸**, which styles itself as the capital of the Fens. The two imposing

★ BIRDWATCHING

Compared to most countries, Britain started early with bird conservation. The Royal Society for the Protection of Birds (RSPB) was formed in 1889 – though it was originally known as the Plumage League, in protest against killing birds to use their feathers in ladies' hats. Since then, hundreds of bird reserves have been created all over the country, breeding programmes have reintroduced rare species, and birdwatching has become a national pastime.

One of the best parts of Britain for birdwatching – and one of the most accessible – is East Anglia. To the north of Cambridge are the Fens, where each winter, two massive drainage channels flood over on to grazing land and create what are known as the Ouse Washes. These marshy areas attract tens of thousands of wildfowl, including all three types of swan. They are also breeding grounds for such rareties as the ruff and the marsh harrier. Centuries ago, all the Fens used to consist of this type of habitat. The draining of most of the region to create farmland in the 17th century caused an ecological disaster. The RSPB (www.rspb.org.uk) and the Wildfowl & Wetlands Trust (www.wwt.org.uk) now manage what's left of the Fenland bogs as nature reserves.

The north Norfolk coast is lined with

Birds flock over the Wash

bird sanctuaries. Vast flocks of waders congregate on the mudflats of the Wash in winter, and when disturbed they wheel about in the air in spectacular swarms. RSPB **Snettisham** is a good place to see them. Meanwhile, reedbeds at Titchwell and Cley provide habitat for warblers and the elusive bittern. In winter, the meadows at Holkham are grazed by thousands of honking geese, great skeins of which fly in in V formations. All along the coast, rare migrants, often blown thousands of miles off course, find temporary sanctuary on the beaches and sand dunes.

A coot nesting with its colourful chicks in the Norfolk Broads

To the south, and inland, are the Norfolk Broads. Among their notable bird residents are the great cranes, probably Britain's rarest breeding species. The **Norfolk Wildlife Trust's Hickling Broad Reserve** (www.norfolk wildlifetrust.org.uk) and the area around Stubb Mill are good places to observe them.

The Suffolk coast also has its attractions for the birdwatcher. The salt marshes at Minsmere are famous for their population of avocets, and nearby Dunwich Heath harbours the Dartford warbler, nightjar and black redstart. Sections of the coast's shingle beaches are roped off in summer for nesting terns. Offshore, the RSPB's **Havergate Island** provides a haven for spoonbills, short-eared owls and spotted redshanks, while the National Trust's **Orford Ness** is renowned for its colonies of gulls and little terns. For both islands, boats leave from Orford Quay.

Birdwatching

Avocets are just one of many species of bird that can be viewed along the Suffolk coast

The city is an excellent place to shop, with Jarrold's department store, the old-fashioned market and the historic **Royal Arcade**, home to Colman's Mustard Shop, where customers can still buy mustard for their foot baths. Also notable are Elm Hill's antiques shops, and St Benedict's Street, lined with independent boutiques.

Today's wealthy grocers are no less munificent than those of yesteryear: in the 1970s a supermarket family commissioned Sir Norman Foster to design the **Sainsbury Centre for Visual Arts** (tel: 01603-593 199; www. scva.org.uk; Tue–Sun 10am–5pm; free), a short bus journey west of the city, on the University of East Anglia campus. Modern works by Francis Bacon and Giacometti are displayed alongside ancient artefacts.

The Norfolk Broads

Northeast of Norwich, the A1161 turns off to the village of Woodbastwick. As you approach it, the buzz of distant tractors fades, and and a pastoral silence prevails. This is the **Broads** ❺ (www.broads-authority.gov.uk). It's a big draw for birdwatchers, though its 200 miles (320km) of navigable waterways are also popular with dinghy sailors. Small cruisers offer tours of the meres and reedbeds, interspersed with church towers and windmills.

North Norfolk

On the north Norfolk coast **Cley-next-the-Sea** is no more than a mile from the shore, but the intervening salt marshes, reedbeds and lagoons attract a remarkable number of wading birds. Nearby **Blakeney Point** is home to common and grey seals that bask on the sands at low tide. Further west are the broad sands of Holkham Beach, and just inland is **Holkham Hall** (tel: 01328-710 227; www.holkham.co.uk;

Colman's Mustard Shop in Norwich

A traditional Punch and Judy show in Southwold

Apr–Oct Sun, Mon, Thur noon–4pm; charge), the neoclassical stately home of the Earl of Leicester.

A few miles to the east is **Wells-next-the-Sea** ❻ – a fishing port, where whelks, crabs and shrimps are deposited on the quay. A narrow-gauge steam railway runs from Wells to **Little Walsingham**, a place of pilgrimage once as important as Canterbury. In addition to the modern shrine, the village has an attractive medieval high street.

The heyday for holidaying in East Anglia was undoubtedly the Victorian era, when the Great Eastern Railway Company's network opened up a dozen resorts on the sunny coastline. A town that particularly retains its Victorian character is **Cromer** ❼, with its grand hotels and pier. This stretch of coastline is lashed by winter storms, and the seabed is strewn with shipwrecks. Even today, almost every village has its own lifeboat.

Suffolk

Suffolk, like Norfolk, is a county largely given over to arable farming, and is fringed with pretty fishing villages. Again, as with its northern neighbour, its sparse population and genteel tranquility belie a livelier past: the Stour Valley was once the hub of the wool trade, and the tiny village of Dunwich was one of Britain's biggest ports.

The coastal towns

The resort of **Southwold** ❽ was largely destroyed by fire in 1659 and later reconstructed in elegant style. The magnificent **Church of St Edmunds** features 'Southwold Jack', a medieval automaton in armour, which rings in the services by striking a bell with his sword. Other landmarks include

Southwold's **Lighthouse** (tel: 01502-726 097; www.southwoldmuseum.
org; tours May–Oct Sat, Sun 2–4pm; free), and the **pier**, reopened in 2001. Despite the dominance of tourism, Southwold has one of the few estuary ports still used by fishermen.

A few miles to the south is the village of **Dunwich** ❾. Back in Roman times this was a major port, and in succeeding centuries the town boasted eight churches. Now the sea has swept all that away. All that is left is a few cottages, the remains of a monastery and a tiny museum.

Further down the coast is **Aldeburgh** ❿, made famous by the composer Benjamin Britten (1913–76), who made this fishing town his home and established a music festival here in 1948 *(see p.14)*. The town has since become fashionable, though the shingle beach still retains its old

tar-soaked huts, where fishermen sell the early morning catch.

Eighteen miles (29km) southwest of Aldeburgh, at Melton, is the site of **Sutton Hoo** ⓫ (tel: 01394-389 700; www.nationaltrust.org.uk; Apr–Oct daily 10.30am–5pm, Nov–Feb Sat–Sun 11am–4pm, Mar Wed–Sun 10.30am–5pm; charge), an Anglo-Saxon royal burial site where ancient treasures were excavated in 1939. Many of the greatest finds are now in the British Museum *(see p.75)*.

Ten miles (16km) to the south-west is the Suffolk county town of **Ipswich**. It has little to recommend it apart from the Victorian docks, complete with lightship and sailing barges on the River Orwell. The Orwell estuary converges with the Stour estuary at its mouth around the North Sea ports of Harwich and Felixstowe.

A quaint Tudor building in Aldeburgh

Constable's *The Hay Wain* depicts the mill at Flatford

the church tower, never finished, are housed in a shed in the graveyard. His father was the mill owner at **Flatford**, just down the hill; it was immortalised in the painting *The Hay Wain*.

The village of **Dedham**, only a few miles upriver, and almost on the border with Essex, has changed little. The row of neoclassical houses that faces the church is pristine.

Constable country
Inland, the countryside along the Stour is known as Constable country (*see p.55*). The painter John Constable (1776–1837) was born in the village of **East Bergholt** ⑫, where the bells of

Lavenham, Bury St Edmunds
Further inland, the villages of Kersey, Hadleigh and Lavenham also remain unspoilt. These towns grew rich from the wool trade, and the fine 16th-century timbered houses that lean over the streets were built by local mill owners and merchants.

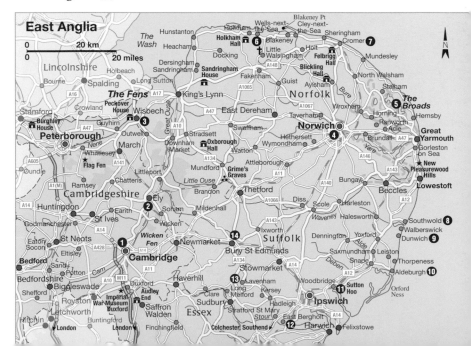

In the remarkably well-preserved village of **Lavenham** ⓭, visitors can see inside the **Little Hall** (tel: 01787-247 019; www.littlehall.org.uk; Apr–Oct Mon 11am–5.30pm, Wed, Thur, Sat, Sun 2–5.30pm; charge) and the **Guildhall** (tel: 01787-247 646; www.nationaltrust.org.uk; Mar Wed–Sun 11am–4pm, Apr–Oct daily 11am–5pm, Nov Sat–Sun 11am–4pm; charge). In the streets, telegraph poles have been removed and the wires buried underground to preserve the village's Tudor appearance.

By contrast, in the small cathedral city of **Bury St Edmunds** ⓮, to the north up the A134, the buildings are mostly of flint and brick. The ancient abbey and **cathedral** (tel: 01284-748 720; www.stedscathedral.co.uk; daily 8.30am–6pm; charge) are surrounded by formal gardens. On Cornhill, the **Moyse's Hall Museum** (tel: 01284-757 160; www.stedmundsbury.gov.uk; Mon–Sat 10am–5pm, Sun until 4pm; charge), built in 1180, is considered the oldest Norman house in East Anglia.

The ruins of the abbey and cathedral at Bury St Edmunds

ACCOMMODATION

While boutique hotels are probably the first choice in Cambridge and Norwich, historic country inns are your best bet in the countryside and on the coast. For more hotel options, visit the regional tourist board websites, www.visitcambridge.org, www.visitnorfolk.co.uk and www.visitsuffolk.com.

Accommodation price categories

Price categories are for a standard double room including breakfast and VAT (value added tax) during high season:

£ = under £80
££ = £80–150
£££ = £150–250
££££ = £250–350
£££££ = over £350

Cambridgeshire

The Varsity Hotel and Spa
Thompson's Lane, Off Bridge Street, Cambridge
Tel: 01223-306 030
www.thevarsityhotel.co.uk
This recently established hotel is by far the most stylish place for a kip while you're in Cambridge. Add in the rooftop garden with views over the colleges, the impressive restaurant, a beautifully designed spa and gym, and even complimentary guided walking tours and punting on the river, and you've got a compelling first choice. **£££**

Hotel du Vin & Bistro
15–19 Trumpington Street, Cambridge
Tel: 01223-227 330
www.hotelduvin.com
Located in the heart of town, just opposite the Fitzwilliam Museum, this elegant boutique hotel occupies a fine historic townhouse. The bistro is one of the best restaurants in Cambridge. **££–£££**

Norfolk

Dunston Hall
Ipswich Road, Norwich
Tel: 01508-470 444
www.devere.co.uk
This grand Elizabethan-style country house offers every facility you could wish for: spa, swimming pool, gym, golf course, bars and restaurants. What's more the prices are reasonable and children are welcome. **££**

Morston Hall
Morston, near Holt
Tel: 01263-741 041

www.morstonhall.com
For a comfortable stay and Michelin-starred cuisine, you can't do better than this flint manor house on the Norfolk coast. **£££**

Suffolk

The Angel
Market Place, Lavenham
Tel: 01787-247 388
www.maypolehotels.com/angelhotel
A 15th-century inn overlooking this old wool town's market place. The excellent restaurant uses only fresh local ingredients. **££**

The Crown
High Street, Southwold
Tel: 01502-722 275
www.adnams.co.uk
This old inn is owned by Adnams Brewery so you know the beer will be good. The rooms are comfortable rooms and the restaurant has a considerable reputation locally. **££**

The lush exterior of Morston Hall

147

Listings

RESTAURANTS

As a region famous for agriculture and edged with fishing towns on the North Sea, East Anglia offers plenty of treats for the epicure. Look out on menus for Cromer crabs, oysters from Brancaster, cockles from Leigh, asparagus in spring, strawberries in the summer, and pheasant during the shooting season. The region also has many good pubs –try beers brewed locally by Adnams, Greene King and Woodforde's.

The garden at Midsummer House

Cambridgeshire

Alimentum
152–4 Hills Road, Cambridge
Tel: 01223-413 000
Ethical values underpin this sleek venture – from being the first UK restaurant to serve humanely produced foie gras right down to the biodegradable cocktail straws. **££–£££**

Midsummer House
Midsummer Common, Cambridge
Tel: 01223-369 299
Chef Daniel Clifford serves elegant, modern European cuisine in the stylish surroundings of a walled Victorian house on the banks of the Cam. The only two-star Michelin restaurant in East Anglia. **£££**

Norfolk

Morston Hall
Morston, near Holt
Tel: 01263-741 041
Owned by Michelin-starred chef, Galton Blackiston, this fine restaurant champions local produce, from Blakeney lobster to Morston mussels. **£££–££££**

The Norfolk Riddle
2 Wells Road, Little Walsingham
Tel: 01328-821 903
With a daily menu of seasonal, local produce (including meat from its own farm shop) and very reasonable prices, this restaurant is hard to beat. **£–££**

Suffolk

The Golden Galleon Fish and Chip Shop
137 High Street, Aldeburgh
Tel: 01728-454 685
If you're prepared to queue, you'll be amply rewarded. Take your fish and chips down to the pebbly beach, or sit upstairs in the restaurant. **£**

Leaping Hare Vineyard Restaurant
Wyken Vineyards, Stanton, near Bury St Edmunds
Tel: 01359-250 287
An elegant restaurant on the edge of a country estate offers Californian-style locally sourced food, accompanied by wines from its own highly respected vineyard. **£–££**

ENTERTAINMENT AND NIGHTLIFE

East Anglia is blessed with an extraordinary range of venues for events and activities.

Cinema City
St Andrews & Blackfriars Hall,
St Andrews Street, Norwich
Tel: 0871-902 5724
www.picturehouses.co.uk
Housed in a gorgeous medieval friary
complex, this is an arts cinema with a
difference.

The Junction
Clifton Way, Cambridge
Tel: 01223-511 511
www.junction.co.uk
This funky venue hosts comedy, music gigs,
theatre, dance and club nights.

Theatre Royal
Westgate Street, Bury St Edmunds
Tel: 01284-769 505
www.theatreroyal.org
Run by the National Trust, this Regency
theatre offers classic and modern drama.

TOURS

Enjoy a tour around the region's picturesque townscapes, countryside and coast.

Beans Boat Trips
Morston Quay, Morston, Norfolk
Tel: 01263-740 505
www.beansboattrips.co.uk
See the seal colonies of the north Norfolk
coast with these year-round boat tours.

Cambridge Guided Tours
Peas Hill, Cambridge
Tel: 0871-226 8006
www.visitcambridge.org

For college, ghost, punting and museum
tours, book up with the local tourist office.

Electric Eel Boat Trip
How Hill National Nature Reserve,
Ludham, Norfolk
Tel: 01603-756 096
www.enjoythebroads.com
What better way to cruise the Norfolk Broads
than in this charming electric boat, which is
so quiet it doesn't disturb the wildlife.

FESTIVALS AND EVENTS

The region's cultural life is celebrated with numerous events throughout the year.

May
Norfolk and Norwich Festival
Various venues in Norwich
www.nnfestival.org.uk
Runs for two weeks, with classical music,
dance, circus, theatre and children's events.

June
Aldeburgh Festival
Snape Maltings Concert Hall, Snape, Suffolk

www.aldeburgh.co.uk
A classical music festival inaugurated in 1948
which still runs for two weeks every June.

July
Cambridge Folk Festival
Cherry Hinton Hall, Cambridge
www.cambridgefolkfestival.co.uk
This long-established event draws big
names in folk music from around the world.

Central England

Central England is a region of stark contrasts. While the Cotswolds and Shropshire, Lincolnshire and the Peak District remain remarkably untouched by the 21st century and offer the allure of a pastoral idyll, the cities of Birmingham and Coventry, Nottingham and Derby combine industrial history with all the attractions of modern metropolitanism.

Oxford

Population: 154,000

Local dialling code: 01865

Tourist office: 15–16 Broad Street; tel: 01865-252 200; www.visit oxfordandoxfordshire.com

Main police station: St Aldate's; tel: 0845-8505 5054

Main post office: 102–110 St Aldate's

Main hospital: John Radcliffe Hospital, Headley Way, Headington; tel: 01865-741 166; www.oxford radcliffe.nhs.uk

Media: *The Oxford Mail*

Train station: Park End Street; tel: 0845-700 0125; www.national rail.co.uk

Bus station: Gloucester Green; www. stagecoachbus.com

Car hire companies: Enterprise Rent-a-car; tel: 01865-202 088; www.enterprise.co.uk

Taxi companies: tel: 01865-240 000; www.001taxis.com

A good hopping-off point for exploring the southern and western parts of central England is Oxford, which is about one hour's drive (60 miles/95km) from both London and Birmingham. Oxford is an unspoilt university town, and a visit here can easily be combined with a tour of the Cotswold countryside to the west, or with a trip to Stratford-upon-Avon, Shakespeare's birthplace, to the north.

For the northern and eastern parts of the region, the city of Nottingham is as good a base as any. From there, day trips to the Peak District National Park or the cathedral city of Lincoln are easily manageable.

Oxford and the Cotswolds

Oxford ❶, the city of dreaming spires, is situated on the edge of the Cotswolds, a region of rolling hills, ancient manors and pretty villages built with honey-coloured stone.

A university city

A good starting point for a tour of Oxford is **Carfax Ⓐ**, the crossroads at the centre of the city. The views from the 14th-century tower on the northwest corner enable you to get your bearings. From Carfax, south along St Aldate's is **Christ Church** , the grandest of the university's colleges (tel: 01865-276 150; www. chch.ox.ac.uk; Mon–Sat 9am–5pm, Sun 2–5.30pm; charge). Founded by Cardinal Wolsey in 1525 on the site of an old priory, its chapel is also Oxford's **cathedral**, with one of the earliest spires in England and exquisite stained glass. The college encompasses the largest quadrangle in Oxford, an enormous **Hall** and a **Picture Gallery** displaying Renaissance paintings (Mon–Sat 10.30am–5pm, Sun 2–5pm).

The tower at Magdalen College is a major landmark

South of the college, extending down to the confluence of the Isis and Cherwell rivers, is bucolic **Christ Church Meadow**. Along the

Taking a stroll around the Radcliffe Camera

Isis are the college boathouses where races take place in the summer. To the northeast of the meadows is Oxford's **Botanic Garden** (tel: 01865-286 690; www.botanic-garden. ox.ac.uk; daily 9am–5pm, May–Aug until 6pm, Nov–Feb until 4.30pm; charge), which is accessed from the High Street.

Across the road is **Magdalen College** (tel: 01865-276 000; www. magd.ox.ac.uk; July–Sept noon–6pm, Oct–June 1–6pm or dusk if earlier; charge), with its landmark tower. The college has a fine Perpendicular-style chapel, picturesque cloisters, and behind them, Magdalen's deer park.

To the west along High Street are **University College** on the south side (with a memorial to the poet Shelley) and, on the north side, **All Souls** (tel: 01865-279 379; www.all-souls.ox.ac.uk; Mon–Fri 2–4pm; free), the only college with no undergraduates. Turning up Queen's Lane to the north, however, you pass **New College**, with its stunning chapel and cloisters, and walk beneath Oxford's **Bridge of Sighs**,

Central England

which connects the old and new buildings of **Hertford College**.

The lane finally emerges on to Catte Street, with the **Bodleian** and Wren's **Sheldonian Theatre** on the far side. The **Bodleian Library** ❸ (tel: 01865-277 162; www.bodley.ox.ac.uk; guided tours: Mon–Sat 10.30am, 11.30am, 2pm, 3pm; charge) is one of the world's largest libraries, with 11 million items on 117 miles (188km) of shelving, mostly underground. Also part of the library is the rotund **Radcliffe Camera** just to the south.

If you actually want to buy a book, **Blackwell's** on Broad Street, to the north, stocks 200,000 titles. Next door is Trinity College with its manicured lawns, and along again is **Balliol College**. A cross in the road outside indicates where the Protestant Martyrs, bishops Cranmer, Latimer and Ridley, were burnt at the stake in 1555 and 1556.

Around the corner at the top end of **St Giles**, they are further commemorated by the **Martyrs' Memorial**, erected in 1841. Around the corner on Beaumont Street is the oldest public museum in Britain, the **Ashmolean Museum** ❺ (tel: 01865-278 000; www.ashmolean.org; Tue–Sun 10am–6pm; free). It is particularly famous for its Renaissance paintings and Egyptian antiquities.

North along St Giles is **St John's College** (tel: 01865-277 300; www.sjc.ox.ac.uk; daily 1–5pm; free), the gardens of which were landscaped by 'Capability' Brown. Behind St John's, at the end of Museum Road, is the **Oxford University Museum** ❻ (tel: 01865-272 950; www.oum.ox.ac.uk; daily 10am–5pm; free),

Oxford

Blenheim Palace's grand exterior and grounds

housing the university's natural history collection.

Blenheim Palace

Eight miles (13km) northwest of Oxford on the A34 is **Blenheim Palace** ❷ (tel: 08700-602 080; www.blenheimpalace.com; mid-Feb–Oct daily 10.30am–5.30pm, Nov–mid-Dec Wed–Sun only; charge), located in the handsome village of Woodstock.

Britain's largest private house, covering 7 acres (2.8 hectares) including the courtyards, was designed by playwright and architect John Vanbrugh (1664–1726). It is famous as the birthplace of Winston Churchill in 1874, and several rooms inside are now devoted to Churchill memorabilia. When the house is closed in the winter, visitors can still enjoy the vast parkland, laid out by Britain's best-known landscape gardener, 'Capability' Brown (1716–83).

Cotswolds' villages

Shaking off the clay of Oxford's vale, the roads west climb gradually to the heights of the Cotswold hills, once made wealthy from the wool trade. The churchyard at **Burford** has tombs in the shape of wool bales and wool merchants' houses of the 14–16th century can often be found hiding behind later fronts.

To the south of Burford is **Kelmscott Manor** ❸ (tel: 01367-252 486; www.kelmscottmanor.co.uk; Apr–Sept Wed and Sat 11am–5pm; charge). William Morris took this typical Cotswold stone-built house with Dante Gabriel Rossetti in 1871, and it became a centre for the pre-Raphaelite movement. His body was carried from here to the churchyard in 1896.

Just across the river is **Buscot Park** (tel: 0845-3453 387; www.buscot-park.com; Apr–Sept Wed–Fri and 2nd and 4th Sat–Sun in month

2–6pm; charge). Lord Faringdon enlarged the Adam-style house in the late 19th century, engaging the pre-Raphaelite artist Edward Burne-Jones to paint panels for the saloon.

To the west on the A417 is **Fairford**. Its church, St Mary's, is renowned for its stained glass; the 'Last Judgment' is a masterpiece. To the north, up the River Coln, is the beautiful village of **Bibury ④**. The weavers' cottages of Arlington Row have gables and high-pitched roofs that are the very essence of the Cotswolds.

To the west, the Cirencester–Northleach road (A429) follows the route of the original Roman road, the Fosse Way. The woods below **Chedworth**, 5 miles (8km) north of Cirencester, shelter a well-preserved **Roman villa** (tel: 01242-890 256; www.nationaltrust.org.uk; Apr–Oct

Wed–Sun 10am–5pm, Mar until 4pm; charge), with mosaics made from local Cotswold stone.

The church tower at **Northleach ⑤**, 10 miles (16km) northeast of Cirencester, soars above the rooftops in the Perpendicular style. The wool merchants who built the church are memorialised in the fine 15th- and 16th-century brasses. In the town centre, **Keith Harding's World of Mechanical Music** (tel: 01451-860 181; www.mechanicalmusic. co.uk; daily 10am–5pm; charge) has antique musical boxes, gramophones and self-playing pianos.

Cirencester

Fosse Way leads south to join two other Roman roads, the Icknield Way and Ermin Street, in **Cirencester ⑥**, the unofficial capital of the

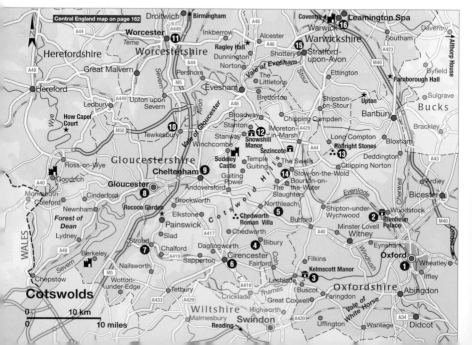

Gloucestershire

Northwest, beyond Tetbury, is **Stroud** ❼ where the country's cloth industry was concentrated in the 16th century. England's armies went to war in uniforms of scarlet and blue cloth from Stroudwater mills.

To the north is **Slad**, the village on which Laurie Lee based his novel *Cider With Rosie*. Lee was born and died here. His cottage and pub are still there, but the school has taught its last children. Further north still is **Painswick**, where the tradition of 'clipping' (meaning 'embracing') is still held every September when children join hands to encircle St Mary's Church.

The nearby county town of **Gloucester** ❽ is a cathedral city and inland port and has been a strategic centre guarding the route to Wales since Roman times. Of the Roman walls, vestiges remain; of the medieval town, very little. The **cathedral** (tel: 01452-528 095; www.gloucester cathedral.org.uk; daily 7.30am–6pm; charge) has the largest east window in England, while the old docks include the child-friendly **Gloucester Waterways Museum** (tel: 01452-

Cotswolds. Here, as well as a fine church, there is the **Corinium Museum** (tel: 01285-655 611; www. cirencester.co.uk; Apr–Oct Mon–Sat 10am–5pm, Sun 2–5pm, Nov–Mar until 4pm; charge) dedicated to the town's Roman past. Substantial remains of the town walls and amphitheatre survive.

Twelve miles (20km) southwest of Cirencester is **Malmesbury**. At the Dissolution of the Monasteries in the 1530s a rich clothier bought the town's abbey in a deal which allowed him to convert it into a weaving shed while the parishioners used the nave for services. The richly decorated porch gives an idea of the abbey's former glory.

Spa water

Cheltenham, with its graceful stuccoed terraces and squares, was once a fashionable spa town. Gentility reigns even today at the **Rotunda** and **Pittville Pump Room** (tel: 01242-521 621; www. cheltenhamtownhall.org.uk; Wed–Sun 10am–4pm; charge) where the mineral waters can still be tasted.

🚗 COTSWOLDS DRIVE

Tetbury, with its royal connections and individual shops, is a good base for car journeys exploring the south Cotswolds, with its pretty villages, narrow country lanes and panoramic views.

Tetbury

In the centre of **Tetbury** is the Market House, dating from 1655, and nearby, the Georgian-Gothic church. Long Street, with its antiques shops, has a **Police Museum** (tel: 01666-504 670; www. visittetbury.co.uk; Mon–Fri 10am–3pm; free), displaying relics of law enforcement in the old cells and courtroom.

Heading southwest on the A433, you pass Prince Charles' home, **Highgrove House** *(see p.23)*, and two miles (3km) further on is **Westonbirt National Arboretum** (tel: 01666-880 220;

(see p.23)

Shopping in Tetbury

www.westonbirtarboretum.com; daily Apr–Nov 9am–8pm or dusk if earlier, Dec–Mar until 5pm; charge), originally planted out in 1829 by the local squire.

Continuing southwest, you pass through the village of Didmarton and on past **Badminton Park**. The domed Palladian **Worcester Lodge** at the entrance is all you will see unless you are here for the horse trials in May.

Just after the A433 joins the A46, take a right turn up France Lane to Hawkesbury Upton and carry on straight through up to Hillseley and Alderley. You will pass the **Somerset Monument**, commemorating General Lord Somerset, who served under Wellington at Waterloo.

Newark Park

Beyond Alderley, a right turn leads along Ozleworth Bottom to the gates of Ozleworth Park. Continue uphill from Ozleworth and take the sharp left to **Newark Park** (tel: 01793-817 666; www. nationaltrust.org.uk; June–Oct Wed–Thur, Sat–Sun 11am–5pm, Mar–May Wed–Thur only; charge). Built as a hunting lodge in 1540, it was remodelled in 1790 with Adam-style interiors.

On leaving, turn left, then left again for Wotton-under-Edge, a bustling former mill town, and onwards via the B4060 to North Nibley. A footpath here leads up through beech woods to the **Tyndale Monument** on Nibley Knoll.

Tips

- **Distance:** 52 miles (84km)
- **Time:** A full day
- **Start/End:** Tetbury

Dedicated to William Tyndale, who was burned at the stake in 1536 for the heresy of translating the Bible into English, the tower offers panoramic views.

Hidden valleys

When you reach the junction with the A4135, continue on to the centre of Dursley, and take the B4066 east to Uley, a former mill village once famous for its blue cloth. From the village green take a detour to the east into the Owlpen Valley to find the 15th-century **Owlpen Manor** (tel: 01453-860 261; www.owlpen.com; reopening in 2012 after restoration; charge). Inside there is Cotswold Arts and Crafts furniture, while outside are 18th-century gardens.

Back in Uley, the steep road out of the village leads to **Uley Bury Iron Age Hillfort**, with extensive views from the summit, and to the north, **Hetty Pegler's Tump**, a neolithic long barrow dating back to 3000BC.

Opposite Coaley Peak is the turning for Woodchester Park (tel: 01452-814 213; daily 9am–dusk; charge) in a hidden valley noted for rare orchids. About 2 miles (1.5km) along stands **Woodchester Mansion** (tel: 01453-861 541; www.woodchestermansion.org. uk; Apr–Oct 11am–5pm, opening days vary; charge), a Pugin-designed house that was left unfinished when the builders were taken off to work on another project. They left their tools behind, expecting to return, but never did, and the house remains frozen in time.

From Woodchester Park, return to Tetbury via Nympsfield, then follow signs to Kingscote to join the A4135; turn left and follow the road back to Tetbury.

Owlpen Manor surrounded by trees

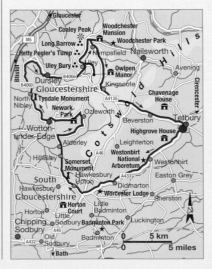

Picturesque cottages in Broadway

318 200; www.gloucesterwaterways
museum.org.uk; daily 11am–4pm,
July–Aug until 5pm; charge).

Northeast of Gloucester is **Cheltenham** ❾ (*see box, p.155*).

Cotswold limits

The Cotswolds's western limit is 10
miles (16km) north at **Tewkesbury** ❿,
where the Avon joins the Severn and
stone gives way to attractive timbered
cottages. In 1471 the Battle of Bloody
Meadow, often regarded as the last of
the Wars of the Roses, was fought here,
spilling over into the Abbey itself.

Twelve miles (20km) northwest
of Tewkesbury is **Great Malvern**,
where the hills offer views over 10
counties, and further north still
is **Worcester** ⓫, home to a 12th-
century **cathedral** (tel: 01905-732
900; www.worcestercathedral.co.uk;
daily 7.30am–6pm; free) and the
Worcester Porcelain Museum (tel:
01905-21247; www.worcesterpor-
celainmuseum.org.uk; Easter–Oct
Mon–Sat 10am–5pm, Nov–Easter
Tue–Sat 10.30am–4pm; charge).

Travelling southeast of Worcester
via the Vale of Evesham is the village
of **Broadway**, where cottages face one
another across the extensive village
green. **Broadway Tower** (tel: 01386-
852 390; www.broadwaytower.co.uk;
Apr–Oct daily 10.30am–5pm; charge)
sits on an escarpment above.

In a valley southwest of Broadway is
Snowshill Manor ⓬ (tel: 01386-852
410; www.nationaltrust.org.uk; Apr–
June and Sept–Oct Wed–Sun noon–
5pm, July–Aug 11.30am–4.30pm;
charge), a Tudor mansion housing
an eclectic collection, from musical
instruments to toys. A little further
southwest still is **Sudeley Castle** (tel:
01242-604 244; www.sudeleycastle.
co.uk; Apr–Oct daily 10.30am–5pm;
charge), a stately home with particularly fine paintings.

Secret valleys

Southeast of Broadway on the A44
is **Moreton-in-Marsh**, which every
Tuesday hosts a large open-air
market. Nearby is **Sezincote** (tel:
01386-700 444; www.sezincote.co.uk;

May–Sept Thur–Fri 2.30–5.30pm; charge), a mansion in the Indian style, which gave the Prince Regent his ideas for Brighton Pavilion.

To the east is the town of **Chipping Norton**, and just to its northwest are the **Rollright Stones** ⑬ (www.rollrightstones.co.uk; site open all year), a large circle of 70 Bronze Age standing stones known as the King's Men, a smaller group called the five Whispering Knights and a lone menhir, the King. According to legend, a local witch turned the king and his knights to stone.

The hill town of **Stow-on-the-Wold** ⑭, 4 miles (6km) south of Moreton-in-Marsh, was once the scene of great sheep fairs. Writer Daniel Defoe recorded as many as 20,000 sheep being sold on one occasion. To the west of the town are the villages of Upper Swell and Lower Swell, and just below are Upper Slaughter and Lower Slaughter, with fords on the tiny Slaughterbrook. Nearby is **Bourton-on-the-Water**, one of the best of the Cotswold stone villages, with miniature footbridges over streams and under willow trees, sweet smells in the perfumery, a motor museum in a barley mill, a model railway and a model village.

The West Midlands

Situated right in the middle of the country, the cities of Birmingham and Coventry, and the rather more beautiful towns of Stratford and Warwick offer history and culture as well as hustle and bustle.

Stratford-upon-Avon

At the northeastern end of the Vale of Evesham is **Stratford-upon-Avon** ⑮,

Resting on one of the bridges in Bourton-on-the-Water

the hometown of Britain's greatest playwright, William Shakespeare. He was born here in Henley Street on 23 April 1564. He was christened in the local **Holy Trinity Church** *(see also p.39)* and went to the local school; at 18 he married 26-year-old Anne Hathaway and they had three children. In 1597, after his extraordinary career in London, he bought New Place in Chapel Street to where he retired. He died on his 52nd birthday and is buried at Holy Trinity.

Shakespeare's Birthplace (tel: 01789-204 016; www.shakespeare. org.uk; daily Apr–May and Sept–Oct 9am–5pm, June–Aug 9am–6pm, Nov–Mar 10am–4pm; charge) is the starting point for a tour of the town. Shakespeare's granddaughter married Thomas Nash in 1626, and they lived in **Nash's House** (contact details as for Birthplace; Apr–Jun and Sept–Oct 10am–5pm, July–Aug 10am–6pm, Nov–Mar 11am–4pm; charge) on Chapel Street, next door to New Place, of which only the foundations remain, preserved in a delightful, Elizabethan-style garden. Between Shakespeare's birthplace and Nash's House is **Harvard House** (tel: 01789-204 507; www.stratford-upon-avon.co.uk; Tue–Sat 10am–4pm, Sun 10.30am– 4.30pm; charge). Built in 1596, this was the home of Katherine Rogers, whose son, John Harvard, funded the famous American university. It now houses the Museum of British Pewter.

The living legacy of the playwright can be found at the **Royal** **Shakespeare Theatre** *(see p.39)*, where a remodelled auditorium includes a thrust-stage; the smaller, galleried Swan Theatre was also reopened after renovation in 2011, and the Royal Shakespeare Company's third theatre is The Other Place.

Midlands towns and cities

Eight miles (13km) north of Stratford, is **Warwick** ⑯. It is home to **Warwick Castle** (tel: 01926-495 421; www.warwick-castle.co.uk; daily Apr–Oct 10am–6pm, Nov–Mar 10am–5pm; charge), England's finest medieval castle. By Warwick's West Gate is the **Lord Leycester Hospital** (tel: 01926-491 422; www.lord leycester.com; Tue–Sun 10am–5pm, winter until 4.30pm; charge),

Warwick Castle, one of Britain's finest medieval fortifications

A sculpture in Coventry Cathedral

founded as a guildhall in 1383, though later renovated as almshouses. Today, the hospital is a museum and the home of ex-servicemen.

A few miles further north is **Coventry** ⑰, once a fine medieval city, though flattened by bombing in World War II. Next to the ruined shell of the old Gothic cathedral, a new **cathedral** (tel: 02476-521 200; www.coventry cathedral.org.uk; Mon–Sat 9am–5pm, Sun noon–3.45pm; charge) was completed in 1962. Nearby, the **Herbert Art Gallery and Museum** (tel: 02476-832 386; www.theherbert.org; Mon–Sat 10am–5.30pm, Sunday 2–5pm; free) houses collections of natural history, social history and paintings.

To the west of Coventry is the city of **Birmingham** ⑱, a manufacturing centre long before the Industrial Revolution of the late 18th century. At the centre is **Victoria Square**, flanked by the classical **Town Hall**, modelled on the Temple of Castor and Pollux in Rome. Around the side of the massive Council House is the **Museum and Art Gallery** (tel: 0121-303 1966; www.bmag.org.uk; Mon–Sat 10am–5pm, Sun 12.30–5pm; free), which has a matchless collection of pre-Raphaelite paintings. A short walk to the west brings you to the new canalside complex, which includes **Symphony Hall** (see p.169) and the **National Sea Life Centre** (tel: 0871-423 2110; www.visitsealife.com; daily Mon–Fri 10am–5pm, Sat–Sun until 6pm; charge).

To the west of Birmingham is the county of Shropshire. The M54 takes you straight to **Telford** ⑲, a new town built in the 1960s but named after the 18th-century engineer Thomas Telford, who was closely associated with the Industrial Revolution, which began in Coalbrookdale just to

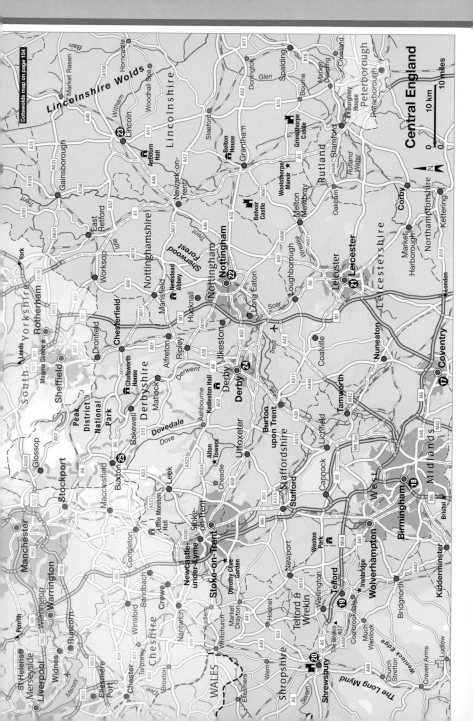

Ironbridge Gorge

Situated on the River Severn in the heart of Shropshire, the **Ironbridge Gorge** is named after the world's first ever cast-iron bridge, constructed over the river in 1779. The Coalbrookdale area had been a centre of mining and ironworking since the time of Henry VIII, but the pioneering use of a furnace to smelt iron with coke made from local coal turned the area into the busiest industrial centre in the world. Today, there are numerous museums around Ironbridge Gorge. The most popular is the **Blists Hill Open Air Museum** (tel: 01952-433 424; www. ironbridge.org.uk; daily 10am–5pm; charge), where a working Victorian town has been created around the original furnaces, foundry and brick works.

the south. Beyond Telford, the motorway becomes the A5 as it approaches the county town of **Shrewsbury** ⑳. The town is notable for its 15th-century houses, fine parks and the sandstone castle which was converted into a house by Telford and now incorporates the **Shropshire Regimental Museum** (tel: 01743-358 516; www. shrewsburymuseums.com; mid-Feb–mid-Dec 10.30am–4pm, closed Thur and Sun; charge).

The East Midlands and the Peak District

The East Midlands includes Leicestershire, Nottinghamshire and Derbyshire. To the east is the farming county of Lincolnshire, while to the north, like a vast rockery garden, is the Peak District National Park, which offers opportunities for walkers, rock climbers and pot holers.

Leicester and Nottingham

Like Birmingham and Coventry to the west, the city of **Leicester** ㉑ was heavily bombed during World War II and largely rebuilt in the 1960s. About the same time, its textile industry attracted large numbers of immigrants from the Indian Subcontinent, who have since made the city one of the most vibrant and cosmopolitan in the region. Vestiges of the city's medieval past remain, with a fine **Guildhall** (tel: 0116-253 2569; charge), the ruins of Leicester Castle, and the **cathedral** (tel: 0116-261 5200; www.cathedral. leicester.anglican.org; Mon–Sat 8am–6pm, Sun 7am–5pm; charge).

Continuing further north, you come to **Nottingham** ㉒, which until the 20th century was world-renowned for its lace making industry. The

Ironbridge

historic Lace Market district has been revamped in recent years, with shops, restaurants and now also **Nottingham Contemporary** (tel: 0115-948 9750; www.nottinghamcontemporary.org; Tue–Fri 10am–7pm, Sat 10am–6pm, Sun 11am–5pm; charge), a stylishly designed art gallery.

Lincolnshire

To the east of Nottingham is the vast county of Lincolnshire, devoted largely to agriculture, and quite sparsely populated. Its county town, **Lincoln** ㉓, has a magnificent **cathedral** (tel: 01522-561 600; www.lincolncathedral.com; daily 7.15am–6pm, July–Aug Sat–Sun until 8pm; donation) built in a mixture of Norman and Perpendicular styles. Its archives hold one of only four surviving copies of the Magna Carta of 1215. Some 47 miles (76km) south of Lincoln is the pretty market town of **Stamford**, with stone-built houses and a 13th-century church clustered around the River Welland. On the outskirts of town is one of Britain's finest Elizabethan stately homes, **Burghley House** (tel: 01780-752 451; www.burghley.co.uk; mid-Mar–Oct Sat–Thur 11am–4.30pm; charge). Its grounds incorporate mazes, fountains, a sculpture garden, and a large deer park.

South of Lincolnshire is **Rutland**, England's smallest county (in terms of population). Highlights include its attractive county town of **Oakham**, and **Rutland Water** nature reserve (www.rutlandwater.org.uk).

Derbyshire

To the west of Nottingham is the city of **Derby** ㉔, once a major industrial centre producing everything from porcelain to Rolls-Royces. Highlights

The elegantly landscaped grounds of Burghley House

The Peak District

From Ashbourne, take the A515 north into the **Peak District National Park**, and continue on through Dovedale. Sheep populate these dales, and sheepdog trials are popular summer distractions. Eventually, the A515 comes to the elegant spa town of **Buxton 25**. At the end of the 18th century, the Duke of Devonshire built a grand crescent here, intending to outshine Bath. Although his aim wasn't quite achieved, visitors flock to the spa-water pool at the Pavilion Gardens. Opera lovers flock here too in July, when Buxton Festival (*see p.171*) is held at the **Opera House**.

East of Buxton on the A6 is **Bakewell**, a stone-built town with two medieval bridges over the Wye and famed for its 'puddings' (a tart with a layer of jam and an almond topping). Two of the town's iron-rich wells survive and a colourful well dressing ceremony is held in June.

in the city centre include the **cathedral** (tel: 01332-341 201; www.derby cathedral.org; daily 8am–6pm; donation), notable for its fine 'Bakewell' wrought iron screen, and the **Derby Museum and Art Gallery** (tel: 01332-641 901; www.derby.gov.uk; Tue–Sat 10am–5pm, Sun 1–4pm; free), which contains important paintings by 18th-century local artist Joseph Wright, Derby porcelain and even Egyptian mummies.

The A52 leads northwest of Derby to **Ashbourne**. This pretty little town has a 16th-century school, 17th-century almshouse, a fine parish church and a gingerbread shop. Noisier attractions are on offer a few miles to the west at **Alton Towers**, a huge theme park with white-knuckle rides (tel: 0871-222 3330; www.altontowers.com; Easter–Oct daily 10am–5pm, later at weekends and until 9pm in summer; charge).

> ### Chatsworth House
>
> Known as 'the Palace of the Peak', **Chatsworth House** (tel: 01246-565 300; www.chatsworth.org; daily 11am–5.30pm; charge) is located to the east of Bakewell, off the A619. This vast Palladian mansion was built between 1687 and 1707 and set in a deer park with gardens landscaped by 'Capability' Brown. The seat of the Duke and Duchess of Devonshire, it contains priceless paintings, furniture and books.

ACCOMMODATION

Visitors to the Cotswolds and the Peak District are spoilt for choice, as almost every town seems to have a venerable old inn or country house hotel. In the cities, the new breed of boutique hotels has taken hold, raising the standards of hospitality enormously.

166

Central England

Accommodation price categories

Price categories are for a standard double room including breakfast and VAT (value added tax) during high season:

£ = under £80
££ = £80–150
£££ = £150–250
££££ = £250–350
£££££ = over £350

Oxford and the Cotswolds

Grapevine Hotel
Sheep Street, Stow-on-the-Wold
Tel: 01451-830 344
www.vines.co.uk
Welcoming hotel in a 17th-century stone building, named after the old vine that shades the conservatory restaurant. **££**

Lords of the Manor
Upper Slaughter, near Bourton-on-the-Water
Tel: 01451-820 243
www.lordsofthemanor.com
This 16th-century former rectory is set in the rolling Cotswold countryside. Many rooms have parkland and lake views. The restaurant is Michelin starred. **£££–££££**

Le Manoir aux Quat'Saisons
Church Road, Great Milton
Tel: 01844-278 881
www.manoir.com
Raymond Blanc's glorious manor house offers the ultimate hotel experience, with elegant and stylish bedrooms, beauty treatments and, of course, his two Michelin-starred restaurant. **£££**

Malmaison
3 Oxford Castle, Oxford
Tel: 01865-268 400
www.malmaison-oxford.com
Occupying the former prison – with each room consisting of three cells knocked into one – this stylish boutique hotel offers luxuries its one-time residents could only have dreamed of. The brasserie is one of Oxford's best restaurants. **££**

The West Midlands

Alveston Manor
Clopton Bridge, Stratford-upon-Avon
Tel: 0844-879 9138
www.macdonaldhotels.co.uk
This 16th-century half-timbered manor on the far bank of the Avon from the Royal Shakespeare Theatre is believed to have been the location of the first performance of *A Midsummer Night's Dream*. **££**

Hotel du Vin
25 Church Street, Birmingham
Tel: 0121-200 0600
www.hotelduvin.com
Occupying a red-brick Victorian hospital, this stylish boutique hotel is generally held to be Birmingham's best hotel. It offers a smart bistro, a spa, gym, billiards room and popular bar. **££**

The Lion
Wyle Cop, Shrewsbury
Tel: 01743-353 107
www.thelionhotelshrewsbury.co.uk

Le Manoir aux Quat'Saisons

Fine dining at the Hotel du Vin

This beamed 16th-century inn in the centre of medieval Shrewsbury has bags of character and a top-notch restaurant. **££**

The East Midlands and the Peak District
The George
71 St Martins, Stamford
Tel: 01780-750 750

www.georgehotelofstamford.com
This old coaching inn is something of an institution in Stamford. It offers homely comforts and hearty food. **££**

Hart's Hotel
Standard Hill, Park Row, Nottingham
Tel: 0115-988 1900
www.hartsnottingham.co.uk
The clean, modern styling of this smart hotel gives it a light and calm atmosphere. In addition to the gym and chic bar, the hotel also benefits from probably Nottingham's finest restaurant. **££–£££**

Old Hall Hotel
The Square, Buxton
Tel: 01298-22841
www.oldhallhotelbuxton.co.uk
A landmark since the 16th century, this dignified hotel is the top choice for Buxton. Rooms overlook Pavilion Gardens and the Opera House is nearby. **££**

RESTAURANTS

The renaissance in British food culture in recent decades has given rise to a style of cuisine that combines the best British ingredients with French cooking techniques. This region boasts many outstanding exponents of this food philosophy, who have quite rightly been recognised with the highest culinary awards.

Restaurant price categories
Prices are for a two-course dinner per person with a glass of house wine.

£ = under £20
££ = £20–30
£££ = £30–50
££££ = over £50

Oxford and the Cotswolds
Bearlands Restaurant and Wine Bar
Bearlands House, Longsmith Street, Gloucester
Tel: 01452-419 966
In a candlelit vaulted cellar dating back to 1740, you will find traditional and contemporary dishes like pan-fried pigeon breast with pancetta and chicken roulade with spinach, wrapped in Parma ham. **££**

Le Champignon Sauvage
24–26 Suffolk Road, Cheltenham
Tel: 01242-573 449
www.lechampignonsauvage.co.uk
David Everitt-Matthias is the chef at this highly acclaimed, two Michelin-starred restaurant. The inventive menu is modern European in style, using locally sourced ingredients such as Gloucester Old Spot pork. **££–£££**

Chiang Mai Kitchen
130a High Street, Oxford
Tel: 01865 202 233
www.chiangmaikitchen.co.uk

Delicious fare at Gee's Restaurant

Stylish and authentic Thai cuisine is served in a beautifully preserved Tudor building. **££**

The Feathers
Market Street, Woodstock
Tel: 01993-812 291
www.feathers.co.uk
The Feathers hotel has won awards for its food. Sunday lunch in the 17th-century panelled dining room is a grand affair, but there is a more informal bistro for lighter meals. **£££**

Gee's Restaurant
61 Banbury Road, Oxford
Tel: 01865-553 540
www.gees-restaurant.co.uk
One of Oxford's most atmospheric restaurants is located within a former flower glasshouse. The food is modern British and relies on top quality seasonal produce, much of it from the owner's Oxfordshire farm. Live jazz on Sunday evenings. **£££**

The West Midlands
Loves Restaurant
The Glasshouse, Canal Square, Browning Street, Birmingham
Tel: 0121-4544 141
www.loves-restaurant.co.uk
Award-winning chef Steve Love offers simple, but accomplished, French-inspired dishes using the freshest ingredients at this stylish restaurant near Brindley Place. **££–£££**

Robbie's Restaurant
74 Smith Street, Warwick
Tel: 01926-400 470
www.robbiesrestaurant.co.uk
This smart bistro in the centre of Warwick combines modern British cooking with an impressive wine list. **££**

The East Midlands and the Peak District
Fischer's at Baslow Hall
Calver Road, Baslow
Tel: 01246-583 259
www.fischers-baslowhall.co.uk
This is an outstanding Michelin-starred restaurant serving traditional British food. Local produce might include Derbyshire spring lamb, wild hare and Chatsworth venison. **£££**

Hambleton Hall
Hambleton, near Oakham
Tel: 01572-756 991
www.hambletonhall.com
Elegant dining room serving modern British cuisine by Michelin-starred chef Aaron Patterson in a gorgeous country house hotel right on the edge of Rutland Water. A great way to 'lunch for less'. Reserve. **£££**

Hart's
Standard Hill, Park Row, Nottingham
Tel: 0115-988 1900
www.hartnottingham.co.uk
Innovative modern British dishes made from superb ingredients are served in this contemporary-styled restaurant. Remarkable value given the quality of the cooking. **££**

MemSaab
59 Highcross Street, Leicester
Tel: 0116-253 243
www.mem-saableics.com
Leicester is renowned for its Indian restaurants, of which this is one of the best. Located within the Highcross shopping centre, it has airy contemporary décor (no flock wallpaper), and the cooking puts the emphasis on fresh ingredients, natural flavours and beautiful presentation. **££**

NIGHTLIFE AND ENTERTAINMENT

Stratford is famous for its theatres, Birmingham for its symphony orchestra, Oxford has the oldest concert hall in Europe and Nottingham has some rocking nightspots.

Nightclubs

Air
Heath Mill Lane, Birmingham
Tel: 0121-766 6646
www.airbirmingham.com
This superclub attracts big-name DJs.

Rock City
8 Talbot Street, Nottingham
Tel: 0845-413 4444
www.rock-city.co.uk
Huge music venue for everything from heavy metal to indie. Within the same vicinity as Stealth and the Rescue Rooms nightclubs.

Superfly
2 King Street, Leicester
Tel: 0116-254 1638
www.superfly-city.com
Four floors of throbbing recorded music, with some live music acts too.

Film

Broadway Cinema
14–18 Broad Street, Nottingham
Tel: 0115-952 6611
www.broadway.org.uk
This arts cinema shows the latest releases and also organises three festivals each year – on screenwriting, horror films and shorts.

Electric Cinema
47–9 Station Street, Birmingham
Tel: 0121-643 7879
www.theelectric.co.uk
Supposedly the oldest working cinema in the UK, this arthouse cinema is a delightfully retro affair.

Theatre

Oxford Playhouse
11–12 Beaumont Street, Oxford
Tel: 01865-305 305
www.oxfordplayhouse.com
The city's main theatre also has an offshoot round the corner – the Burton-Taylor Studio – which stages many of the best student productions.

Nottingham Playhouse
Wellington Circus, Nottingham
Tel: 0115-941 9419
www.nottinghamplayhouse.co.uk
Stages a high-quality mixture of drama, comedy, dance, and some excellent children's shows too.

Royal Shakespeare Theatre
Stratford-upon-Avon
Tel: 0844-800 1110
www.rsc.org.uk
The home of the Royal Shakespeare Company has three theatres: in addition to the main theatre, there is the Swan Theatre on Waterside and the Courtyard Theatre on Southern Lane.

Music

Holywell Music Room
Holywell Street, Oxford
Tel: 01865-276 133
www.music.ox.ac.uk
The oldest purpose-built concert hall in Europe is a lovely venue for chamber music.

02 Academy Oxford
190 Cowley Road, Oxford
Tel: 0844-477 2000
www.o2academyoxford.co.uk
Oxford's premier venue for touring bands, with an emphasis on indie music.

Symphony Hall
Broad Street, Birmingham
Tel: 0121-780 3333
www.thsh.co.uk
The home of the City of Birmingham Symphony Orchestra is one of the finest concert halls in the country, boasting excellent acoustics.

Listings

SPORTS AND ACTIVITIES

The region's natural assets lend themselves to various activities, from gliding down the canal on a narrowboat to trekking across the Oxford countryside on horseback.

Capital Sport Cycling Tours
The Red House, Aston Clinton
Tel: 01296-631 671
www.capital-sport.co.uk/gentle-cycling
Guided cycle rides of Oxford take place Sunday mornings from May and throughout the summer. Cycle hire is included, and children are welcome.

College Cruisers Narrow Boats
Combe Road Wharf, Oxford
Tel: 01865-554 343
www.collegecruisers.com
Offers 2- to 12-berth canal boats for short breaks and longer holidays.

Footpath Holidays
Tel: 01985-840 049
www.footpath-holidays.com
This company runs walking vacations, and can also tailor trips to a theme (eg. literary, historical).

Standlake Equestrian Centre and Ranch
Downs Road, Standlake, near Oxford
Tel: 01865-300 099
www.standlakeranch.co.uk
In addition to riding lessons, this centre offers residential 'Ranch Riding' holidays and family ranch holidays in self-catering chalets.

TOURS

There's no better way to see the rolling country of the Cotswolds or the dreaming spires of Oxford than from a hot-air balloon or a light aircraft. But for those who don't have a head for heights, there are also plenty of tours by bus, boat or on foot.

Avon Air Centre
Loxley Lane, Wellesbourne Airfield, Wellesbourne
Tel: 01926-678 093
www.avonaircentre.com
This centre offers pleasure flights over Stratford and the Cotswolds in Cessna aircraft.

City Sightseeing Stratford Tours
Avenue Farm Road, Stratford-upon-Avon
Tel: 01789-412 680
www.citysightseeing-stratford.com
Hop-on-hop-off open-top bus tours of Stratford make regular departures from the tourist information centre.

Oxford Balloon Company
97 Whitecross, Wootton, Abingdon
Tel: 01235-537 429
www.oxfordballoon.com

Morning and evening flights in summer offer an extraordinary opportunity to see Oxford and the surrounding countryside from a different angle.

Oxford Water Walks
12 Hythe Bridge Arm, Oxford Canal, Oxford
Tel: 01865-798 254
www.oxfordwaterwalks.co.uk
Group walks along the towpaths of Oxford's waterways, guided by a local historian and narrowboat resident, offer an insight into the non-university side of the city.

Rutland Belle
Rutland Water, Oakham
Tel: 01572-787 630
www.rutlandwatercruises.com
Cruise from Whitwell to Normanton on the southern shore of Rutland Water most afternoons between April and October.

FESTIVALS AND EVENTS

In addition to music festivals and sporting events, some parts of the region still celebrate bizarre traditions that have their origins in folklore. The people of Tetbury run up a hill carrying a bale of wool, while the inhabitants of Ashbourne organise a football match on an epic scale.

February
Four-Four Time Festival
Buxton Opera House and Pavilion Arts Centre
www.buxtonoperahouse.org.uk
This mid-February festival of live music showcases rock, pop, folk, blues, jazz and world music.

February/March
Royal Shrovetide Football Match
Ashbourne
www.ashbourne-town.com
Three hundred players a side try to score goals by touching the walls of Sturston Mill and Clifton Mill, 3 miles (5km) apart, every year on Shrove Tuesday and Ash Wednesday.

May
Badminton Horse Trials
Badminton, Gloucestershire
www.badminton-horse.co.uk
This prestigious equestrian event is held in the beautiful setting of the Badminton Estate in early May.

June
Woolsack Race
Gumstool Hill, Tetbury
www.tetburywoolsack.co.uk
Early June (the Monday after Whitsun) sees contestants run up a hill carrying a bale of wool – a race that probably started as a trial of strength between young farmers, designed to impress local girls.

July
Buxton Festival
Various venues in Buxton
www.buxtonfestival.co.uk
For three weeks in mid-July, operas are staged in the Opera House and literary events at other venues around town.

October
Goose Fair
Forest Recreation Ground, Nottingham
www.nottinghamcity.gov.uk
This four-day event early in October has graduated over the centuries – once a goose market, it is now a funfair of exhilarating rides.

October/November
Diwali
Belgrave Road, Leicester
www.leicester.gov.uk
This is the biggest celebration of the Hindu Festival of Lights outside India, and is celebrated with the switching on of decorative lights, and fireworks.

Take in the Oxfordshire countryside from a hot air balloon

Wales and the Borders

Traditionally, Wales is a land of green hills and welcoming valleys, of Welsh Cakes, crumbling castles, poets and song. It is less populous than England, though its accessibility from southern, central and northern parts of the country also make it a very popular holiday haunt.

Cardiff

Population: 340,000

Local dialling code: 02920

Tourist office: Old Library, The Hayes; tel: 02920-873 573; www.visitcardiff.com

Main police station: King Edward VII Avenue; tel: 02920-222 111

Main post office: 2–4 Hill's Street

Main hospital: University Hospital of Wales, Heath Park; tel: 02920-747 747; www.wales.nhs.uk

Media: *The Western Mail*

Airport: Cardiff Airport; tel: 01446-711 111; www.tbicardiffairport.com

Train station: Cardiff Central Station, Central Square; tel: 0870-121 1258; www.arriva trainswales.co.uk

Bus station: Wood Street; tel: 0870-121 1258; www.first group.com

Taxis: tel: 02920-555 555; www.premiertaxis.net

Wales is little more than 135 miles (216km) long and at one part less than 35 miles (56km) wide. The border runs from the mouth of the Dee in Liverpool Bay in the north to the mouth of the Wye on the Severn estuary in the south. It roughly follows the lines of the dyke built to contain the Celts by Offa, the powerful Anglo-Saxon king of Mercia from 757 to 796. Some 300 years after Offa, the Normans drove the Welsh further into the hills, establishing the Marches and the powerful Marcher Lordships along the border.

Cardiff and environs

Between the mountains and the industrial south coast run the valleys – Merthyr, Ebbw Vale, Rhondda, Neath – which were once synonymous with mining, and made **Cardiff ❶** the world's greatest coal port. Today, only a few deep mines remain, but Cardiff, the capital of Wales, is a thriving centre for business, government and tourism.

The city's museums

Cardiff Castle (tel: 02920-878 100; www.cardiffcastle.com; daily, Mar–Oct 9am–6pm, Nov–Feb 9am–5pm; charge) brings together all the strands of the city's history. The outer walls contain Roman stonework and the Norman keep still stands tall. At the height of Cardiff's prosperity, in the 1860s, the Marquis of Bute (responsible for building the docks) added to the castle, with a clock tower and banqueting halls. Nearby, the **National Museum and Gallery** (tel: 02920-397 951; www.museumwales.ac.uk; Tue–Sun 10am–5pm; free) covers science, history and archaeology, and has galleries for its collection of Impressionist, English and Welsh paintings.

But for those who really want to know about Wales, the **National History Museum** (tel: 02920-573 500; www.museumwales.ac.uk; daily

Reconstructed buildings exhibited at the National History Museum

10am–5pm; charge), just to the west of the city, is a must. Set in parkland around an Elizabethan manor house, it collects together reconstructed buildings from across the country – a toll gate, a chapel, a school room, a quarryman's cottage, a cock pit – and there are demonstrations by craftspeople.

Cardiff Bay

Europe's largest urban renewal scheme at **Cardiff Bay** is reuniting the city with its seafaring past. The waterfront now centres on the new **Cardiff Bay Barrage**, which has created a vast lake and 8 miles (13km) of coastline.

Close by, there's **Techniquest** (tel: 02920-475 475; www.techniquest. org; Mon–Fri 9.30am–4.30pm, weekends 10am–5pm; charge), a science museum, with hands-on exhibits that enable you to launch a hot-air balloon, fire a rocket and much more. The bay is also the site of the new Welsh Assembly Building, the **Senedd**. Visitors can see debates from the public gallery (tel: 0845-010 5500; www.assemblywales.org; debates: Tue 2pm, Wed 12.30pm; free).

The Norman keep of Cardiff Castle

Wales and the Borders

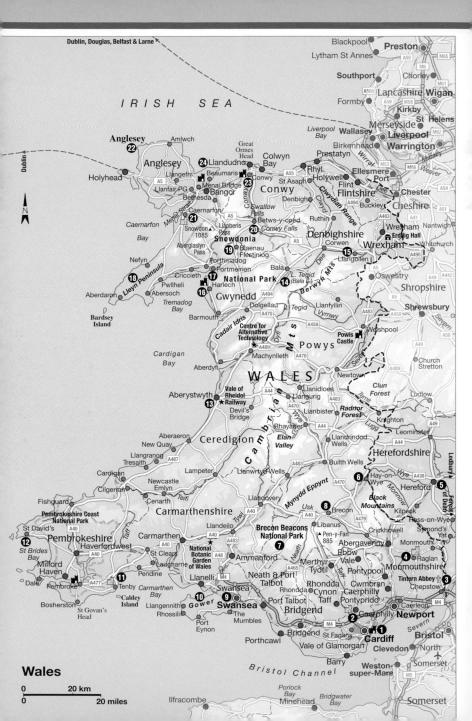

A carpet of wild flowers in the Forest of Dean

Caerphilly and Carleon

Five miles (8km) north of Cardiff, guarding the southern approaches to the valleys is **Caerphilly Castle** ❷ (tel: 02920-883 143; www.caerphilly.gov.uk; Apr–Oct daily 9am–5pm, Nov–Mar Mon–Sat 9.30am–4pm, Sun 11am–4pm; charge). The 13th-century fortress, with its concentric fortifications and leaning tower, is Britain's biggest castle after Windsor.

East of Cardiff is **Newport**, Wales' third-largest conurbation. Like Cardiff, this drab industrial city on the mouth of the River Usk was the product of industrial expansion in the 19th century. Of more interest is nearby **Caerleon** (tel: 01633-423 134; www.museumwales.ac.uk; Mon–Sat 10am–5pm, Sun 2–5pm; free), a Roman military town with impressive remains of baths, barracks and an amphitheatre.

The Welsh Borders

The border between England and Wales has remained largely unchanged since Henry VIII effectively annexed Wales in the 1540s. Ruined fortifications from ancient conflicts remain to this day amidst some of the most lush and picturesque countryside in Britain.

The Wye Valley

To the east of Caerleon, is the mouth of the River Wye. It empties into the River Severn at **Chepstow**, unremarkable but for its Norman fortress, set high on a rock. Just to the north is **Tintern Abbey** ❸ (tel: 01291-689 251; www.cadw.wales.gov.uk; Apr–Oct daily 9am–5pm, Nov–Mar Mon–Sat 9.30am–4pm, Sun 11am–4pm; charge), the romantic 13th-century ruins that inspired Wordsworth and Turner.

Further north still is **Monmouth**, famous as the birthplace of Henry V, who won the battle of Agincourt. A few miles to the southwest is **Raglan Castle** ❹ (tel: 01291-690 228; www.cadw.wales.gov.uk; Apr–Oct daily 9am–5pm, Nov–Mar Mon–Sat 9.30am–4pm, Sun 11am–4pm; charge), with a hexagonal moated keep.

On the other side of Monmouth is the **Forest of Dean**, a 40-sq-mile (105-sq-km) former royal hunting ground criss-crossed by trails. The **Dean Heritage Centre** (tel: 01594-822 170; www.deanheritagecentre.com; daily

Mar–Oct 10am–5pm, Nov–Feb until 4pm; charge) is sited on the forest's northeast side at Camp Mill.

Just to the north is **Symonds Yat**, a dramatic outcrop over a loop in the Wye valley. The river twists along to the east to **Ross-on-Wye**, a pretty town centred on an arcaded 17th-century market hall which is still used every Thursday and Saturday.

Black-and-white, half-timbered Tudor buildings are a speciality of these border towns. Above Ross is **Ledbury**, which has a herring-bone patterned Market House, and **Hereford** ❺, with its **cathedral** (tel: 01432-374 202; www. herefordcathedral.org; daily 9.15am–5.30pm, Sun until 3.30pm; donation) founded by King Offa (AD757–96). Its greatest treasure is the **Mappa Mundi**, one of the first maps of the world,

dating from around 1300. There's also a medieval chain library.

Twenty-three miles (38km) west of Hereford is **Hay-on-Wye** ❻. It was transformed into a 'book town' in the 1960s, and its many book shops have helped make it the biggest second-hand book centre in the world. The next major town on the Wye is **Builth Wells** to the west. This is hiking and fishing country, and the site of the Royal Welsh Agricultural Show each July *(see p.189)*. Just to the north is **Llandrindod Wells**, a Victorian spa town. In August the Victorian Festival returns the town to the days of hansom cabs, frock coats and mutton-chop whiskers.

Further west, near to the source of the Wye, lies the attractive town of **Rhayader,** where many Welsh crafts are on sale. Beyond is the **Elan Valley**, where in the late 19th century reservoirs were built to supply water to the thirsty city of Birmingham.

The Black Mountains

On the south side of Hay-on-Wye is **Hay Bluff**, which heralds the **Black Mountains**. To the south, the Black Mountains are cut off from the neighbouring Brecon Beacons by the Usk Valley, which the A40 follows between Abergavenny and Brecon. **Abergavenny**, the area's main town, sits in a hollow surrounded by hills: the Sugar Loaf, Skirrid Fach and Skirrid Fawr, and the Blorenge.

The Brecon Beacons

Covering 529 sq miles (1,370 sq km) and stretching south to Merthyr Tydfil is the **Brecon Beacons National Park** ❼. These old red sandstone mountains

Hereford's cathedral is home to the Mappa Mundi

The Brecon Mountain Railway offers a picturesque route through the Beacons

are the highest in south Wales, rising to 2,906ft (885m) at Pen-y-Fan; they take their name from their use as locations for signal fires.

Brecon ❽ itself is an old market town, at the confluence of the Usk and the Honddu. William the Conqueror's half-brother built Brecon Castle; its surviving tower is in the garden of the Castle Hotel. He also had a hand in the building of **Brecon Cathedral** (tel: 01874-623 857; www.breconcathedral.org.uk; daily 8.30am–6pm; donation), which was heavily restored in the 19th century.

Just off the A465, known as the Heads of the Valleys road, along the park's southern boundary, is the narrow-gauge **Brecon Mountain Railway** (tel: 01685-722 988; www.breconmountainrailway.co.uk). It runs a scenic round trip into the Beacons.

Southwest Wales

The pride of southwest Wales is its coastline, especially around Pembrokeshire, where long-distance footpaths guide visitors over spectacular jagged cliffs.

The Gower Peninsula

Although scarred by industrialisation and World War II bombs, **Swansea ❾**

Offa's Dyke

Offa's Dyke, a bank of earth running 142 miles (227km) from Prestatyn in the north to Sedbury in the south, was built by King Offa as the first official boundary between England and Wales. A deep ditch was dug on the Welsh side. Above this, an earthwork barrier rose up to 20ft (6m) high. Walkers can trace its course on the Offa's Dyke Path (www.offas-dyke.co.uk).

Villages and farmsteads cling to the edges of this 'empty quarter' and mountain roads transect the area providing an opportunity to experience the roof of Snowdonia from the security of a vehicle.

The old wool town of **Bala** is situated at the northern end of Bala Lake (Llyn Tegid), the largest natural area of water in Wales, with its very own species of fish, the alpine gwyniad.

The steam and diesel engines of the narrow-gauge Bala Lake Railway (www.bala-lake-railway.co.uk) haul visitors along the eastern shore of the lake down to the village of Llanuwchllyn.

A drowned village

Sticking to the roads, though, the A4212 leads west of Bala via the village of Frongoch and the National White Water Centre (tel: 01678-521 083; www.ukrafting.co.uk) to **Llyn Celyn**, a large reservoir. Not so many years ago Llyn Celyn was just a marshy valley containing the long-established community of Capel Celyn and the old railway line from Blaenau Ffestiniog to Bala. During the 1960s, the Afon Tryweryn was dammed to form Llyn Celyn as a holding reservoir for the Liverpool Corporation. Despite much public opposition, the village of Capel Celyn, with its school, post office, chapel and farms, was lost to the dam. Many of the community subsequently emigrated to Pennsylvania. All that remains today is a bronze commemoration plaque on a boulder just beyond the grass-covered dam.

Rhaeadr Cynfal

Continuing west, the road leads to the decommissioned nuclear power station on the shore of Llyn Trawsfynydd, where you turn right on the A470 towards **Llan Ffestiniog**, a large village of terraced stone houses. Blaenau Ffestiniog, famous for its slate quarries and railway lies some 3 miles (5km) to the north. Back in Llan Ffestiniog, however, a footpath leads from near the old railway station to the **Rhaeadr Cynfal**, or Cynfal Falls. Another fine waterfall on the Afon Cynfal – Rhaeadr y Cwm – can be reached on foot 1½ miles (2.5km) upstream from Bont Newydd where the A470 bends left to cross the river.

Steam train on the Bala Lake Railway

Tips

- **Distance:** 38 miles (61km)
- **Time:** Half a day
- **Start:** Bala
- **End:** Pentrefoelas

The Migneint

The road route from Llan Ffestiniog continues by turning right on to the B4391. Soon after passing a superb viewpoint into the Cynfal ravine, take a left turn onto the B4407. In every direction the land rolls out into bog and heather moorland. This is the **Migneint** (Swampy Place), where acid ground has encouraged the growth of mat-grass, cotton-grass and deer's hair-sedge.

The ribbon of tarmac snakes over this desolate, lake-dotted wilderness, and in about 3 miles (5km), at Pont ar Conwy, it crosses the infant River Conwy not far from its source in Llyn Conwy. To the southeast rises the peak of Arenig Fach (2,261ft/689m), while downstream is the sleepy village

The B4391 crossing over the Migneint

of Ysbyty Ifan, centre of the National Trust's Penrhyn Estate.

Forking right on an unclassified road over the River Conwy, the route continues to **Pentrefoelas** on the A5. From here, on a clear day, visitors are recommended to extend the tour a little to the north along the B5113. After the village of Nebo, the B5421 branches off to Llanrwst, but just beyond this fork in the road is a lay-by offering stunning views down into the Conwy Valley and up to the distant summits of Snowdonia.

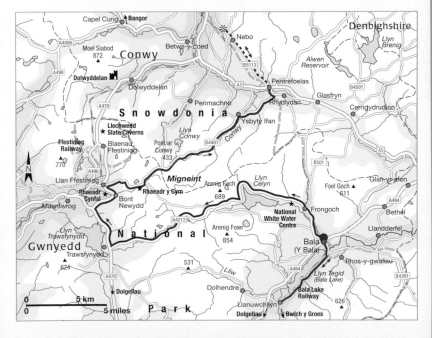

A scenic spot on the Gower Peninsula

is nevertheless a pleasant city. It has an indoor market, offering everything from antiques to laverbread, and to the west, a sea wall skirts the bay to the Victorian pier at **The Mumbles** a popular sailing centre and resort.

This is the start of the **Gower Peninsula ⑩**, a small finger of land which juts out into Carmarthen Bay. It has three National Nature Reserves and 21 Sites of Special Scientific Interest. At the western end is the 3-mile (5km) sweep of **Rhossilli** beach. The spectacular **Worms Head** promontory at one end has a large seabird colony. Meanwhile, on the northern coast, the cockle women of Penclawdd traipse across the mudflats to collect the cockles and seaweed for laverbread.

On the mainland behind the peninsula, the River Tywi forces the road inland to the market town of **Carmarthen**. To the east is the **National Botanic Garden of Wales** (tel: 01558-668 768; www.gardenofwales.org.uk; daily Apr–Sept 10am–6pm, Oct–Mar 10am–4.30pm; charge). Its centrepiece is a glasshouse designed by Norman Foster.

To the southwest of Carmarthen is **Laugharne**. This tranquil town provided Dylan Thomas with inspiration for Llareggub (spell it backwards) in *Under Milk Wood,* his 'play for voices'. You can see the boathouse where he spent his last years.

The Pembrokeshire coast

The spectacular coastline of Pembrokeshire, in the extreme southwest of Wales, is now part of a National Park stretching up to Cardigan Bay. Its major resort is **Tenby ⑪**, with castle ruins, pastel-shaded Georgian townhouses, medieval walls and beaches. From the harbour you can take a boat out to **Caldey Island**, where monks make perfume from the gorse and lavender that grows there.

The coast around **St Govan's Head**, west of Tenby, offers stunning scenery. Behind the cliffs lie the man-made lakes of **Bosherston**, covered in water-lilies in June. A few miles north in the natural harbour of **Milford Haven** (a major oil terminal) is the Georgian town of **Pembroke** with its imposing medieval castle.

To the north of Milford Haven is sandy **St Bride's Bay** with Britain's smallest city, **St David's** ⓬ on the far side. Its **cathedral** (tel: 01437-720 202; www.stdavidscathedral.org.uk; daily 8.40am–6pm; donation) and Bishop's

Palace were built into a grassy hollow, half a mile from the sea to keep it out of sight of marauders.

Aberystwyth

The coastline continuing north into Cardigan Bay features a chain of pretty seaside towns – first Fishguard, then Cardigan, then New Quay and Aberaeron – before reaching the university town of **Aberystwyth** ⓭. Aberystwyth's Alexandra Road Station is the terminal of the steam-powered **Vale of Rheidol Railway** (see www.rheidolrailway.co.uk for timetable). The line culminates 12 miles (20km) inland at **Devil's Bridge**, where three bridges, built one over the other, span the gorge of the River Mynach.

North Wales

Snowdonia's crags and gullies have long attracted hikers and mountaineers. Equally deserving, though less well publicised, is the region's glorious coastline, stretching north from the Dovey estuary around Anglesey to the River Conwy.

Towns around Snowdonia

Continuing north from Aberystwyth, visitors come to the market town of **Machynlleth** on the southern edge of Snowdonia. Its main attraction is the **Owain Glyndwr Centre** (tel: 01654-702 932; www.canolfanglyndwr.org; daily Mar–Sept 10am–5pm, Oct–Dec 11am–4pm; charge) on the site where Glyndwr established the country's first Parliament in 1404.

To the north is **Dolgellau**, and from there the A494 leads to **Bala Lake** ⓮

The lifeboat station at St Bride's Bay

(Llynn Tegid), the largest natural expanse of water in Wales and a centre for watersports. Alternatively, you can take the A458 east from Dolgellau to **Welshpool** and nearby **Powis Castle**, built by Welsh princes around 1300.

To the north of Welshpool is **Llangollen ⓯**, home of the International Musical Eisteddfod. Its two most famous residents, Lady Eleanor Butler and the Hon. Sarah Ponsonby, scandalised contemporary society by setting up home together in 1780 at **Plas Newydd Cottage** (tel: 01978-862 834; www.denbighshire.gov.uk; Apr–Oct Wed–Sun 10am–5pm; charge).

Heading for the coast again via Dolgellau, you reach **Harlech ⓰**, renowned for its **castle** (tel: 01766-780 552; www.cadw.wales.gov.uk; daily Apr–Oct 9.30am–5pm, Nov–Mar Mon–Sat 10am–4pm, Sun 11am–4pm; charge). It was besieged during the Wars of the Roses, and later inspired the marching song *Men of Harlech*.

A few miles further up the coast is **Portmeirion ⓱** (tel: 01766-770 000; www.portmeirion-village.com; daily 9.30am–7.30pm; charge), nestling beside **Porthmadog** on the Dwyryd estuary. This elaborate folly was created by architect Sir Clough William Ellis, who decided in 1926 to create a village using architectural salvage: he bought, for example, the ballroom ceiling from a Flintshire mansion that was being torn down and brought it in 100 different pieces to use in Portmeirion's village hall.

The Lleyn Peninsula

To the southwest of Snowdon, and outside the bounds of the national park, a

A group enjoying the sunshine outside a tea room in Llangollen

large spit of land, the **Lleyn Peninsula ⓲**, juts out into the sea. On its southern side is the resort of **Criccieth**, and just to the west, **Llanystumdwy**, childhood home of David Lloyd George, prime minister during World War I.

At the tip of the peninsula is **Aberdaron**, from where you can see across to **Bardsey Island**, where monks settled in the 7th century and gave it its soubriquet 'Island of 20,000 saints.'

Railway and mountains

Returning to Porthmadog, the steam-powered **Ffestiniog Narrow Gauge Railway** (tel: 01766-516 000; www.festrail.co.uk; all year) sets out on its 13½-mile (22km) journey to **Blaenau Ffestiniog ⓳**, providing spectacular mountain views along the way. The railway was originally built to carry slate from the quarries at Blaenau Ffestiniog, where the **Llechwedd Slate Caverns** (tel: 01766-830 306; www.llechwedd-slate-caverns.co.uk; daily Apr–Sept 10am–6pm, Oct–Mar until 5pm; charge) now offer visitors a tour of Britain's deepest underground railway.

North of Blaenau Ffestiniog up the A470 is **Betws-y-coed** ⑳, situated at the meeting point of three valleys – Lledr, Llugwy and Conwy. This is a popular centre for outdoor enthusiasts. Two miles (3km) to the west on the A5 are the renowned **Swallow Falls**.

To the Isle of Anglesey
Returning to the coast north of the Lleyn Peninsula is **Caernarfon Castle** ㉑ (tel: 01286-677 617; www.cadw. wales.gov.uk; Mar–Oct daily 9.30am–5pm, Nov–Feb Mon–Sat 10am–4pm,

> ### Mount Snowdon
> Much of northwest Wales is covered by the Snowdonia National Park. Snowdon itself is its highest summit at 3,560ft (1,085m). The easiest and most popular path to the summit starts on its northern side at Llanberis and is 5 miles (8km) long. Near the eastern end of Llanberis is the **Snowdon Mountain Railway** (tel: 0844 493 8120; www.snowdonrailway. co.uk; late Mar–Oct daily, subject to weather and demand), which takes an hour each way with 30 minutes at the top.

Sun 11am–4pm; charge). Begun in 1283, it was the largest of Edward I's fortifications; the walls and three towers remain intact even today.

Offshore is the **Isle of Anglesey** ㉒, separated from the mainland by the Menai Strait, which runs north from Caernarfon to the university town of

Wales and the Borders

Caenarfon Castle is well-preserved and sits beside the coast

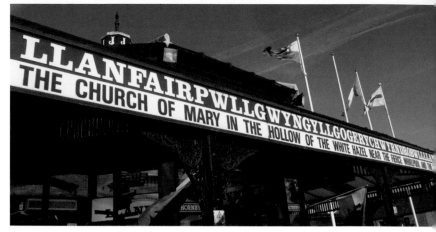

Llanfairpwllgwyngyllgogerychwyrndrobwllllantysiliogogogoch

Bangor. From here, the **Menai Suspension Bridge**, built by Thomas Telford in 1826, makes the crossing.

Just after reaching the island, the A5 passes the village of **Llanfairpwllgwyngyllgogerychwyrndrobwllllantysiliogogogoch** (Llanfair PG); its name is an accurate description of the place: 'St Mary's Church in the hollow of the white hazel near the rapid whirlpool of St Tysilio, close to the red cave'. To the east is **Beaumaris**, with its fine moated castle, while in the extreme northwest is **Holyhead**, from where ferries depart for Ireland.

The North Wales coast

East along the mainland coast from Bangor is **Conwy ㉓**, enclosed by medieval battlemented walls. The **castle** (tel: 01492-592 358; www.cadw.wales.gov.uk; Mar–Oct daily 9.30am–5pm, Nov–Feb Mon–Sat 10am–4pm, Sun 11am–4pm; charge) was built by Edward I as part of his campaign to conquer Wales between

1277 and 1284. Conwy is also home to Britain's finest Elizabethan townhouse, **Plas Mawr** (tel: 01492-580 167; www.cadw.wales.gov.uk; Tue–Sun Apr–Sept 9am–5pm, Oct 9.30am–4pm; charge), notable for its elaborate plasterwork.

Opposite Conwy, at the other end of Telford's **Conwy Suspension Bridge** is **Llandudno ㉔**, with the summit of the Great Orme looming behind. Llandudno is the finest of a string of sandy resorts along the A55 North Wales Coast Expressway that also include **Rhyl** and **Prestatyn**.

Denbighshire

South of Rhyl in the tranquil Vale of Clwyd is St Asaph. Its small cathedral dates back to the 1st century AD and was restored in the 19th-century by Gilbert Scott. Further south is the castle town of Denbigh, and further south still is the bustling town of Ruthin, which was besieged by Owain Glyndwr in 1400.

ACCOMMODATION

Accommodation in Wales runs over the full spectrum, from cheap and cheerful B&Bs to country house estates with championship golf courses. Wherever you choose to stay, one thing you should be assured of is a fine view – whether over the mountains and valleys, or over the picturesque coastline.

Cardiff and environs

Celtic Manor
Coldra Woods, Usk Valley, Newport
Tel: 01633-413 000
www.celtic-manor.com
This 19th-century manor offers landscaped gardens, three golf courses (venue for the 2010 Ryder Cup), an indoor pool, tennis and shooting. **£££–££££**

St David's Hotel and Spa
Havannah Street, Cardiff
Tel: 02920-454 045
www.principal-hayley.com
Spectacular views over Cardiff Bay, luxurious rooms and an excellent restaurant make this a strong choice. **£££**

The Welsh Borders

Llanthony Priory Hotel
Llanthony, Abergavenny
Tel: 01873-890 487
www.llanthonyprioryhotel.co.uk
This small country inn is part of an

The deluxe suite at Celtic Manor

Augustinian priory and the four rooms in the tower are furnished in historic style. **££**

Peterstone Court
Llanhamlach, Brecon
Tel: 01874-665 387
www.peterstone-court.com
Comfortable 18th-century manor with a prime location in the Brecon Beacons National Park. **££**

Southwest Wales

Conrah Hotel
Chancery, Aberystwyth
Tel: 01970-617 941
www.conrah.co.uk
This peaceful place offers traditional country comfort a few miles south of Aberystwyth. **££**

Fairyhill
Reynoldston, Swansea
Tel: 01792-390 139
www.fairyhill.net
Situated close to the beaches of the Gower Peninsula, this 18th-century house is set in beautiful parkland and has one of the best restaurants in the area. **££–£££**

North Wales

The Old Rectory
Llansanffraid Glan, near Conwy
Tel: 01492-580 611
www.oldrectorycountryhouse.co.uk
Georgian guesthouse overlooking a bird reserve with views towards Conwy Castle. **££**

Hotel Portmeirion
Portmeirion
Tel: 01766-770 000

www.portmeirion-village.com
Eccentric hotel at the heart of this model
village above Tremadog Bay. **£££**

Ye Olde Bull's Head Inn
Castle Street, Beaumaris, Isle of Anglesey
Tel: 01248-810 329
www.bullsheadinn.co.uk
This historic coaching inn has oak-beamed
rooms and a fine restaurant. **££**

Hotel Portmeirion has a coastal location

RESTAURANTS

The major towns and cities in Wales
can be dominated by chain restaurants,
but delve deeper and you can find some
gems. In the countryside and on the
coast, many inns serve local produce
and bistros offer the catch of the day.

Restaurant price categories

Prices are for a two-course dinner per
person with a glass of house wine.

£ = under £20
££ = £20–30
£££ = £30–50
££££ = over £50

Cardiff and environs
Bosphorus
31 Mermaid Quay, Cardiff Bay
Tel: 02920-487 477
www.bosphorus.co.uk
Located on a small pier in the bay, this Turkish
restaurant serves fresh food with flavour. **££**

Sir Henry Morgan
635 Newport Road, Cardiff
Tel: 02920-361 311
www.sirhenrymorganrumney.com
Characterful old pub serving well-executed
comfort food in the Rumney area of town. **£**

The Welsh Borders
The Walnut Tree
Llandewi Skirrid, Abergavenny
Tel: 01873-852 797
www.thewalnuttreeinn.com
A well-known restaurant serving quality fish,
local meat and game, and vegetables from its
garden. Good value set lunches. **£££–££££**

Southwest Wales
The Blue Ball Restaurant
Upper Frog Street, Tenby
Tel: 01834-843 038

www.theblueballrestaurant.co.uk
This informal restaurant serves good honest
grub, offering local produce and smoking its
own fish, meat and cheese. **££**

The Old Pharmacy
5 Main Street, Solva
Tel: 01437-720 005
www.theoldpharmacy.co.uk
Good restaurants in Pembrokeshire are
hard to find – this one in a coastal village
serves excellent fish and seafood. **££**

North Wales
Ynyshir Hall
Eglwysfach, near Machynlleth
Tel: 01654-781 209
www.ynyshirhall.co.uk
Local ingredients such as Cardigan Bay
seafood, wild salmon, venison, game and
farmhouse cheeses will grace your dinner
plate at this country house hotel. **££**

Pant-yr-Ochain
Old Wrexham Road, Gresford, near Wrexham
tel: 01978-853 525
www.pantyrochain-gresford.co.uk
This 16th-century manor house offers a

reasonably priced menu with options for vegetarians, and a terrace overlooking pretty gardens is ideal for dining in the summer. **££**

Tyddan Llan
Llandrillo, near Corwen

Tel: 01490-440 264
www.tyddynllan.co.uk
A Michelin star means you will need to book here in advance. Its tasting menu offers a sample of Welsh produce.
£££–££££

NIGHTLIFE

Cardiff has an active nightlife and *Buzz* magazine (www.buzzmag.co.uk) has listings of events. Elsewhere, there are impromptu venues for club nights, and good pubs.

Club X
35 Charles Street, Cardiff
www.clubxcardiff.net
This dance club is a well-established part of Cardiff's gay scene.

Globe at Hay
Newport Street, Hay-on-Wye
Tel: 01497-821 762
www.globeathay.co.uk

This former Methodist chapel has a new purpose and holds a variety of events including regular club nights.

Pier Pressure
Pier, Marine Terrace, Aberystwyth
Tel: 01970-636 104
www.royalpier.co.uk
Cheesy nightclub, cheap booze. It occasionally hosts bands.

ENTERTAINMENT

Wales has a varied cultural scene with its own orchestras, theatre companies, and its male-voice choirs, so there is every chance you'll catch a good show.

Film
Coliseum Cinema
Wheat Street, Brecon
Tel: 01874-622 501
www.coliseumbrecon.co.uk
Offers blockbusters and arthouse cinema.

Commodore Cinema
Bath Street,
Aberystwyth
Tel: 01970-612 421
www.commodorecinema.co.uk
Independent cinema showing the latest films.

Music
Aberystwyth Male Voice Choir
RAFA Club, Bridge Street, Aberystwyth
www.aberchoir.co.uk

The heart-stopping sound of this Welsh male voice choir can be heard at 7pm every Thursday.

Clwb Ifor Bach
11 Womanby Street, Cardiff
Tel: 02920-232 199
www.clwb.net
This is the place to find up-and-coming bands before they become rich and famous.

St David's Hall
The Hayes, Cardiff
Tel: 02920-878 444
www.stdavidshallcardiff.co.uk
The national concert hall of Wales is the setting for the Welsh Proms and major classical concerts throughout the year.

Theatre

Sherman Theatre
Senghennydd Road, Cathays, Cardiff
Tel: 02920-646 900
www.shermancymru.co.uk
Stages theatre, from classics to new work.

Swansea Grand Theatre
Singleton Street, Swansea
Tel: 01792-475 715
www.swanseagrand.co.uk
Swansea's main venue for theatre, musicals and comedy.

SPORTS AND ACTIVITIES

Wales is perfect for outdoor pursuits; Pembrokeshire (www.pembrokeshire coast.org.uk), the Brecon Beacons (www.breconbeacons.org) and Snowdonia (www.eryri-npa.gov.uk) all have visitor centres advising on routes and attractions.

Holey Trail
31 Maengwyn Street, Machynlleth
Tel: 01654-700 411
www.theholeytrail.co.uk
This bicycle shop rents out mountain bikes so that you can try out one of the local trails.

Gwydir Stables
Penmachno, Betws-y-Coed, Snowdonia
Tel: 01690-760 248
www.horse-riding-wales.co.uk
Half-day, full-day, summer-evening and even 'pub' rides are organised within Snowdonia.

Paddles and Pedals
15 Castle Street, Hay-on-Wye
Tel: 01497-820 604
www.paddlesandpedals.co.uk
Hire a kayak or a canoe and paddle in the clear waters of the River Wye.

Canolfan Tryweryn National White Water Centre
Frongoch, Bala
Tel: 01678-521 083
www.ukrafting.co.uk
Hold on tight when rafting down this white water stretch of the River Tryweryn.

TOURS

See Wales from above in a cable-car, from the sea onboard a boat, or from the top of a bus touring round the streets of Cardiff.

City Sightseeing
Cardiff Castle
Tel: 02920-473 432
www.city-sightseeing.com
Tickets are valid for 24 hours for these hop-on-hop-off tour buses around Cardiff.

Horse Drawn Boat Centre
Llangollen Wharf, Wharf Hill, Llangollen
Tel: 01978-860 702
www.horsedrawnboats.co.uk
Two-hour or 45-minute horse-drawn boat

trips take you along the canal towpath.

Great Orme Cable Car
Happy Valley Gardens, Llandudno
Tel: 01492-876 413
www.greatorme.org.uk
Britain's longest cable-car ride takes you over a mile up to the summit of the Great Orme.

Puffin Island Cruises
The Anchorage, Rosemary Lane, Beaumaris, Anglesey

Canoeing in Snowdonia

Tel: 01248-810 746
www.beaumarismarine.com
Tickets for cruises to see the seabird colonies of Puffin Island can be purchased from the kiosk on Beaumaris pier. The same company also organises sea fishing trips.

FESTIVALS AND EVENTS

The Welsh are an artistic lot, evident at the Eisteddfod – part competition, part expression of national identity and part affirmation of peace and friendship.

May
Hay Festival
www.hayfestival.com
This high-profile literary festival in late May attracts well-known international authors and celebrities.

June
Escape into the Park
Singleton Park, Swansea
www.escapefestival.com
This one-day outdoor festival in mid-June features big-name DJs playing the latest dance music.

July
Cardiff Festival
Various venues in the city
www.cardiff-festival.com
Lasting until early September, this mix of festivals includes the Welsh Proms (two weeks of classical concerts at St David's Hall), the Big Weekend (a three-day music festival), the Lord Mayor's parade, and others.

International Musical Eisteddfod
Royal International Pavilion, Llangollen
www.international-eisteddfod.co.uk
Thousands of music and dance performers attend this festival in early July, culminating in the Choir of the World competition.

Royal Welsh Agricultural Show
Builth Wells

www.rwas.co.uk
Huge fair at the start of the month featuring livestock and exhibitions.

August
Jazz Festival
Various venues in Brecon
www.breconjazz.co.uk
An international jazz festival wakes up this sleepy Welsh town on the second weekend in August.

September
Abergavenny Food Festival
Various venues in Abergavenny
www.abergavennyfoodfestival.co.uk
The largest food festival in Wales features demonstrations, tastings and exhibitions. The action happens on the third weekend of the month.

Great British Cheese Festival
Cardiff Castle
www.greatbritishcheesefestival.co.uk
A weekend in late September of cheese master classes and tastings creates a big pong in Cardiff Castle.

October/November
Dylan Thomas Festival
Dylan Thomas Centre, Swansea
www.dylanthomas.com
Annual festival (27 October–9 November) with readings and lectures.

The north

The region the British simply call 'the north' covers a vast tract of country, from Liverpool and Manchester via Leeds and York right up to Newcastle in the northeast and the Lake District in the northwest. While the distances between these areas are quite long, the variety and the wealth of attractions make the journey all the more worthwhile.

Liverpool

Population: 435,000

Local dialling code: 0151

Tourist office: Anchor Courtyard, Albert Dock; tel: 0151-707 0729; www.visitliverpool.com

Main police station: Canning Place, Albert Dock; tel: 0151-709 6010

Main post office: 1 Monument Place

Main hospital: The Royal Liverpool University Hospital, Prescot Street; tel: 0151-706 2000; www.rlbuht.nhs.uk

Media: *Liverpool Echo*

Airport: Liverpool John Lennon; tel: 0871-521 8484; www.liverpool airport.com

Train station: Lime Street; tel: 08457-114 141; www.national rail.co.uk

Bus station: Queen Square; tel: 0151-476 8000; www.arriva bus.co.uk

Car hire companies: Car Hire Liverpool; tel: 0151-808 0010; www.car-hire-liverpool.com

Taxi companies: tel: 0151-298 2222; www.merseycabs.co.uk

As in many European countries, there is a tendency to differentiate broadly – and controversially – between the north and the south. In Britain, the north is associated with the old heavy industries of shipbuilding, steel and coal mining. These industries have long been in decline, and many of the Victorian factory towns have since been plagued by unemployment. Recent decades have, however, brought regeneration, with hi-tech businesses, new universities, cultural centres and tourism.

Another widely held perception in the north versus the south debate is that people from the north are more outgoing, forthright and gregarious and southerners are more wary, noncommittal and reserved. Join a bus queue in London, it is said, and you'll stand in silence; join one in Liverpool and you'll soon strike up a conversation. It's a claim that's difficult to verify, but many visitors find some truth in it.

Merseyside

Despite post-industrial decline, Liverpool remains a proud city, famed for its football club, its contribution to pop music, and its community solidarity. Just to the south are the more sedate towns of Port Sunlight and Chester, each with their own distinctive style of architecture.

Liverpool

While the shipping industry of **Liverpool ❶** has now disappeared, a great deal of rejuvenation has since taken place and the waterfront is now designated a Unesco World Heritage Site. The Albert Dock warehousing area now accommodates small shops, bars and restaurants as well as several museums. Foremost among the museums is **Tate Liverpool** (tel: 0151-702 7400; www.tate.org.uk; daily 10am–5.50pm, closed on Mondays in winter; free), which

A view of the Royal Liver Building at night

specialises in modern and contemporary art.

Nearby, in the Britannia Pavilion, is the **Beatles Story** (tel: 0151-709 1963; daily 9am–7pm; charge), which offers a fun exhibition on the city's most famous musical export. An altogether more serious story is told at the dockside **Merseyside Maritime Museum** (tel: 0151-478 4499; www.liverpoolmuseums.org.uk; daily 10am–5pm; free) which also incorporates the International Slavery Museum, which offers a thought-provoking view of the slave trade. Also in the vicinity is the newly opened **Museum of Liverpool** (tel: 0151-207 0001; www.liverpoolmuseums.org.uk; daily 10am–5pm; free), dedicated to telling the city's history.

Liverpool's architecture is on a grand scale. The docks accommodate the **Royal Liver Building** (with the mythical liver birds sitting atop the two clock towers), the Cunard Building and the Port of Liverpool Building. Collectively, they are known as 'The Three Graces' and were built in the early 20th century, at the height of the city's prosperity.

Tate Liverpool

Liverpool also has two modern churches. The Roman Catholic **Metropolitan Cathedral** (tel: 0151-709 9222; www.liverpoolmetrocathedral.org.uk; daily 8am–6pm; free), consecrated in 1967, is a circular structure topped with a spire that represents the Crown of Thorns. The neo-Gothic **Anglican Cathedral** (tel: 0151-709 6271; www.liverpoolcathedral.org.uk; daily 8am–6pm; free), Britain's largest, by Giles Gilbert Scott, was begun in 1904 and completed in 1978 after two world wars delayed its construction.

On William Brown Street, in the city centre, is the **World Museum** (tel: 0151-478 4393; www.liverpool museums.org.uk; daily 10am–5pm; free), with collections of archaeology and ethnology as well as an aquarium. Nearby is the **Walker Art Gallery** (tel: 0151-478 4199; www.liverpoolmus eums.org.uk; daily 10am–5pm; free), which has an outstanding collection of paintings from Rembrandt to Hockney.

On the peninsula known as the Wirral – across the Mersey via Queens Way – is the delightful model village of **Port Sunlight ❷**, built by a soap magnate for his workforce. Here, at the **Lady Lever Art Gallery** (tel: 0151-478 4136; www.liverpoolmuseums.org.uk; daily 10am–5pm; free), there is a good Pre-Raphaelite collection, along with some Turners and Constables.

Chester

South of Port Sunlight is the city of **Chester ❸**, the most northerly of the timbered Tudor towns of the Welsh Marches. In the centre of town, Eastgate, Watergate and Bridge Street all have their 'rows' – double tiers of shops and covered walkways, one on top of the other. The oldest dates from 1486.

Merseyside to Lancashire

> **Black and white**
>
> Perhaps the greatest half-timbered building in Britain is **Little Moreton Hall** (tel: 01260-272 018; www.nationaltrust.org.uk; mid-Mar–Oct Wed–Sun 11am–5pm, Nov–mid-Mar Sat–Sun 11am–4pm, closed Jan–Feb; charge), east of Chester via the A54 and A34, south of Congleton. This half-timbered, moated Tudor manor has a delightful knot garden.

Lake District map on page 198
Yorkshire and the northeast map on page 207

In Roman times Chester was an important stronghold called Deva and part of an amphitheatre can be seen just outside the city walls by St John's Street. This offers the best access to the 2-mile (3km) round trip of the medieval **city walls**.

The **cathedral** (tel: 01244-324 756; www.chestercathedral.com; Mon–Sat 9am–5pm, Sun 1–4pm; charge), off St Werburg Street, was a Benedictine Abbey until Henry VIII's Dissolution of the Monasteries. Unusually squat, it has a short nave and a massive south transept with a Victorian stained-glass window.

At Upton, 2 miles (4km) north of the city, is **Chester Zoo** (tel: 01244-380 280; www.chesterzoo.org; daily 10am–5pm, winter until 4pm; charge), the largest outside London, set in 80 acres (32 hectares) of gardens and home to more than 7,000 animals.

Manchester and Lancashire

The Victorian city of Manchester is the capital of northern England. It was in the vanguard of the Industrial Revolution and is still a relatively prosperous city. Around it is rolling green countryside, and not far away are the city's favourite holiday resorts on the Lancashire coast.

Manchester

In **Manchester ❹**, the neo-Gothic **Town Hall** stands proudly on **Albert Square**. The Sculpture Hall, with a roof of Bath stone, is open to the public during working hours. Just to the east is **Chinatown**, packed with restaurants. It's also home to the **Chinese Arts Centre** (tel: 0161-832

Manchester's Town Hall is a highlight of the city skyline

7271; www.chinese-arts-centre.org; Tue–Sat 10am–5pm; free), featuring changing exhibitions by contemporary Chinese artists.

At Castlefield, a few minutes' walk west of the city centre, is the **Museum of Science and Industry** (tel: 0161-832 2244; www.mosi.org.uk; daily 10am–5pm; free). It has an impressive collection of technology from Victorian

⭐ THE BEATLES

Formed in Liverpool in 1960, The Beatles – John Lennon, Paul McCartney, George Harrison and Ringo Starr – became arguably the most successful pop group the world has ever seen. They are the best-selling band in history, the album *Sgt. Pepper's Lonely Hearts Club Band* is widely regarded as a pop-art masterpiece, and their enormous popularity (or 'Beatlemania') is seen as integral to the social history of Britain in the 1960s.

Liverpool's pride in its four famous sons is much in evidence. The National Trust has bought **Mendips**, the house where John Lennon grew up, as well as Paul McCartney's child-hood home, **20 Forthlin Road**. Both can also be visited by guided tour (tel: 0844-800 4791; www.nationaltrust.org.uk; book online; charge).

The Beatles played many of their early gigs at the **Cavern Club** on Liverpool's Mathew Street. The original Cavern Club closed in 1973, but was reconstructed in 1984 and is now going strong again as a venue for local bands (tel: 0151-236 1965; www.cavernclub.org). It also stages a Beatles tribute show on Beatles Day, 10 July, each year. This was the memorable day in 1964 when the band returned to Liverpool from their US tour just in time for the premiere of their film *A Hard Day's Night*.

Mathew Street also holds its own

The Cavern Club, the venue for some of the Beatles' earliest gigs

festival (tel: 0151-239 9091; www.
mathewstreetfestival.org) in the last
week of August, when there are six
days of live music, markets and even
boat cruises. For the rest of the year,
Beatles groupies can get their fix by
buying memorabilia at the Beatles
Shop and at From Me To You at nos. 31
and 9 Mathew Street respectively.

On Liverpool's dockside, the Britannia Pavilion houses the **Beatles
Story** (tel: 0151-709 1963; www.
beatlesstory.com), an 'experience'
of the city's illustrious sons which is
naturally open 'eight days a week'
and features the Yellow Submarine
and a stroll down Penny Lane. Buses
for the Magical Mystery Tour (tel:
0151-709 3285; www.beatlestour.
org) leave from Albert Dock's Tourist
Information Centre daily, and take in
all the important landmarks, including
Strawberry Field, Penny Lane, Eleanor
Rigby's grave and the Cavern Club.
Most tours last two hours, though
dedicated fans can also join a full-day
tour, which includes visits to Mendips
and 20 Forthlin Road.

The Beatles finally broke up in
1970 and thereafter pursued individual music careers. Lennon and
McCartney each chalked up several
more hits of long-lasting appeal, and
George Harrison brought out a successful triple album, *All Things Must
Pass*. Ringo Starr achieved some success as a solo artist in the 1970s, but
his post-Beatles career is now chiefly
remembered for his narration of the
Thomas the Tank Engine children's
television series.

The Cavern Club wall of fame

A chance to buy fab-four
memorabilia at the Beatles Shop

The Lowry Centre, a theatre and gallery space in Salford Quays

times to the Space Age, with lots to interest children.

Pre-Raphaelite art and 20th-century British artwork can be enjoyed in the **Manchester Art Gallery** (tel: 0161-235 8888; www.manchestergalleries.org; Tue–Sun 10am–5pm; free), along with an extensive collection of decorative art. On the University of Manchester campus to the south is the **Whitworth Art Gallery** (tel: 0161-275 7450; www.

whitworth.manchester.ac.uk; Mon–Sat 10am–5pm, Sun 2–4pm; free) which has an outstanding collection of British watercolours and a sculpture gallery that includes major works by Hepworth, Epstein and Frink.

At **Salford Quays**, to the west of the city centre, is the **Lowry Centre** (tel: 0843-208 6000; www.thelowry.com; daily 11am–5pm, Sat from 10am; free). It has the world's largest collection of

Manchester

Population: 465,000

Local dialling code: 0161

Tourist office: Piccadilly Plaza, Portland Street; tel: 0871-222 8223; www.visitmanchester.com

Main police station: 31 Bootle Street; tel: 0161-872 5050

Main post office: 26 Spring Gardens

Main hospital: Manchester Royal Infirmary, Oxford Road; tel: 0161-276 1234; www.cmft.nhs.uk

Media: *Manchester Evening News*

Airport: tel: 08712-710 711; www.manchesterairport.co.uk; 9 miles (14km) southwest of Manchester; direct train to city centre (journey time: 20 minutes); fare: £4

Train station: Manchester Piccadilly Station; tel: 0161-820 7579; www.nationalrail.co.uk

Bus and tram station: Piccadilly Gardens; buses: www.firstgroup.com; trams: www.metrolink.co.uk

Car hire companies: Manchester Car Hire; tel: 0161-273 1807; www.manchestercarhire.com

Taxi companies: tel: 0161-236 8033; www.radiocarsmanchester.co.uk

work by local artist, L.S. Lowry (1887–1976). The stunning, asymmetrical building opposite, designed by American architect Daniel Libeskind, houses the **Imperial War Museum North** (tel: 0161-836 4007; www.iwm.org.uk; daily 10am–5pm; free).

Lancashire's resorts

On the coast to the north of Manchester are Lancashire's traditional sandy resorts.

Blackpool ❺ is Britain's most popular seaside resort, and up to 6 million people come here each year – even though, sadly, it has seen better days. The **promenade**, all 7 miles (11km) of it, is centred on the 518ft (160m) Eiffel-style **Blackpool Tower**. Famous for its 'illuminations', it is lit up from the end of August to October. With its fairground rides, **Blackpool Pleasure Beach** (tel: 0871-222 1234; www.blackpoolpleasurebeach.com; Apr–Oct daily 10.30am–5pm, July–Aug until 8pm, mid-Feb–Mar and Nov weekends only; charge) is among the resort's most popular attractions. Tickets must be booked in advance, up to 12 hours before your visit.

The beaches all down this coast are wide and long, and sand yachting is popular at the resort of **Lytham St Anne's. Morecambe**, to the north, is now largely known for the walk across the sands of the bay, a trip of about 8 miles (5km). The walk must be done with the official guide, or 'Queen's Sand Pilot' (tel: 01539-534 026), as it is fraught with the twin dangers of quicksand and unusually rapid rising tides.

The Lake District

The Lake District in northwest England is protected by England's largest National Park, at 885 square miles (2,292 sq km). The central area of mountains was never much affected by

A busy street in Blackpool and the Blackpool Tower

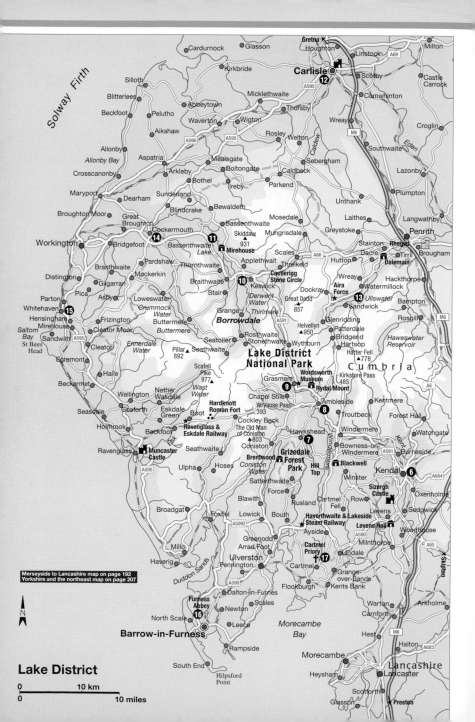

A war memorial on Kendal's high street

industry or quarrying, and sheep farming has long been the traditional way of life of the hill folk, making it ideal terrain for walkers.

Kendal

Approaching the Lake District from the south along the M6, a turn off at junction 36 leads to the town of **Levens**. Here, **Levens Hall** (tel: 01539-560 321; www levenshall.co.uk; Apr–mid-Oct Sun–Thur noon–4.30pm; charge), a 16th-century house built around a 13th-century pele tower (distinctive square keep), has a famous topiary garden. Nearby, **Sizergh Castle** (tel: 01539-560 951; www.national-trust.org.uk; mid-Mar–Oct Sun–Thur noon–5pm; charge) is a stately home built around a medieval tower.

Just to the north is **Kendal ❻**, a working town that forms a good centre for the Lakes. Beside the fine church is **Abbot Hall Art Gallery** (tel: 01539-722 464; www.abbothall.org.

uk; Mon–Sat, Apr–Oct 10.30am–5pm, Nov–Mar 10.30am–4pm; charge), which exhibits works by local artists such as George Romney and John Ruskin. Next door is the **Museum of Lakeland Life** (www.lakeland museum.org.uk; other details as for the gallery), which includes two rooms devoted to the *Swallows and Amazons*, author Arthur Ransome (1884–1967).

Beatrix Potter

The A591 runs from Kendal to the Victorian town of **Windermere**, a Victorian town that owes its growth to the visitors who arrived here by train on their way to **Bowness-on-Windermere**, just below. Bowness is home to **The World of Beatrix Potter** (tel: 0844-504 1233; www.hop-skip-jump.com; daily summer 10am–5.30pm, winter 10am–4.30pm; charge) which includes a re-creation of the kitchen garden from the Peter Rabbit tales. To the south of Bowness just off the A5074 is **Blackwell** (tel: 01539-446 139; www.blackwell.org.uk; daily Apr–Oct 10.30am–5pm, Nov–Mar until 4pm; charge), the Arts and Crafts house designed by M.H. Baillie Scott for a wealthy Manchester brewer.

From Bowness, a car ferry crosses Lake Windemere to Far Sawrey, near which is Beatrix Potter's house, **Hill Top** (tel: 01539-436 269; www.nationaltrust.org.uk; Sat–Thur mid-Feb–Mar 10.30am–3.30pm, Apr–May and Sept–Oct 10.30am–4.30pm, June–Aug 10am–5pm; charge). This traditional Lakeland farmhouse has the archetypal cottage garden.

In nearby **Hawkshead ❼** is the **Beatrix Potter Gallery** (tel: 01539-436 355; www.nationaltrust.org.uk; Sat–Thur mid-Feb–Mar 11am–3.30pm, Apr–May and Sept–Oct 11am–5pm, June–Aug 10.30am–5pm; charge) in the office of her solicitor husband William Heelis. It displays many of the original sketches and watercolour paintings from Potter's books.

Other notable buildings in Hawkshead include the **Old Grammar School** (tel: 01539-436 735; www.hawksheadgrammar.org.uk; Apr–Sept Mon–Sat 10am–1pm and 2–5pm, Sun 1–5pm, Oct Mon–Sat 10am–1pm and 2–3.30pm, Sun 1–3.30pm; charge), established in 1585. The poet William Wordsworth was a pupil here in the 1780s, and carved his initials on his desk.

The Lake Poets

At the northern end of Lake Windermere is **Ambleside ❽**, and just beyond it, **Rydal Water**, a reedy lake with several islands. At the head of the village is **Rydal Mount and Gardens** (tel: 01539-433 002; www.rydalmount.co.uk; Mar–Oct daily 9.30am–5pm, Nov–Dec and Feb Wed–Sun 11am–4pm; charge), home of the Wordsworths from 1813 until William's death in 1850.

To the north lies **Grasmere ❾**, where Wordsworth and his sister Dorothy first settled in 1799 in a simple white cottage. **Dove Cottage** and the neighbouring **Wordsworth Museum** (tel: 01539-435 544; www.wordsworth.org.uk; daily Mar–Oct 9.30am–5.30pm, Nov–Feb 9.30am–4pm; charge) display the poet's personal possessions and manuscripts. Nearby St Oswald's Church has the Wordsworth family tombstones in the graveyard.

The World of Beatrix Potter, in Bowness-on-Windermere

The *Gondola* on Coniston Water

Keswick

The 17-mile (28km) journey north-west to Keswick on the A591 passes **Thirlmere**, a reservoir, and **Helvellyn**, the third-highest mountain in England (3,120ft/950m). Close to Keswick you can turn off to **Castlerigg Stone Circle**, an ancient monument of 48 large stones commanding tremendous views.

Keswick ❿ itself has been popular since the poet Thomas Gray stayed there in the 1760s to explore its lake, **Derwent Water**. A favourite excursion since Gray's time is the Bowder Stone, balanced on the side of the hill a little way up the Borrowdale valley,

to the south of the lake. Another attraction is the waterfall at Lodore, near the head of Derwent Water.

Borrowdale was famed among early tourists for the 'wad' or black lead mine that enabled the manufacture of pencils in Keswick. The **Cumberland Pencil Museum** (tel: 01768-773 626; www.pencilmuseum.co.uk; daily 9.30am–5pm; charge) charts the history of this industry.

A few minutes' walk to the east, in Fitz Park, is Keswick's **Museum and Art Gallery** (tel: 01768-773 263; www.allerdale.gov.uk; Tue–Sat 10am–4pm; charge), which includes displays of letters by Wordsworth

Coniston Water

Coniston Water, to the west of Windermere, is notable as the home of artist and critic John Ruskin (1819–1900), and later as the scene of the world water speed record attempts of Donald Campbell, who died in the last attempt in 1967. Ruskin's house, Brantwood (tel: 01539-441 396; www.brantwood.org.uk;

daily mid-Mar–mid-Nov 11am–5.30pm, mid-Nov–mid-Mar 11am–4.30pm; charge) remains much as he left it. Nowadays, a safer way of taking to the water is on the Victorian steam yacht *Gondola* (tel: 01539-432 733; www.nationaltrust.org.uk; Apr–Oct daily, call for times; charge), which departs from Coniston Pier.

🚗 LAKE DISTRICT DRIVE

The western Lake District offers stern peaks, secluded valleys, isolated hill farms and a Roman hill fort. The first part of this route – to the end of Eskdale – follows public roads, which can be negotiated by bus or on foot. The gradients make the ascents strenuous, and the descents hair-raising. Beyond Eskdale, your efforts are rewarded with a charming journey by steam train to the coast at Ravenglass.

Beginning in Ambleside, the A593 leads westwards, and along the way offers glimpses of the River Brathay, which gathers up near the Three Shires Stone on Wrynose Pass and eventually presents a white-water spectacle near Skelwith Bridge. Near Loughrigg Tarn it is a short walk to **Skelwith Force** ('the noisy fall') which, though only 15ft (4.5m) high, is a cheerful sight.

The Langdale Pikes

At Skelwith Bridge take the road for Great Langdale, which bursts into view near Elterwater. Across the common and beyond the woodland rise the Langdale Pikes, one of the most distinctive landforms in the district. The evidence of slate quarrying is everywhere, and a terrace of slate dwellings overlooking the common is particularly attractive.

Great Langdale

Great Langdale doesn't have a lake, but it has all the other attributes of a picturesque Lakeland valley – a beck, green fields hatched by dry-stone walls, and mountains blocking out more than half the sky. It is entered from the pretty village of Chapel Stile, with its church on a hill above. To the west, the waters of Dungeon Ghyll enter the valley from the north. Walk a little way up the beck to see the impressive 60ft (18m) waterfall of **Dungeon Ghyll Force**.

The Langdale Pikes dominate the view beyond. The 'Langdale Round', starting from the ascent of Pavey Ark, is one of the finest outings on the fells. This 13-mile (21km) walk takes you over Harrison Stickle, around the head of the valley by Angle Tarn and up Bow Fell (2,960ft/902m). After enjoying the views from Bow Fell

Tips

- **Distance:** 60-mile (97km)
- **Time:** A full day
- **Start:** Ambleside
- **End:** Ravenglass

over to Scafell, England's highest mountain (3,206ft/977m), you either descend into the side valley of Oxendale, or carry on to the peak of Pike o' Blisco (2,303ft/702m), from where you can make your way back to Dungeon Ghyll.

The Wrynose and Hardknott Passes
A road leaves Langdale heading south near Wall End Farm and climbs to **Blea Tarn** in its own secluded little valley. Then, to the south, the route joins the road westwards over the Wrynose and Hardknott Passes.

The **Wrynose Pass** has a steep gradient, taking little time to attain 1,289ft (393m), before descending again to the head of the Duddon Valley, where the **Hardknott Pass** begins its course to Eskdale. A succession of hairpin bends leads the traveller up again before finally descending to Eskdale. On the way down, the remains of the Roman fort of Mediobogdum can be seen on a plateau beside the road.

The Wrynose Pass

Eskdale
Lakeless **Eskdale** extends with a quiet charm down to Boot. Just beyond the village at Dalegarth visitors' centre is the station for the narrow-gauge Ravenglass and Eskdale Steam Railway (www.ravenglass-railway.co.uk). The line runs for 7 miles (11km) down to Ravenglass harbour. Ravenglass was once an important Roman naval base, and it marks the west end of Hadrian's Wall. A large bath house remains.

Lake District drive

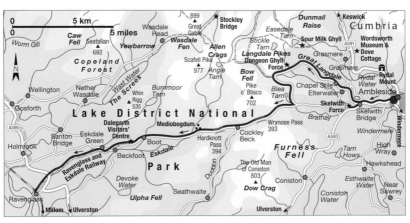

and his fellow poet Robert Southey. Another local, the poet Samuel Taylor Coleridge, settled at Greta Hall on the outskirts of Keswick in 1800 and persuaded Southey (his brother-in-law) to join him there.

Northwards, the churchyard looks towards **Bassenthwaite Lake** ⓫, the

Rowing a boat on Lake Windermere on a sunny day

eastern side of which is dominated by **Skiddaw** (3,050ft/931m).

The A66 going eastwards from Keswick leads to Penrith, a staging post for **Carlisle** ⓬ (*see box*) further north. To the south is **Ullswater** ⓭, the second-largest lake after Windermere. There are steamers on the lake from which to enjoy the views of Helvellyn and other surrounding mountains. On the north shore beneath Gowbarrow Fell is **Aira Force**, one of the most impressive waterfalls in the Lake District.

The western seaboard

On the western side of the Lake District is the old-fashioned town of **Cockermouth** ⓮. On its main street is the Wordsworth House (tel: 01900-820 884; www.wordsworthhouse.org.uk; Mar–Oct Sat–Thur 11am–5pm; charge), where William and Dorothy spent their earliest years. Actors in period costume play the parts of the servants, cooking, cleaning and working in the garden.

Further west towards the Solway Firth is **Workington**, a town at the mouth of the River Derwent. On the outskirts, on the A66, is the **Helena Thompson Museum** (tel: 01900-64040; www.helenathompson museum.co.uk; Tue–Sun 1.30–4.30pm; charge), an exhibition about local maritime and social history located within a Georgian mansion.

South along the coast is **Whitehaven** ⓯. You can delve into this port's history at **The Beacon** (tel: 01946-592 302; www.thebeacon-whitehaven.co.uk; daily 10am–4.30pm; charge), with its five floors of interactive

Limestone crag at Malham Cove

exhibits and galleries. A footpath leads from behind the Beacon to the **Haig Colliery Mining Museum** (tel: 01946-599 949; www.haigpit.com; daily 9am–4.30pm; charge) on the former site of the Haig Pit.

The south coast

The southern tip of Lakeland was in medieval days the heart of the great Cistercian estate farmed by the monks of **Furness Abbey** ⑯ (tel: 01229-823 420; www.english-heritage.org.uk; Apr–Sept Thur–Mon 10am–5pm, Oct until 4pm; charge). The impressive ruins are set in the picturesque Vale of Deadly Nightshade, on the northside of the shipbuilding town of Barrow-in-Furness. Just to the east is the 12th-century **Cartmel Priory** ⑰ (tel: 01539-536 536; www.cartmelpriory.org.uk; daily summer 9am–5.30pm, winter until 3.30pm; donations), near the resort of **Grange-over-Sands** on a finger of land pointing down into Morecambe Bay.

Yorkshire

Although the lands of the north are wild open spaces, littered with evidence of a turbulent history, they do also shelter picture-book villages, bustling towns and the historic city of York.

West Yorkshire

Although many of the north's heavy industries have all but died out, traditional life lives on. At **Huddersfield** ⑱, to the north of the Peak District, the famous choral society has performed Handel's *Messiah* in the Town Hall just before Christmas every year since 1836. On the A642, halfway between Huddersfield and Wakefield, the **National Coal Mining Museum** (tel: 01924-848 806; www.ncm.org.uk; daily, 10am–5pm; free) illustrates the industry's history with an underground tour of a disused mine.

In nearby **Bradford** ⑲, the 19th-century textile barons built solid dependability into every brick of the city's Italianate Town Hall and its Gothic Wool Exchange. One of the richest, Sir Titus Salt, enshrined his ideals in the nearby model village of **Saltaire**. The giant **Salts Mill** (tel: 01274-531 163; www.saltsmill.org.uk; daily 10am–5.30pm, weekends until 6pm; free) now provides gallery space for artwork by David Hockney, who was born in Bradford in 1937.

In the town centre is the **National Media Museum** (tel: 0844-856 3797; www.nationalmediamuseum.org.uk; Tue–Sun 10am–6pm; charge). Its three cinemas include an IMAX screen, five storeys high by 96ft (30m) wide.

Yorkshire's main city, **Leeds 20**, is a bustling university city and business centre. Its big tourist attraction is the **Royal Armouries Museum** (tel: 0113-220 1999; www.royalarmouries. org; daily 10am–5pm; free) at Clarence Dock. It displays 3,000 years of arms, from musket balls to parts of Saddam Hussein's supergun.

The picturesque ruins of Bolton Abbey

The Dales

Northwest of Bradford is the market town of **Skipton 21**, the 'gateway to the Dales' and home to the 12th-century **Skipton Castle** (tel: 01756-792 442; www.skiptoncastle.co.uk; daily 10am–6pm, Sun from noon, Oct–Feb until 4pm; charge). Dating from about the same time is the ruined **Bolton Abbey** (tel: 01756-718 000; www.boltonabbey.com; daily 9am–9pm, mid-Mar–May and Sept–Oct until 7pm, Nov–mid-Mar until 6pm; parking charge), located just off the A59 to the east.

Striking out northwest from Skipton into the **Yorkshire Dales National Park 22**, winding lanes lead to **Malham Cove**, an enormous limestone crag with the largest area of limestone pavement in Britain at its top. Further west is the small town of **Settle** the beginning of the scenic **Settle to Carlisle Railway** (see www. settle-carlisle.co.uk for timetables), which crosses the spectacular Ribblehead Viaduct along its route.

Situated to the north, at the heart of the National Park, **Wensleydale** is broad and wooded. In the village of Hawes is the **Dales Countryside Museum** (tel: 01969-666 210; www. yorkshiredales.org.uk; daily 10am–5pm, Jan Tue and weekends only; charge) housed in the former railway station. Nearby is **Hardraw Force**, England's largest single-drop waterfall, where water cascades an impressive 100ft (30m) over the cliff.

Buttertubs Pass, ('buttertubs' are deep limestone shafts) is a road that climbs 1,730ft (530m) high and links Wensleydale with Swaledale to the

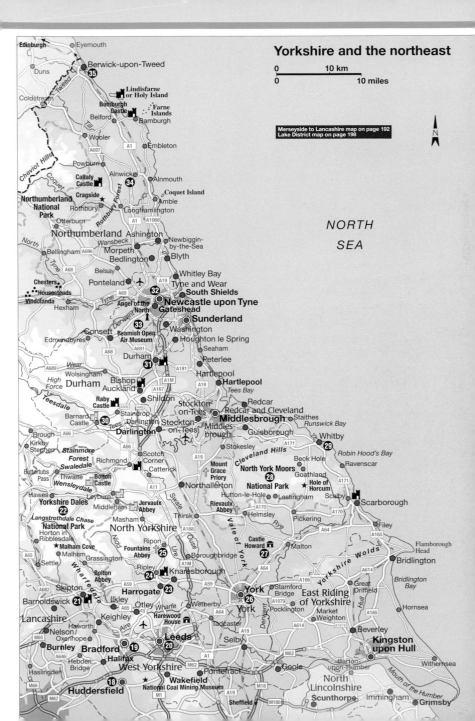

Yorkshire and the northeast

0   10 km
0   10 miles

Merseyside to Lancashire map on page 192
Lake District map on page 198

N

NORTH

SEA

Edinburgh
Eyemouth
Berwick-upon-Tweed ㉟
Duns
Coldstream
Tweed
Lindisfarne
or Holy Island
Bamburgh Castle
Belford
Farne Islands
Bamburgh
Wooler
Till
A1
Embleton
A697
Powburn
Cheviot Hills
Alnwick ㉞
Alnmouth
Callally Castle
Cragside ★
Rothbury
Coquet Island
Amble
Longframlington
Coquet
Northumberland National Park
Otterburn
A1 A1068
North
Bellingham
A696
Wansbeck
Newbiggin-by-the-Sea
Northumberland
Ashington
Morpeth
Bedlington
Blyth
Tyne
A68
Belsay
Whitley Bay
Ponteland
Tyne and Wear
South Shields
Chesters
Housesteads
Vindolanda
Hexham
A69
A19 ㉜
Angel of the North
Newcastle upon Tyne
Gateshead
Sunderland
Derwent
Consett ㉝ Beamish Open Air Museum
Washington
Edmundbyres
Houghton le Spring
Seaham
A68 A691
Durham ㉛
Peterlee
Wear
A689
Wolsingham
Hartlepool
High Force
Durham
A181
Bishop Auckland
Hartlepool
A1M
Tees Bay
Raby Castle
A167
Shildon
A19
Teesdale
Staindrop
Stockton-on-Tees
Redcar
Redcar and Cleveland
Barnard Castle ㉚
Darlington Stockton-on-Tees
Middlesbrough
Staithes
Brough
A66
Middlesbrough
Guisborough
Runswick Bay
Darlington
A66
Kirkby Stephen
Stainmore Forest
Richmond
Scotch Corner
Stokesley
A19
Cleveland Hills
A171
Whitby ㉙
Robin Hood's Bay
Swaledale
Catterick
Ravenscar
Butterbubs Pass
Thwaite
Bolton Castle
A11
Mount Grace Priory
Beck Hole
North York Moors ㉘
Goathland
Hawes
Wensleydale
Northallerton
National Park
Hole of Horcum
Yorkshire Dales ㉒
Jervaulx Abbey
Leyburn
Middleham
Rievaulx Abbey
Hutton-le-Hole
Lastingham
Scalby
Langstrothdale Chase
National Park
Masham
Thirsk
A170
Helmsley
Pickering
Scarborough
Horton in Ribblesdale
Fountains Abbey ㉕
Ripon
A168
Rye
Filey
★ Malham Cove
Ure
Vale of York
Castle Howard ㉗
A64
A165
Malham
Grassington
Nidd
Boroughbridge
Ouse
Malton
Flamborough Head
A65
Settle
Ripley
A1M
A166
Yorkshire Wolds
A614
Bridlington
Bolton Abbey
Knaresborough ㉔
A59
A64
Bridlington Bay
Skipton
㉓ Harrogate
Ilkley
A59
Wetherby
York ㉖
Stamford Bridge
Great Driffield
Barnoldswick ㉑
A65
Otley
Wharfe
York
A1079
East Riding of Yorkshire
Hornsea
Lancashire
Keighley
Harewood House
A64
Pocklington
Market Weighton
A165
Haworth
Aire
Tadcaster
A19
Derwent
Hull
Nelson
Oxenhope
Leeds ㉛
Selby
A614
Beverley
Burnley
M65
Bradford ⑲
West Yorkshire
Halifax
A646
Hebden Bridge
Kingston upon Hull
Haslingden
M66
Huddersfield ⑱
Wakefield
National Coal Mining Museum ★
Pontefract
M62
Goole
M62
Barton-upon-Humber
Withernsea
M1
M18
North Lincolnshire
Mouth of the Humber
M62
Sheffield
A19
M180
Scunthorpe
Immingham
Grimsby

The Royal Pump Room in Harrogate serves Europe's strongest sulphur water

northeast. **Swaledale** is steep and rocky, with intricate patterns of drystone walls and field barns. Its market town, **Richmond** has a cobbled square and a Norman **castle** (www.english-heritage.org.uk; Mar–Sept daily 10am–6pm, Oct Thur–Mon 10am–4pm; charge).

North from Leeds

North of Leeds just off the A61 is **Harewood House** (tel: 0113-218 1010; www.harewood.org; mid-Apr–Oct daily noon–4pm; charge), a stately home with Robert Adam interiors, Thomas Chippendale furniture and landscaped gardens by 'Capability' Brown.

A little further up the A61 is **Harrogate** ㉓, a handsome spa town. The **Royal Pump Room** (tel: 01423-556 188; www.harrogate.gov.uk; Mon–Sat 10.30am–5pm, Sun 2–5pm; charge) still serves the strongest sulphur water in Europe. The **Royal Hall**, Britain's last surviving Kursaal (Cure Hall) was built in 1903 by the theatre designer Frank Matcham.

Four miles (6.5km) north is **Ripley** ㉔, a village of cobbled squares and stone cottages conceived in the style of Alsace-Lorraine, after the French region took the fancy of the local landowner on his travels. The squire's home, **Ripley Castle** (tel: 01423-770 152; www.ripley-castle.co.uk; guided tours: Apr–Sept daily 10.30am–3pm; Mar and Oct–Nov closed Mon, Wed, Fri; Dec–Jan closed weekdays; charge) has fine collections of art and armour.

Ripon, further along the A61, developed around the Saxon cathedral founded by St Wilfrid in the 7th century. Three miles (5km) to the southwest is **Fountains Abbey** ㉕ (tel: 01765-608 888; www.

Brontë country

Just a few miles to the west – though a world away – from the vast conurbation around Bradford and Leeds is the hill village of Haworth, with its steep cobbled streets and grey stone houses. Scorched in summer and lashed by rain and wind in winter, this atmospheric place is home to the **Brontë Parsonage** (tel: 01535-642 323; www.bronte.org.uk; daily Apr–Sept 10am–5.30pm, Oct–Mar 11am–5pm; charge), where Charlotte, Emily, Anne and their brother Branwell grew up, and masterpieces such as *Wuthering Heights* and *Jane Eyre* were written.

fountainsabbey.org.uk; daily Apr–Sept 10am–5pm, winter until 4pm; charge). The abbey was once part of Britain's richest Cistercian monastery, and the atmospheric remains are the largest monastic ruins in the country. Adjacent to the abbey grounds is Studley Royal, an estate with Georgian water gardens and a deer park.

York

The Yorkshire Dales are separated from the North York Moors by the broad Vale of York, and at its centre is **York** ㉖, a city of partly Roman, but mainly medieval, walls and streets, centred around the country's largest cathedral.

York Minster (tel: 0844-939 0011; www.yorkminster.org; Mon–Sat 9am–5pm, Sun noon–3.45pm; charge) is a fusion of classical, Norman, Saxon and English influences. Constantine the Great was declared Roman emperor here, providing an improbable link between Yorkshire and the founding of

Constantinople. In the shelter of the cathedral, to the south, is a maze of medieval streets and alleys, including the **Shambles**, the former butchers' quarter. Surrounding the old centre are the **city walls**, in some parts wide enough for horses to pass – though it can take two hours to complete the circuit on foot.

Eight centuries after the Romans arrived in York, the Vikings came, renaming the settlement Jorvik. A routine archaeological dig in 1976 turned up a treasure trove of 15,000 artefacts, now the core of the **Jorvik Viking Centre** (tel: 01904-615 505; www.jorvik-viking-centre.co.uk; daily Easter–Oct 10am–5pm, winter until 4pm; charge). Visitors ride in electric buggies down a 'time tunnel' into a reconstructed 10th-century Viking village. The buggies then pass through the actual excavation site.

There is also a historical survey on offer at the **Yorkshire Museum** (tel: 01904-687 687; www.yorkshire museum.org.uk; daily 10am–5pm;

The north

York Minster, where Constantine the Great was declared Roman emperor

charge) near the railway station to the north of the old town. Among the Roman, Anglo-Saxon and Viking treasures is the Middleham Jewel. You can picnic in the museum's botanical gardens, where peacocks roam.

Nearby is the **National Railway Museum** (tel: 08448-153 139; www.nrm.org.uk; daily 10am–6pm; free). This is the world's largest such museum, and includes the famous *Flying Scotsman* as well as Queen Victoria's luxurious carriage.

North Yorkshire

North of York off the A64 is **Castle Howard** ❷ (tel: 01653-648 333; www.castlehoward.co.uk; Apr–Oct daily 11am–4pm; charge), one of the grandest Baroque stately homes in Britain. It is also famous since it featured heavily in the television adaptation of Evelyn Waugh's *Brideshead Revisited*.

Further north lies the **North York Moors National Park** ❷. Approaching from the west or the south, many visitors arrive in the park via the market town of Helmsley. Nearby, deep in the Rye Valley, are the romantic ruins of **Rievaulx Abbey** (tel: 01439-798 228; www.english-heritage.org.uk; Apr–Sept daily 10am–6pm, Oct Thur–Mon 10am–4pm; charge), another of Yorkshire's great medieval monasteries.

Where the park's moorland heather is penetrated by dales of lush pasture, there are sometimes dramatic natural features, such as the Hole of Horcum above the Vale of Pickering; elsewhere the dales enfold villages and farmhouses of honey-coloured sandstone. On the northern flanks, above Eskdale, are Goathland and Beck Hole, the latter a delightful hamlet with an arc of cottages facing a green. Across it all, from Pickering to Whitby, runs the steam-powered

Old farm building on the North York Moors

Scarborough spa town and its 12th-century castle

lies **Scarborough**, a Victorian spa resort with a 12th-century **castle** (tel: 01723-372 451; www.english-heritage.org.uk; Apr–Sept daily 10am–6pm, Oct Thur–Mon 10am–4pm; charge).

The northeast

The northeast of England feels like border country. The presence of grand castles and Hadrian's Wall reminds the visitor of historic boundaries, and the great ports of Teesside and Tyneside emphasise that the North Sea is a barrier of a different kind.

To County Durham

Heading north from Whitby and leaving Yorkshire behind, the beach resort of **Redcar** is a playground for the former Teesside industrial centres of **Middlesbrough**, **Stockton-on-Tees** and **Darlington**. The region boomed in the 19th century, as coal and iron were discovered and railways were built. George Stephenson's Locomotion No. 1 (1825) is displayed at Darlington's railway museum, **Head of Steam** (tel: 01325-460 532; www.darlington.gov.uk; Apr–Sept Tue–Sun 10am–4pm, Oct–Mar Wed–Sun 11am–3.30pm; charge), near where it once ran on the world's first railway line, between Stockton and Darlington.

Sixteen miles (25km) to the west, on the River Tees, is the the old market town of **Barnard Castle** ❸⓪. Here the château-like **Bowes Museum** (tel: 01833-690 606; www.thebowesmuseum.org.uk; daily 10am–5pm; charge) has a superb

North Yorkshire Moors Railway (see www.nymr.co.uk for timetable).

Coastal highlights

The Moors end at the east coast, where breaks in the cliffs provide space for pretty villages and the occasional town. **Whitby** ❷⓽ is a fishing port noted for its ruined 13th-century **abbey** (tel: 01947-603 568; www.english-heritage.org.uk; Apr–Sept daily 10am–6pm, Oct Thur–Mon 10am–4pm; charge). The Pacific explorer Captain James Cook (1728–79) also lived in this former whaling port, and the **Captain Cook Memorial Museum** (tel: 01947-601 900; www.cookmuseumwhitby.co.uk; Apr–Oct daily 9.45am–5pm, Mar 11am–3pm; charge) is the focal point of a Cook heritage trail.

To the south, **Robin Hood's Bay**, was once a smugglers' haunt. Today its cobbled streets and sandy beaches are popular with families. Further south

The north

collection of fine and decorative arts, including a clockwork silver swan.

Further north is the university city of **Durham ③**, with a spectacular Romanesque **cathedral** (tel: 0191-386 4266; www.durhamcathedral.co.uk; Mon–Sat 7.30am–6pm, Sun 7.45am–5.30pm; donations). The city's splendid **castle** (for guided tour tel: 0191-334 3800) was the only northern stronghold not to fall to the marauding Scots, and is now occupied by University College.

Many American visitors continue north to **Washington** to see the 17th-century **Old Hall** (tel: 0191-416 6879; www.nationaltrust.org.uk; mid-Mar–Oct Sun–Wed 11am–5pm; charge). This handsome stone manor house is the ancestral home of the USA's first president.

Newcastle upon Tyne

Dominating the northeast is **Newcastle upon Tyne ③**, a sprawling former shipbuilding city, celebrated for its resilient locals ('Geordies'), whose dialect borders on impenetrability. Approaching from the south by the A1 or A167, a 66ft (20m) -tall steel giant marks the entry into Tyneside. The **Angel of the North** stands on the site of a former coal mine and was created by artist Antony Gormley. For a realistic look at how life used to be in the northeast, visit the **Beamish Open Air Museum ③** (tel: 0191-370 4000; www.beamish.org.uk; Apr–Oct daily 10am–5pm, Nov–mid-Mar Tue–Thur and Sat–Sun 10am–4pm; charge), 8 miles (13km) southwest of Newcastle. It has a working 1913 village with buildings and artefacts collected from the region.

The Millennium Bridge in Newcastle leads to the developments in Gateshead Quays

In the city itself, the striking **Millennium Bridge** links Newcastle Quayside with the new developments on Gateshead Quays. These include the **Baltic Centre for Contemporary Art** (tel: 0191-478 1810; www.balticmill.com; Mon–Sat 9am–6pm; free) and the **Sage** concert hall and music education centre (*see p.218*). The latter's shimmering shell-like form was designed by Norman Foster.

Coastal strongholds

About 34 miles (54km) north of Newcastle is **Alnwick Castle ③** (tel: 01665-511 100; www.alnwickcastle.com; Apr–Oct daily 11am–5pm; charge), home of the Dukes of Northumberland and backdrop of Harry Potter and many other films. The grounds have fun for children, with the Poison Garden, Serpent Garden, Bamboo Labyrinth and a Tree House complex linked by walkways.

Further up the coast is another stunning fortress, **Bamburgh Castle** (tel: 01668-214 515; www.bamburghcastle.com; mid-Feb–Oct daily 10am–5pm, Nov–mid-Feb Sat–Sun 11am–4.30pm;

Hadrian's Wall

Begun during the reign of Emperor Hadrian in AD122, **Hadrian's Wall** runs 73 miles (117km) across the north of England. The strategic importance of the site of Newcastle was first recognised at this time, and a minor fort and bridge were built on the wall here. At nearby South Shields, archaeologists have excavated the **Arbeia Roman Fort** (tel: 0191-232 6789; www.twmuseums.org.uk; Easter–Sept Mon–Sat 10am–3pm, Sun 1–5pm, Oct–Easter 10am–3.30pm, closed Sun; charge). To the west, near Hexham, **Housesteads Roman Fort** (tel: 01434-652 220; www.english-heritage.org.uk; Apr–Sept daily 10am–6pm, Oct until 4pm; charge) is the best preserved of the 16 forts along the wall, and nearby is the major site of **Vindolanda** and the **Roman Army Museum** (tel: 01434-344 277; www.vindolanda.com; Apr–Nov daily 10am–6pm, Oct until 5pm; charge).

charge). From here, on a clear day, you can see the **Farne Islands**, 4½ miles (7km) offshore. Boats for this former saints' sanctuary of seabirds and seals leave from Seahouses harbour (tel: 01665-720 308; www.farne-islands.com; daily, every hour 10am–3pm; charge).

Further north still is **Lindisfarne** (or 'Holy Island'), which can be reached at low tide via a causeway. Monks from the Scottish Isle of Iona, led by St Columbine, settled here in the 7th century and founded a **priory** (tel: 01289-389 200; www.english-heritage.org.uk; daily Apr–Sept 9.30am–5pm, Oct until 4pm; charge) that achieved renown as a centre of scholarship. The illuminated Lindisfarne Gospels, now in the British Museum, were produced here.

On the border with Scotland is the seaport of **Berwick-upon-Tweed** ⑮, England's most northerly town. Walk along the Elizabethan ramparts and you can gaze down on its cobbled streets and out towards the shoreline.

Alnwick Castle has been featured in several films, including the Harry Potter franchise

ACCOMMODATION

Visitors can look to cities such as Liverpool and Manchester for stylish boutique hotels, while in rural areas such as the Lake District or Northumberland they can expect to find peaceful country house hotels with fine cuisine and coaching inns with old-fashioned informality.

Merseyside

Britannia Adelphi Hotel
Ranelagh Place, Liverpool
Tel: 0151-709 7200
www.adelphi-hotel.co.uk
This grand neoclassical stone block building is one of Liverpool's major landmarks, next to Lime Street station. **££**

Hope Street Hotel
40 Hope Street, Liverpool
Tel: 0151-709 3000
www.hopestreethotel.co.uk
Boutique hotel with large, light rooms, wood floors, friendly staff and an excellent restaurant. **££–£££**

Manchester

Malmaison Manchester
1–3 Piccadilly, Manchester
Tel: 0161-2781 000
www.malmaison-manchester.com
Occupying a former warehouse, this boutique hotel's red-and-black decor recalls the Moulin Rouge and is decadently luxurious. **££**

Malmaison Manchester

Yorkshire

Devonshire Arms Country House Hotel
Bolton Abbey, Skipton
Tel: 01756-710 441
www.thedevonshirearms.co.uk
This hotel is renowned for quality and service, and even boasts antique furniture from Chatsworth. **£££**

Minster Hotel
60 Bootham, York
Tel: 01904-621 267
www.yorkminsterhotel.co.uk
A skilful conversion of two Victorian houses, four minutes from the Minster, has created a stylish hotel with a rooftop garden and superb views. **££**

The northeast

The Blue Bell Hotel
Market Place, Belford
Tel: 01668-213 543
www.bluebellhotel.com
Located on the coast near Lindisfarne, this charmingly old-fashioned 17th-century coaching inn is furnished in a quaint period style. **£–££**

The County Hotel
Priestpopple, Hexham
Tel: 01434-603 601
www.thecountyhexham.co.uk
This is a family-run inn which offers excellent hospitality in a market town close to Hadrian's Wall. **£**

Three Tuns Hotel
New Elvet, Durham
Tel: 0191-3864 326

www.swallow-hotels.com
With its wooden-panelled restaurant and old-fashioned service, this is a grand place to stay. **££**

The Lake District

Fayrer Garden House Hotel
Lyth Valley Road, Bowness-on-Windermere
Tel: 01539-488 195
www.fayrergarden.com
For comfort and service, this hotel cannot be bettered. The restaurant's menu is based on locally sourced ingredients, and the dishes are executed with style and intelligence. **££–£££**

Sharrow Bay
Sharrow Bay, Ullswater
Tel: 01768-486 301
www.sharrowbay.co.uk
This Italianate luxury hotel is set in formal gardens overlooking Ullswater. The fine food on offer has won its restaurant a Michelin star. **£££**

RESTAURANTS

Fortunately, the days of north-country chip butties, and vegetables boiled for hours are long gone. Today, the north of England boasts some excellent eateries, and the Lake District in particular is renowned for its Michelin-starred restaurants.

Merseyside

Arkle Restaurant
Chester Grosvenor Hotel, Eastgate Street, Chester
Tel: 01244-324 024
www.chestergrosvenor.co.uk
This Michelin-starred restaurant is situated within a grand hotel in central Chester. Its British cuisine is beautifully cooked and exquisitely presented. **£££**

Yuet Ben Restaurant
1 Upper Duke Street, Liverpool
Tel: 0151-709 5772
www.yuetben.co.uk
A local institution serving well-cooked northern Chinese food at reasonable prices. **£**

Manchester and Lancashire

Chaophraya Thai Restaurant
15–17 Chapel Walks, Manchester
Tel: 0161-832 8342
www.chaophraya.co.uk
For excellent Thai food and friendly service, this bustling restaurant is a reliable option. **££**

Oliver's Restaurant
Lancaster House Hotel, 272 Central Drive, Blackpool
Tel: 01253-341 928
www.oliversblackpool.co.uk
No, not Jamie Oliver, but another chef who knows what to do with good fresh ingredients, including Morecambe Bay shrimps. **££**

Yorkshire

Box Tree
35-37 Church Street, Ilkley
Tel: 01943-608 484
www.theboxtree.co.uk
Young Marco Pierre White cut his culinary teeth at this 18th-century farmhouse serving modern French classics. **££**

The Magpie Café
14 Pier Road, Whitby
Tel: 01947-602 058
www.magpiecafe.co.uk
Legendary harbourside restaurant, best known for superb fish and chips. **££**

L'Enclume interior

Robust French country cooking in a 16th-century farmhouse on the edge of the city. **££**

Blackfriars Restaurant
Friars Street, Newcastle
Tel: 0191-261 2945
www.blackfriarsrestaurant.co.uk
Reputedly the oldest purpose-built restaurant in Britain, with a medieval banqueting hall. Actor Kevin Spacey declared it served 'the best roast dinners in England'. **££**

The Lake District
L'Enclume
Cavendish Street, Cartmel, near Grange-Over-Sands
Tel: 01539-536 362
www.lenclume.co.uk
This Michelin-starred restaurant is one of the most creative restaurants in the Lakes. The food is a combination of traditional and modern, using many ingredients foraged from the wild. **£££**

Nawaab
32 Manor Road, Bradford
Tel: 01274-730 371
www.nawaabs.net
With scores of curry houses in Bradford, you couldn't do better than start at this city-centre evergreen. **£–££**

The northeast
Bistro 21
Aykley Heads House, Aykley Heads, Durham
Tel: 0191-384 4354
www.bistrotwentyone.co.uk

Miller Howe
Rayrigg Road, Windermere
Tel: 01539-442 536
www.millerhowe.com
With Lancashire cheese, Cumbrian ham and Herdwick mutton, this restaurant within a country house hotel is a great place to try some well-cooked, imaginative local food. **££–£££**

NIGHTLIFE

Some of the best centres for nightlife in the UK are to be found in the north. Manchester has long had a big reputation to live up to, but Liverpool, Leeds and Newcastle also boast high-quality venues, good music and a happy atmosphere.

Merseyside
The Masque
90 Seel Street, Liverpool
Tel: 0151-707 6171
www.masque-liverpool.com
Thursdays, Fridays and Saturdays are big nights out at this well-established club. The music ranges from hip-hop to house.

Manchester and Lancashire
Club Alter Ego
105–7 Princess Street, Manchester
Tel: 0161-236 9266
www.clubalterego.co.uk
Perhaps Manchester's best known club on the gay scene holds club nights Thursday to Saturday, starting late and finishing early.

FAC 251: The Factory
112-8 Princess Street, Manchester
Tel: 0161-272 7251
www.factorymanchester.com
The former premises of Factory Records
is now a club and live music venue. Gigs
are usually at 9pm and DJ sets follow on
afterwards.

Sankeys
Radium Street, Manchester
Tel: 0161-236 5444
www.sankeys.info
This is one of Manchester's top dance clubs,
hosting top-end DJs and featuring the latest
sound systems.

Yorkshire
Mission
8-13 Heaton's Court, Leeds
Tel: 08701-220 114

www.clubmission.com
This well-established club throws some of
the biggest parties in Leeds. It also hosts
gay club nights.

The northeast
Powerhouse Nightclub
9-19 Westmorland Road, Newcastle
Tel: 0191-261 5348
www.clubph.co.uk
Cheesy music, video screens and lots of
lights make this perfect for dancing.

World Headquarters
Curtis Mayfield House, Carliol Square,
Newcastle
Tel: 0191-2813 445
www.welovewhq.com
One of Newcastle's best clubs plays most
styles of black music, from funk to soul to
R&B and reggae.

ENTERTAINMENT
Victorian industrial wealth in the north of England left many grand theatres and
fine orchestras in its wake. In recent decades these have been supplemented
with stylish new venues, dedicated to theatre, film and music of all kinds.

Film
Brewery Arts Centre
Highgate, Kendal
Tel: 01539-725 133
www.breweryarts.co.uk
This arts complex made out of a beautiful
old brewery has two cinemas as well as a
theatre.

City Screen
13-17 Coney Street
Tel: 0871-902 5726
www.picturehouses.co.uk
This smart new cinema is built out of the shell
of the old Yorkshire Evening Press building.

Cornerhouse
70 Oxford Street, Manchester
Tel: 0161-200 1500
www.cornerhouse.org

Manchester's premier arts cinema screens
the latest releases, and also offers film
courses, Q&As and themed festivals.

Hyde Park Picture House
Brudenell Road, Headingley, Leeds
Tel: 0113-275 2045
www.hydeparkpicturehouse.co.uk
This beautiful old cinema was built in 1914,
and offers a dedicated clientele of cineastes
all the latest arthouse flicks.

Rheged Centre
Redhills, Penrith
Tel: 01768-868 000
www.rheged.com
Housed in Europe's largest grass-covered
building, this arts centre houses a state-of-
the-art cinema, children's play areas and
places to eat.

Tyneside Cinema
Pilgrim Street, Newcastle
Tel: 0845-217 9909
www.tynesidecinema.co.uk
As well as a beautiful Art-Deco auditorium, the same building houses two other, more modern, movie theatres. Free guided tours and old newsreel screenings are also on offer.

Theatre
Royal Exchange Theatre
St Ann's Square, Manchester
Tel: 0161-833 9833
www.royalexchange.org.uk
This extraordinary glass-walled theatre-in-the-round is situated within the historic Victorian Cotton Exchange Buildings in Manchester city centre.

Stephen Joseph Theatre
Westborough, Scarborough
Tel: 01723-370 541
www.sjt.uk.com
Scarborough has an enviable theatrical reputation, built around Alan Ayckbourn, the local-born playwright who has premiered most of his 70-plus plays at this theatre.

Theatre Royal
100 Grey Street, Newcastle
Tel: 08448-112 121
www.theatreroyal.co.uk
The winter home of the Royal Shakespeare Company offers classic drama as well as more light-hearted fare, from musicals to comedy.

York Theatre Royal
St Leonard's Place, York
Tel: 01904-623 568
www.yorktheatreroyal.co.uk
This fine old theatre stages a varied diet of classic plays, musicals, children's shows and dance.

Music
Band on the Wall
25 Swan Street, Manchester

Tel: 0161-834 1786
www.bandonthewall.org
This stylish not-for-profit venue presents a varied programme of world music, jazz and folk.

Bridgewater Concert Hall
Lower Mosley Street, Manchester
Tel: 0161-907 9000
www.bridgewater-hall.co.uk
This modern sculptural structure on the waterfront houses a 2,400-seat concert hall for performances by the resident orchestra, the Hallé.

Grand Theatre and Opera House
46 New Briggate, Leeds
Tel: 0844-848 2706
www.leedsgrandtheatre.com
Opera North, the resident opera company, handles the classical side of things, while a range of touring productions offer audiences lighter musical theatre.

Philharmonic Hall
Hope Street, Liverpool
Tel: 0151-709 3789
www.liverpoolphil.com
This beautiful Art-Deco building is home to the renowned Liverpool Philharmonic Orchestra.

Royal Hall
Ripon Road, Harrogate
Tel: 01423-500 500
www.royalhall.co.uk
This opulent Edwardian theatre offers a programme featuring top orchestras, brass bands, choirs, jazz outfits and ballet companies.

Sage Gateshead
Gateshead Quays
Tel: 0191-443 4666
www.thesagegateshead.org
This Norman Foster-designed venue is home to both the Northern Sinfonia and Folkworks, a company dedicated to traditional music, song and dance. There are a variety of concerts, classes and workshops on offer.

SPORTS AND ACTIVITIES

Probably the most popular outdoor activity among visitors to the north of England is walking, and with four national parks offering moors, fells, lakes and forests, it's not difficult to see why. There are other options, though, including horse riding, sailing, cycling and canoeing.

Activities on the Water

Browns Boathouse
Elvet Bridge, Durham
Tel: 0191 386 3779
Between April and October you can hire a rowing boat and paddle up the River Wear.

Low Wood Watersports Centre
Low Wood Bay, Windermere
Tel: 015394-39441
www.elh.co.uk
Between April and October, this watersports centre offers rowing boats, kayaks, canoes, sailing dinghies and water-skiing.

Cycling

Grizedale Mountain Bikes
Grizedale Visitor Centre, Hawkshead
Tel: 01229-860 369
www.grizedalemountainbikes.co.uk
The Lake District provides plenty of challenging routes for the mountain biking enthusiast, and this shop rents out all the necessary equipment.

Purple Mountain Bike Hire
Low Dalby, Pickering, Northumberland
Tel: 01751-460 011
www.purplemountain.co.uk
Hire a bike and try out one of the local trails in the Kielder Forest either on your own or on one of the evening group rides.

Horse riding

Friars Hill Stables
Sinnington, near Pickering, North Yorkshire
Tel: 01751-432 758
www.friarshillstables.co.uk
Friars Hill have an indoor school, and offer a range of lessons and accompanied hacks. They also run children's 'learn about ponies' morning sessions, as well as longer residential and non-residential courses.

Lakeland Pony Trekking
Limefitt Park, Patterdale Road, Troutbeck, Windermere
Tel: 015394-31999
www.lakelandponytrekking.co.uk
From half-hour rides for small children to full-day trail rides through the Troutbeck Valley, this company caters for all ages and all levels of experience.

Gliding

Yorkshire Gliding Club
Sutton Bank, Thirsk, North Yorkshire
Tel: 01845-597 237
www.ygc.co.uk
For a bird's-eye view of Yorkshire, this club offers trail lessons, as well as one- and five-day courses.

Horse riding in the Lake District

TOURS

Whatever your preferred means of travel – boat, train, bus or on foot – there is no shortage of tours being offered around the major cities and beauty spots of the north. And besides the usual sightseeing, there are plenty of themed tours too – from ghosts to ABBA, and from *Swallows and Amazons* to The Beatles.

Walking tours

Shiverpool Tours
Unit C, Baltic Creative Centre,
22 Jordan Street, Liverpool
Tel: 0151-709 2030
www.shiverpool.co.uk
These evening ghost tours take you to some of Liverpool's eeriest quarters. Many of the tours are accessible to wheelchair users.

Yorkwalk
3 Fairway, Clifton, York
Tel: 01904-622 303
www.yorkwalk.co.uk
Historical, literary, pub, and even 'choccy and sweetie' tours leave from Museum Gardens Gates on Museum Street.

Train tours

Keighley and Worth Valley Railway
The Railway Station, Haworth
Tel: 01535-645 214
www.kwvr.co.uk
The film of *The Railway Children* was shot on this 5-mile (8km) steam railway line that chugs along between Keighley and Oxenhope.

Bus and car tours

Beatles Fab Four Taxi Tour
Liverpool
Tel: 0151-601 2111
www.thebeatlesfabfourtaxitour.co.uk
Up to five people can cram into a black cab for a three-hour tour of Beatles landmarks.

City Sightseeing Newcastle
Departs from Newcastle railway station
Tel: 0191-228 8900
www.city-sightseeing.com
A 24-hour ticket enables you to hop on and off this open-top bus as it tours the city.

Boat trips

ChesterBoat
Boating Station, Souters Lane,
The Groves, Chester
Tel: 01244-325 394
www.chesterboat.co.uk
Enjoy boat trips up the River Dee with an informative commentary. Alternatively, on summer evenings you can dance to ABBA songs on disco cruises.

Coniston Launch
29 Manor Park, Keswick
Tel: 017687-75753
www.conistonlaunch.co.uk
Solar-powered launches offer trips on Coniston Water, stopping at jetties on the way.

Windermere Lake Cruises
Winander House, Glebe Road, Bowness-on-Windermere
Tel: 015394-43360
www.windermere-lakecruises.co.uk
Vintage and modern cruisers offer trips to various attractions around Windermere.

Yellow Duckmarine Tour
32 Anchor Courtyard, Albert Dock, Liverpool
Tel: 0151-708 7799
www.theyellowduckmarine.co.uk
The first half-hour of a tour on this World War II amphibious vehicle takes you round the city centre, for the second half, you take to the water for a cruise around Liverpool docks.

The Yellow Duckmarine Tour

FESTIVALS AND EVENTS

Several events in the north of England celebrate the particularities of the region's culture and landscape, whether it's the Lake District's mountains, York's Viking past, Manchester's gay scene or the people of Bradford's south Asian heritage.

February

Jorvik Viking Festival
Various venues in York
www.vikingjorvik.com
A week-long programme of battle re-enactments, talks, themed walks and exhibitions; coincides with schools' half-term holidays in mid-February.

April

Aintree Festival
Aintree, Liverpool
www.aintree.co.uk
The main event is the Grand National Steeplechase, probably the biggest race in the British horse racing calendar. The festival takes place on the first weekend of the month.

May

Whitby Spring Session
Whitby Rugby Club, White Leys Road
www.moorandcoast.co.uk
This three-day folk festival over the Spring Bank Holiday weekend features prominent practitioners of the genre and food stalls.

June

Bradford Mela
Peel Park, Bradford
www.bradfordmela.org.uk
A one-day festival in mid-June celebrating Indian heritage with music, dance, street theatre and crafts.

Keswick Beer Festival
Near the town centre
www.keswickbeerfestival.co.uk
On the first weekend in June marquees offer over 250 different ales, and bands provide the music.

July

Great Yorkshire Show
Showground, Harrogate
www.greatyorkshireshow.co.uk
This vast three-day agricultural show in mid-July features livestock competitions, show jumping, food tastings and hot-air balloon rides.

Manchester Jazz Festival
Various venues in Manchester
www.manchesterjazz.com
From lunchtime until late at night each day for a week at the end of the month, jazz enthusiasts can mellow at over 50 venues throughout the city.

August

Leeds Festival
Bramham Park, near Leeds
www.leedsfestival.com
This well-established festival over the August Bank Holiday weekend features a big line-up of rock bands, from relative newcomers to the world famous.

Manchester Pride
www.manchesterpride.com
This 10-day festival of gay pride in mid-August includes music, comedy, theatre, and a parade.

October

Manchester Comedy Festival
Various venues in Manchester
www.manchestercomedyfestival.co.uk
For two weeks in the second half of October Manchester welcomes old hands from the circuit and exciting new talent.

November

Kendal Mountain Festival
Brewery Arts Centre and venues in Kendal
www.mountainfest.co.uk
Four days of book signings, talks and exhibitions, and the mountain film competition. It all happens in mid-November.

Listings

Scotland

Scotland is a place of endless variety. The Lowlands offer hills and seascapes, impressive stately homes and the country of Robert Burns, as well as the vibrant cities of Edinburgh and Glasgow. The Highlands form one of the last great wildernesses of Europe – endless stretches of mountains, glens and moorlands probed by the long fingers of sea lochs.

Edinburgh

Population: 480,000

Local dialling code: 0131

Tourist office: Edinburgh and Scotland Information Centre, 3 Princes Street; tel: 0845-225 5121; www.edinburgh.org

Main police station: 2 Gayfield Square; tel: 0131-556 9270

Main post office: 40 Frederick Street

Main hospital: Royal Infirmary of Edinburgh, Little France Crescent, Old Dalkeith Road; tel: 0131-536 1000; www.nhslothian.scot.nhs.uk

Media: *The Scotsman; The Skinny*

Scotland is a quite different experience from England. The Scots themselves have a keen sense of identity, different values, and their own history and traditions. The Scots joined England in the Union of the Crowns in 1603 – James VI of Scotland became James I of England, the first 'British' monarch – and then in 1701 joined England in the Union of the Parliaments, whereby the two parliaments met jointly at Westminster. Scotland regained its own independent parliament in 1999. Throughout all, the Scots maintained their own legal and educational systems, widely regarded as superior to those in England, and continued to print their own design of bank notes – often the first clue to visitors that this is a different country within Britain.

Occupying the north of Great Britain, two Roman emperors built walls across the country to keep in place the region's Celtic warriors, the Picts and the Scots: Hadrian's Wall, across what is now northern England, and the Antonine Wall, on a line between Glasgow and Edinburgh. Scotland's 30,400 sq miles (78,740 sq km) cover one-third of Great Britain yet its population, of which over 30 percent live in or around the three most populous cities, Edinburgh, Glasgow and Aberdeen, is less than one-tenth of the whole.

Edinburgh and environs

Between the Pentland Hills and the Firth (estuary) of Forth, **Edinburgh** ❶ has one of the most stunning settings in the world.

Edinburgh Castle

On the south side of its main thoroughfare, Princes Street, rises the basalt ridge on which medieval Edinburgh is built. It is dominated by **Edinburgh Castle**  (tel: 0131-225 9846; www.edinburghcastle.gov.uk; daily, Apr–Sept 9.30am–6pm, Oct–Mar until 5pm; charge).

Inside the castle complex is the 12th-century St Margaret's Chapel, the Great Hall – which has a magnificent hammerbeam ceiling – and the tiny room where in 1566 Mary Queen of Scots gave birth to James VI of Scotland (James I of England). There is also the crown jewels and the Stone of Destiny, or Stone of Scone, the coronation seat of Scottish kings.

The Royal Mile

Four streets – Castlehill, Lawnmarket, High Street and Canongate – make

A view of impressive Edinburgh Castle and its lush surrounds

Shopping along the Royal Mile

up the **Royal Mile**, which descends from the vast esplanade in front of the castle (where the spectacular Tattoo is held in August) and ends in the Palace of Holyroodhouse. Along its route are some of the best examples of 16th- and 17th-century domestic architecture in Scotland.

At the top is the **Scotch Whisky Experience** (tel: 0131-220 0441; www.scotchwhiskyexperience.co.uk; daily 10am–6pm; charge), which offers a thorough briefing on the national drink and a free dram at the end of the tour. Nearby is a **Camera Obscura** (tel: 0131-226 3709; www.camera-obscura.co.uk; daily July–Oct 9.30am–7.30pm, Apr–June 9.30am–6pm, Nov–Mar 10am–5pm; charge), where an extraordinary contraption projects live images of the surrounding city.

Further along stands Parliament House – now the law courts – and the **High Kirk of St Giles**  (tel: 0131-225 9442; www.stgilescathedral.org.uk; May-Sept Mon–Fri 9am–7pm, Sat 9am–5pm, Sun 1–5pm, Oct–Apr Mon–Sat 9am–5pm, Sun 1–5pm; charge)

Scotland

with the magnificent Thistle Chapel. There is also the **John Knox House Museum** (tel: 0131-556 9579; www. scottishstorytellingcentre.co.uk; Mon–Sat 10am–6pm, Sun Jul–Aug only noon–6pm; charge); the fiery Protestant reformer preached from the windows here.

For Scottish history, the newly renovated **National Museum of Scotland** (tel: 0300-123 6789; www.nms. ac.uk; daily 10am–5pm), in Chambers Street, is worth a visit.

At the end of the Royal Mile is the **Palace of Holyroodhouse** (tel: 0131-556 5100; www.royalcollection. org.uk; daily, Apr–Oct 9.30am–5pm, Nov–Mar until 3.30pm; charge), the official residence of the Queen when she visits Scotland. The palace was begun in 1498 by James IV, and was to have close associations with Mary Queen of Scots. Situated in front of the palace is the **Queen's Gallery** (opening times as above; joint ticket available), which offers changing exhibits of artwork from the Royal Collection.

Across the road is the controversial **Scottish Parliament** (tel: 0131-348 5200; www.scottish.parliament.uk; Mon–Sat, see website for times; free), completed in 2004 after exceeding its £40 million construction budget more than 10 times over.

To the south of the palace is the volcanic peak known as **Arthur's Seat**, 823ft (251m) in height. The vantage point at the summit offers wonderful views of the city and across the Firth of Forth to the north.

Princes Street and the New Town

Edinburgh's main shopping street is **Princes Street**, which runs roughly

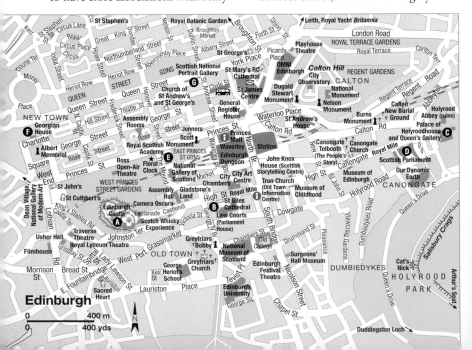

Airports: Edinburgh (tel: 0844-481 8989; www.edinburghairport.com) is 8 miles (13km) west of the city centre. Airlink 100 buses (www.flybybus.com) run into town every 10–20 minutes between 4.50am and 00.20am (journey time 25 minutes). Fare: £3.50 single. A taxi takes 20 minutes and costs around £20

 Trains: Waverley Station is the main train hub, with good connections to London, Glasgow (every 15 minutes daily) and much of the rest of Scotland (www.nationalrail.co.uk). Tickets can be purchased in advance online or at stations at the time of travelling

 Buses: Lothian Buses (www.lothianbuses.com) operate services throughout the city and the region. The flat fare is £1.20. Nightbuses operate on ten routes across the city (see www.nightbuses.com). Unlimited night travel is £3. Tickets can be purchased from the driver

 Taxis: Licensed taxis ('black cabs') can be hailed on the street; they display the regulated charges on the meter. For booking ahead, try Central Taxis, tel: 0131-229 2468; www.taxis-edinburgh.co.uk

 Car hire: All the major companies (see p.267) have branches at the airports

parallel with the Royal Mile on the far side of the gardens below the Castle. It's most conspicuous landmark is the huge Gothic **monument to Sir Walter Scott** opposite Jenners department store. A little to the west is the turning for The Mound, which harbours the **Royal Scottish Academy ❺** (tel: 0131-225 6671; www.royalscottishacademy.org; Mon–Sat 10am–5pm, Sun noon–5pm; charge) and the **National Gallery of Scotland** (tel: 0131-624 6200; www.nationalgalleries.org; daily 10am–5pm, Thur until 7pm; free).

On the north side of Princes Street is the **New Town**, a splendid example of 18th-century town planning, in marked contrast to the chaotic street plan of the medieval **Old Town**. Both the Old and the New Town are Unesco World Heritage Sites. Visitors can learn more about the building of the New Town and its first residents at the **Georgian**

House ❻ (7 Charlotte Square; tel: 0844-493 2117; www.nts.org.uk; Mar–Nov daily, see website for times; charge). At the eastern end of Queen's Street is the **Scottish National Portrait Gallery ❼** (details as for National Gallery; *see left*).

To the east of Princes Street is **Calton Hill**, another volcanic outcrop, which is crowned by the

The Royal Botanic Garden in Edinburgh

old **City Observatory**, with its Grecian-style dome, together with the **National Monument**, an unfinished copy of the Parthenon in Athens, and the **Nelson Monument** (tel: 0131-556 2716; www.edinburghmuseums.org.uk; Mon–Sat Apr–Sept 10am–6pm, Oct–Mar 10am–3pm; charge).

Beyond the New Town

North of the New Town is the **Royal Botanic Garden** (tel: 0131-552 7171; www.rbge.org.uk; daily Feb–Oct 10am–6pm, Nov–Jan 10am–4pm; free), with its woodland, flora and glass-houses. Following the Water of Leith northeast leads on to the old docklands of **Leith**, where the decommissioned **Royal Yacht Britannia** (tel: 0131-555 5566; www.royalyachtbritannia.co.uk; daily 10am–4.30pm, 3.30pm in winter; charge; *see also p.27*) is permanently moored at the Ocean Terminal. In recent decades, the district around has been given a thorough makeover. It is now home to many of the city's most fashionable bars and restaurants.

Back upstream to the west of the New Town lies **Dean Village**. On Belford Street are the **Scottish National Gallery of Modern Art** and its sister museum, the **Dean Gallery** (details as for National Gallery; *see previous page*; *see also p.55*).

The Firth of Forth

East Lothian, to the east of Edinburgh, has a littoral dotted with golf courses, castles and nature reserves and, beyond the Lammermuir Hills, a wide hinterland of lush farmland. Some of the best links are the four Gullane courses (including Muirfield – an Open Championship course), North Berwick, Longniddry, Luffness and Dunbar.

Charming **Dirleton Castle** (tel: 01620-850 330) stands in the centre of a lovely eponymous village on the A198 between Gullane and North Berwick while **Tantallon Castle** (tel: 01620-892 727) is an imposing ruin on a headland above the North Sea off the A198 between North Berwick and Dunbar (both sites: www.historic-scotland.gov.uk; Apr–Sept daily 9.30am–5.30pm, until 4.30pm in winter; charge).

Enormous colonies of gannets and other seabirds populate the spectacular **Bass Rock** that stands 2 miles (3km) offshore from North Berwick; boat excursions are available between May and September (tel: 01620-890 202; www.seabird.org). Alternatively, state-of-the-art technology in the Scottish Seabird Centre shows all that is happening on Bass Rock on giant video screens (10am–6pm, shorter hours in winter). Closer to Edinburgh is **Aberlady Bay**, where a splendid dune-backed beach has been designated as a nature reserve (tel: 01620-827 847; www.aberlady.org).

Linlithgow and Falkirk

On Edinburgh's western fringe is South Queensferry, the location of **Hopetoun House** (tel: 0131-331 2451; www.hopetoun.co.uk; late-Apr–Oct daily 10.30am–5pm; charge), a glorious Georgian pile belonging to the Marquess of Linlithgow. The work of several great Scottish architects, including the Adam family, it has a sumptuous interior and vast grounds where deer and four-horned St Kilda's sheep graze. The observatory affords a splendid view of the **Forth Bridge** nearby.

From here the M9 leads to **Linlithgow ❷**, where, above a loch and park, stands the roofless shell of **Linlithgow Palace** (tel: 01506-842 896; www.historic-scotland.gov.uk; daily, 9.30am–5.30pm, 4.30pm in winter; charge), home of the Stuart kings, where Mary Queen of Scots was born. The adjacent Church of St Michael is the largest pre-Reformation church to survive in Scotland. Here, James IV saw the ghost that warned him of his defeat at Flodden Field.

A further ❸ 10 miles (16km) leads to **Falkirk ❸** and the Falkirk Wheel, the world's first rotating boat-lift. In 2003, converging moribund canals at different levels were linked, not by customary locks, but by a 135ft (35m)-high rotating wheel which lifts boats in gondolas between the two canals. Visitors can enjoy the ride, too.

Fife

Across the wide estuary of the Firth of Forth is Fife, or 'the Kingdom of Fife' as it is still known. On its western fringes, along the north bank of the Forth, is **Culross**, a perfectly preserved example of a small Scottish borough of the 16th and 17th centuries. It was once one of Scotland's major ports trading in coal, salt and griddle pans for making scones. Visitors can go inside the **Palace, Study and Town House** (tel:

The Scottish National Gallery of Modern Art

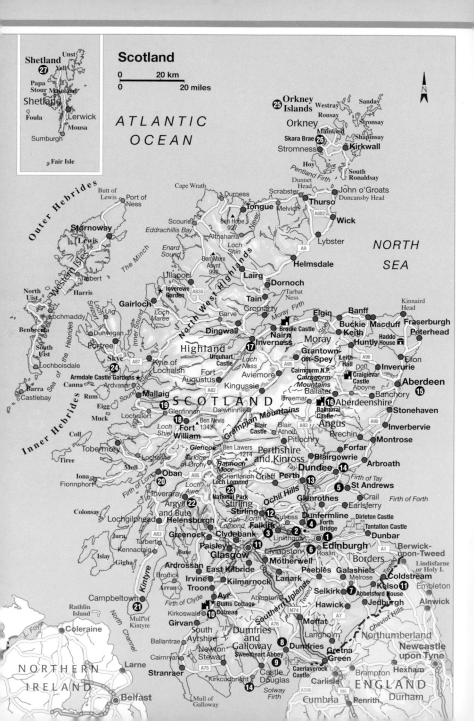

Scotland

0   20 km
0   20 miles

ATLANTIC OCEAN

NORTH SEA

Shetland

Unst
Yell
Shetland 27
Papa Stour Mainland
Foula
Lerwick
Mousa
Sumburgh
Fair Isle

Orkney Islands

Orkney Islands 25
Westray
Rousay
Sanday
Stronsay
Shapinsay
Orkney
Mainland
Skara Brae 26
Stromness
Kirkwall
Hoy
South Ronaldsay
Pentland Firth
Dunnet Head
Duncansby Head
John o'Groats

Cape Wrath
Durness
Scrabster
Thurso
Melvich
Wick
Tongue
Ben Hope 927
Scourie
Eddrachillis Bay
Altnaharra
Lybster
Enard Sound
Loch Shin
Helmsdale
Ben More Assynt 998
Lairg
Ullapool
Dornoch
Tain
Tarbat Ness
Inverewe Garden
Garve
Cromarty
Moray Firth
Gairloch
Dingwall
Elgin
Banff
Kinnaird Head
Loch Maree
Brodie Castle
Buckie
Macduff
Fraserburgh
Nairn
Keith
Peterhead
Inverness
Moray
Huntly
Haddo House
Highland
Urquhart Castle
Grantown-on-Spey
Leith Hall
Ellon
Skye
Loch Ness
Aviemore
Cairngorm N.P.
Craigievar Castle
Inverurie
Dunvegan
Kyle of Lochalsh
Fort Augustus
Kingussie
Cairngorm Mountains
Aboyne
Aberdeen
Portree
Ballater
Banchory
Armdale Castle Gardens
Braemar
Aberdeenshire
Stonehaven
Ardvasar
Mallaig
SCOTLAND
Balmoral Castle
Angus
Inverbervie
Glenfinnan
Ben Nevis 1343
Grampian Mountains
Brechin
Montrose
Fort William
Blair Castle
Blair Atholl
Forfar
Loch Shiel
Glencoe
Pitlochry
Arbroath
Ben Lawers 1214
Blairgowrie
Bridge of Orchy
Perthshire and Kinross
Dundee 14
Tobermory
Rannoch Moor
Dundee
Firth of Tay
Crianlarich
Perth
St Andrews
Loch Lomond
Crail
Oban
Crieff
Earlsferry
Loch Awe
National Park
Ochil Hills
Glenrothes
Inveraray
Stirling
Firth of Forth
Argyll and Bute
Stirling
Dunfermline
Dirleton Castle
Helensburgh
Falkirk
Forth Bridge
Tantallon Castle
Lochgilphead
Greenock
Clydebank
Linlithgow
Edinburgh
Dunbar
Paisley
Glasgow
Roslin
Berwick-upon-Tweed
Ardrossan
East Kilbride
Motherwell
Peebles
Galashiels
Lindisfarne or Holy I.
Irvine
Kilmarnock
Lanark
Melrose
Kelso
Embleton
Troon
Selkirk
Abbotsford House
Jedburgh
Alnwick
Ayr
Burns Cottage
Hawick
Campbeltown
Kirkoswald
Colzean
Moffat
Cheviot Hills
Girvan
Langholm
Northumberland
South Ayrshire
Dumfries and Galloway
Gretna Green
Newcastle upon Tyne
Ballantrae
Newton Stewart
Sweetheart Abbey
Dumfries
Hexham
Cairnryan
Caerlaverock Castle
Brampton
Stranraer
Castle Douglas
Carlisle
ENGLAND
Kirkcudbright
Solway Firth
Cumbria
Penrith
Durham
Mull of Galloway
Coleraine
Larne
Belfast
NORTHERN IRELAND

Falkirk Wheel, Britain's first rotating boat-lift

0844-493 2189; www.nts.org; Apr–May and Sept Thur–Mon noon–5pm, June–Aug daily noon–5pm, Oct Fri–Mon noon–4pm; charge).

To the east is **Dunfermline ❹**, the ancient Scottish capital, with a 12th-century **abbey** (tel: 01383-739 026; www.historic-scotland.gov.uk; Apr–Sept daily 9.30am–5.30pm, Oct until 4.30pm, Nov–Mar Mon–Wed and Sat–Sun 9.30am–4.30pm; charge) where Robert the Bruce was buried in 1329. Dunfermline is also the location of the **Andrew Carnegie Birthplace Museum** (tel: 01383-724 302; www.carnegiebirthplace.com; Mar–Nov Mon– Sat 10am–5pm, Sun 2–5pm; free), commemorating the weaver's son who went on to become America's greatest steel baron.

On the coast of the easternmost promontory of the Neuk are the pretty fishing ports of Earlsferry, St Monans, Pittenweem, Anstruther and Crail. A few miles northwest is Fife's most famous town, **St Andrews ❺**, with its famous golf courses and the **British Golf Museum** (tel: 01334-460 046; www.britishgolfmuseum.co.uk; daily Apr–Oct Mon–Sat 9.30am–5pm, Nov–Mar 10am–4pm; charge). The city is also famed for its ancient university (founded in 1412) and ecclesiastical and castle ruins.

South to the Borders

Beyond the hills ringing Edinburgh to the south lie the Borders. This is Scotland along the frontier with England, north of the Cheviot Hills and the mouths of the rivers Esk and Tweed, the first part of Scotland to encounter the Romans, the Angles and the English on their fruitless thrusts northwards. Today, it is gentle,

Real tennis

Inland from St Andrews is **Falkland Palace** (tel: 0844-493 2186; www.nts.org.uk; Mar–Oct Mon–Sat 11am–5pm, Sun 1–5pm; charge). It is notable as a hunting lodge of the Stuarts, from James IV to Mary Queen of Scots, and also for having a 'real' (or 'royal') tennis court which is still in use.

pastoral country with rolling green hills and bright clear streams where farming, knitwear and tweed remain the principal industries, and the passions are for trout and salmon fishing, and rugby, of which the Border towns are the great Scottish stronghold.

Literary associations

Leaving Edinburgh by the A703, the village of **Roslin** ❻ is soon reached. The interior of the 15th-century **Rosslyn Chapel** (tel: 0131-440 2159; www.rosslynchapel.org.uk; Mon–Sat 9.30am–6pm, Sun noon–4.45pm; charge) is covered with an abundance of fascinating stone carvings – 'a Bible in Stone'. It gained added renown when the novel *The Da Vinci Code* reiterated the long-held belief that within the chapel lies the Holy Grail.

Further south, 36 miles (44km) from Edinburgh, overlooking the River Tweed outside Galashiels, is **Abbotsford House** ❼ (tel: 01896-752 043; www.scottsabbotsford.co.uk; daily mid-Mar–mid-Sept 9.30am–5pm; Sundays Mar–May 11am–4pm only; charge), which was the home of the popular historical novelist Sir Walter Scott (1771–1832) and which is full of Scott memorabilia. His family were Border people, and his romantic imagination was first stirred by the derring-do of his ancestors defending their land against England, the 'Auld Enemy'.

Abbeys and castles

Sitting beneath the triple mounds of the Eildon Hills, **Melrose**, 2 miles (3km) east of Abbotsford, was the haunt of poet and seer Thomas de Rhymer (*c.*1220–97). From the highest

The grand interior of Rosslyn Chapel, which features unusual stone carvings

hill, a breathtaking view of the Cheviots and the hills running westwards towards Galloway can be enjoyed. In the town stand the ruins of the 12th-century **Melrose Abbey** (tel: 01896-822 562; www.historic-scotland.gov.uk; Apr–Sept daily 9.30am–5.30pm, winter until 4.30pm; charge), which despite its sacking by the English in 1544 remains an architectural poem in red sandstone.

Nearby are other glorious medieval abbeys: at Dryburgh, 4 miles (6km) beyond Melrose where Scott is buried; at Kelso, 10 miles (16km) east on the A699 (Mon–Sat and Sun pm); and at Jedburgh, 8 miles (13km) south of Dryburgh on the A68 (all three abbeys: www.historic-scotland.

gov.uk; daily, 9.30am–5.30pm, winter until 4.30pm; charge).

Just outside **Kelso** there are several impressive stately homes. **Floors Castle** (tel: 01573-223 333; www.roxburghe.net; late-Apr–Oct daily 11am–5pm; charge) is the largest inhabited castle in Scotland and seat of the Duke of Roxburgh. Also worth visiting are the Duke of Buccleuch's house, **Bowhill**, near Selkirk (tel: 01750-22 204; www.bowhill.org; July–Aug only, daily 1–4.30pm; charge), and **Mellerstain**, one of the finest Adam houses in Scotland (tel: 01573-410 225; www.mellerstain.com; July–Aug Sun, Mon, Wed, Thur 12.30–5pm; May–June and Sept Sun, Wed 12.30–5pm; Oct Sun only 12.30–5pm; charge).

Dumfries and Galloway

In the southwestern-most corner of Scotland lies Dumfries and Galloway, a region with pretty towns along the Solway Firth and wild moorlands inland. It culminates in the west in the Mull of Galloway, a hammerhead peninsula with sandy beaches, cliffs and hills.

Dumfries ❽ is the largest town in southwest Scotland, and Robert Burns, the national poet, spent the last years of his life here. The house where he died in 1796 is now a museum, the **Burns House** (tel: 01387-255 297; www.dumfries museum.demon.co.uk; Apr–Sept Mon–Sat 10am–5pm, Oct–Mar Tue–Sat 10am–1pm, 2–5pm; free).

South of Dumfries, on the banks of the Neith where it debouches into the Solway Firth, are the red sandstone ruins of **Sweetheart Abbey** ❾ (tel: 01387-850 397; www.historic-scotland.gov.uk; Apr–Sept daily 9.30am–5.30pm, Oct daily 9.30am–4.30pm, Nov–Mar Mon–Wed and

Scotland

Floors Castle is the largest inhabited castle in Scotland

Sat–Sun 9.30am–4.30pm; charge), founded in the 14th century by Devorgilla, Lady of Galloway, in memory of her husband John Balliol, founder of Balliol College, Oxford. Also here are the dramatic ruins of moated **Caerlaverock Castle** (tel: 01387-770 244; www.historic-scotland.gov.uk; Apr–Sept daily 9.30am–5.30pm, winter until 4.30pm; charge).

West of Dumfries on the A75 is **Kirkcudbright** (pronounced care-coo-bree), formerly an artists' colony, the essence of which is distilled in **Broughton House** (tel: 0844-493 2246; www.nts.org.uk; Apr–Oct daily noon–5pm; charge), home of artist E.A. Hornel (1864–1933), one of the so-called 'Glasgow Boys' *(see also p.54)*.

Ayrshire

The land of Robert Burns, Ayrshire is also home to several famous seaside resorts and championship golf courses. Starting on the coast, close to Kirkoswald, is **Culzean Castle** ❿ (tel: 0844-493 2149; www.culzeanexperience.org; Apr–Oct daily 10.30am–5pm; charge), one of the greatest achievements of the 18th-century Scottish architect, Robert Adam. General Dwight Eisenhower was given life tenure of a suite on the top floor. In addition to paintings, weapons and porcelain, a museum commemorates the US President's achievements. At Kirkoswald itself is **Souter Johnnie's Cottage** (tel: 0844-493 2147; www.nts.org.uk; Apr–Sept Fri–Tue 11.30m–5pm; charge), home of the 'ancient, trusty, druthy crony' featured in Burns' poem *Tam O'Shanter* and now a museum.

Next up the coast is the seaside resort of **Ayr**. On the edge of the town is Alloway and the **Burns National Heritage Park**, where the centrepiece is the **Burns Cottage** (tel: 0844-493 2601; www.burnsmuseum.org.uk; daily, Apr–Sept 10am–5.30pm, Oct–Mar 10am–5pm; charge), the 'auld clay biggin' where the poet was born. Continuing north from Ayr, the road reaches **Troon**, famous for its Open Championship golf course (tel: 01292-311 555; www.royaltroon.com).

Glasgow

The major city on the western side of Scotland is **Glasgow** ⓫, straddling the River Clyde 14 miles (23km) from the estuary. It grew rich on shipbuilding and heavy engineering and by the end of the 19th century was Britain's

The Dumfries residence where Robert Burns died is now the Burns House museum

Argyle Street is one of Glasgow's main shopping thoroughfares

second-largest city. However, the solid manufacturing base on which the city was founded was whipped from under it during the recession of the 1970s. Although unemployment rose distressingly and the population has declined to just over 600,000, an extraordinary renaissance occurred in the 1990s and Glasgow has become famous for its tourist attractions, cultural scene and nightlife. It also has Scotland's national football stadium,

at Hampden Park, which will be used as part of the 2012 Olympics.

The city's great buildings and museums

Glasgow's 12th-century **cathedral** (tel: 0141-552 6891; www.historic-scotland.gov.uk; Apr–Sept Mon–Sat 9.30am–5.30pm, Sun 1–5.30pm, winter daily until 4pm; free) was the only Scottish medieval cathedral to escape the destruction of the

Glasgow

 Population: 593,000

 Local dialling code: 0141

 Tourist office: Tourist Information Office, 11 George Square; tel: 0141-204 4400; www.seeglasgow.com

 Main police station: 173 Pitt Street; tel: 01465-811 222

 Main post office: 47 St Vincent Street

 Main hospital: Glasgow Royal Infirmary, 84 Castle Street; tel: 0141-211 4000; www.nhsggc.org.uk

 Media: *The Scotsman*; *The Skinny*

⭐ WHISKY

Some historians believe that the art of distilling was brought to Scotland by Christian missionaries. But it is just as likely that Highland farmers discovered how to distil spirits from their surplus barley. The earliest reference to whisky dates from 1494, when the Scottish Exchequer records that a friar purchased a quantity of malt 'to make aquavitae'. The 'water of life' has been giving pleasure to drinkers ever since.

Scotch whisky is one of Britain's top five export items, contributing £2 billion annually to the balance of trade. Even the Vatican, on one recent annual reckoning, bought 18,000 bottles. More than 2,500 brands of Scotch whisky are now sold around the world with the major export market being the United States.

These days, there are two kinds of Scotch: malt, made from malted barley only; and grain, made from malted barley together with unmalted barley, maize or other cereals. Most popular brands are blends of both types of whisky – typically 60 percent grain to 40 percent malt.

A single malt, the product of one distillery, has become an increasingly popular drink, thanks largely to the aggressive marketing by William Grant & Sons of their Glenfiddich brand. But sales of single malts still account for only one bottle in 20 sold around the world, and most of the production of single-malt distilleries is used to add flavour to a blended whisky.

The trick with whisky-making is to

A Bell's whisky barrel

Inside a distillery

know when the whisky has distilled sufficiently. Although scientific measuring devices are universally employed, the judgement of experienced experts still plays a part. Once distilled, the liquid is poured into oak casks, which, being porous, allow air to enter. Evaporation takes place, removing the harsher constituents of the new spirit and enabling it to mellow. Legally, it can't be sold as whisky until it has spent three years in the cask, and a good malt will stay casked for at least eight years. As much as 4 million gallons (20 million litres) evaporate into the air each year.

While blended whiskies are often hard to tell apart in a blind tasting, malt whiskies are more readily identifiable. Experienced drinkers can differentiate between Highland malts, Lowland malts, Campbeltown malts and Islay malts. A good malt whisky should be drunk neat (especially after dinner) or with the addition of a little spring water, which can prevent the strength of the whisky numbing your senses and reducing your enjoyment of the subtler characteristics. Single malts should not be drunk with a mixer as this destroys the drink's complexities.

Enthusiasts can participate in tours of distilleries on the Malt Whisky Trail (www.maltwhiskytrail.com). There is also the Speyside Whisky Festival (www.spiritofspeyside.com) in May each year. If you're not visiting Scotland, there is an outpost in London, where you can join the Whisky Society; its members' rooms are above the Bleeding Heart Restaurant in Hatton Garden, Clerkenwell (tel: 020-7831 4447; www.smws.co.uk).

A very Scottish offering: haggis and whisky

Airports: Glasgow International (tel: 0844-481 5555; **www.glasgow airport.com**) is 8 miles (13km) west of the city centre. Glasgow Shuttle buses (**www.firstgroup. com**) run to Buchanan Street bus station every 10 minutes, 24 hours a day (journey time 25 minutes). Fare: £4.50 single. A taxi takes 20 minutes and costs around £20. Glasgow Prestwick (tel: 0871-223 0700; **www.glasgowprestwick.com**) is 30 miles (48km) south of the city centre. Trains (**www.nationalrail. co.uk**) run to Glasgow Central Station every 30 minutes (hourly on Sundays) between about 6am and 11.30pm (journey time 45 minutes). Fare: £7 single

 Trains: Glasgow Central Station is the city's main train hub, with good connections to Edinburgh (every 15 minutes daily) and much of the rest of Scotland (**www.nationalrail.**

co.uk). The West Highland line to Fort William and Mallaig is a particularly popular tourist route. Tickets can be purchased in advance online or at stations at the time of travelling

 Buses: Bus routes run throughout the city (see **www.firstgroup.com**). Tickets cost from £0.90 and step up according to a zoning system. Tickets can be purchased from the driver. At night there is a reduced service, with flat fares of £2.65

 Taxis: Licensed taxis ('black cabs') can be hailed on the street; they display the regulated charges on the meter. To book ahead, try Glasgow Taxis, tel: 0141-429 7070, **www.glasgowtaxis.co.uk**

Car hire: All the major companies (see p.267) have branches at the airports

Reformation. Adjacent to it is the **St Mungo Museum of Religious Life & Art** (tel: 0141-276 1625), which faces the **Provand's Lordship** (tel: 0141-552 8819), the city's oldest house (1471) and now a museum (both museums: www.glasgowlife.org.uk/museums; daily 10am–5pm, Fri and Sun from 11am; free).

In the city centre is the **School of Art** (tel: 0141-353 4500; www. gsa.ac.uk; guided tours Apr–Sept daily 10am–5pm; charge) designed by Charles Rennie Mackintosh. On nearby Sauchiehall Street stands the Willow Tea Rooms with an immaculate Mackintosh setting. More Mackintosh can be seen in the Glasgow University area where a reconstruction

of his home is an integral part of the **Hunterian Art Gallery** (tel: 0141-330 4221; www.hunterian.gla.ac.uk; Mon–Sat 9.30am–5pm; free). Also in this part of town is the **Kelvingrove Art Gallery & Museum** (tel: 0141-276 9599; www.glasgowlife.org.uk; daily 10am–5pm, Fri and Sun from 11am; free; see also p.54).

On the south bank of the River Clyde stand the futuristic buildings of the **Science Centre** (tel: 0141-420 5000; www.glasgowsciencecentre.org; daily 10am–5pm; charge) together with the 423ft (127m), 360-degree revolving **Glasgow Tower**, which, to minimise wind resistance, can turn along its entire height into the wind. At the top is a viewing platform.

The outskirts of town

Much further to the south is **Pollok Country Park** (accessible by train from Central Station). As well as wildlife gardens, a mountain bike circuit and play areas, the park accommodates two important museums. The **Burrell Collection** (tel: 0141-287 2550; www.glasgowlife.org.uk/museums; daily 10am–5pm, Fri and Sun from 11am; free) displays the extraordinary bequest of shipowner Sir William Burrell (1861–1958), and includes everything from ancient artefacts to Impressionist paintings. **Pollok House** (tel: 0844-493 2202; www.nts.org.uk; daily 10am–5pm; charge) contains paintings by masters from El Greco to William Blake.

Isle of Arran

Adrossan on the Ayrshire coast is the departure point for ferries to the **Isle of Arran**. Apart from knitwear, Arran is best known as the location of **Brodick Castle** (tel: 0844-493 2152; www.nts.org.uk; Apr–Sept daily 11am–4pm, Oct until 3pm; grounds daily all year 9.30am–sunset; charge), parts of which date from the 14th century and have associations with Robert the Bruce.

Stirling

Equidistant between Edinburgh and Glasgow is the city of **Stirling ⑫** with its winding streets and medieval cobblestones. **Stirling Castle** (tel: 01786-450 000; www.historic-scotland.gov.uk; daily Apr–Sept 9.30am–6pm,

Scotland

Making education fun at the Science Centre

Looking out over Stirling Castle

winter until 5pm, charge) featured prominently in the Scottish wars of succession in the Middle Ages, passing between English and Scots until the Scots finally won it for keeps in 1342. It was the home of the Stuart kings from 1370 to 1603. Today it contains the regimental museum of the Argyll & Sutherland Highlanders.

At the foot of the castle is the oldest part of Stirling, which includes historic buildings such as **Argyll's Lodging** (tel: 01786-450 000; www.historic-scotland.gov.uk; Apr–Sept daily 9.30am–5.30pm, winter until 4.30pm; charge), the fine 17th-century town-house, and **Cowane's Hospital**, once the Guildhall and now a public venue.

Also worth visiting are two religious sites: the **Church of the Holy Rude** (tel: 01786 475 275; www.holy rude.org) and the **Cambuskenneth Abbey** (www.historic-scotland.gov.uk; both attractions open daily Apr–Sept;

donations). As a child, Mary Queen of Scots was crowned in the former, and following her abdication, it was the scene of the coronation of her son, James. The abbey, by the River Forth east of the town, was the site of Robert the Bruce's first Scottish Parliament in 1326.

The Tayside and Grampian regions

The historic regions of Tayside and Grampian occupy the northeast section of Scotland between the Firth of Tay in the south and the Firth of Moray to the north. The Tay, which flows through the cities of Perth and Dundee, offers excellent salmon and trout fishing, while the Grampian region boasts many of Scotland's greatest castles.

Perth and Pitlochry

On the way to Perth, up the A9, is Gleneagles (*see p.250*), probably

Scotland's grandest hotel, with its own championship golf courses. **Perth** ⓭ itself is generally considered the gateway to the Highlands (the first line of high hills rise over the horizon), and is notable for its fine Georgian terraces. Its road connections make it an excellent base for exploring the surrounding area.

Continuing north on the A9, there is the pretty town of **Dunkeld**, with its ruined abbey, and a little further north still, the Victorian resort of **Pitlochry**. The latter hosts Highland Games in September (www.pitlochryhighlandgames.co.uk), and is also noted for the Pitlochry

Festival Theatre *(see p.254)*. Eight miles (13km) northwest of Pitlochry is 12th-century **Blair Castle** (tel: 01796-481 207; www.blair-castle.co.uk; Apr–Oct daily 9.30am–5.30pm, Nov–Mar Tue and Sat 9.30am–2.30pm; charge). This is the seat of the Duke of Atholl, the last noble in Britain licensed to have a private army.

North Sea ports

The Tay river drains into the North Sea at **Dundee** ⓮, a port known for its jam, jute and journalism industries. Its harbour is the mooring place of Captain Scott's Antarctic ship *Discovery* and the *Unicorn*, a 24-cannon frigate launched in 1824.

From Dundee, the A92 coast road goes through the historic ports of Montrose and Arbroath on the way to Aberdeen. At **Arbroath** are the ruins of a 12th-century **abbey** (tel: 01241-878 756; www.historic-scotland.gov.uk; daily Apr–Sept 9.30am–5.30pm, winter until 4.30pm; charge) where Scotland declared its independence in 1320.

Further up the coast is **Aberdeen** ⓯, the greatest of the North Sea ports. The granite city is the oil capital of Britain, bustling with oil-related shipping in its busy harbour, set between the rivers Don and Dee. It has a prestigious university, of which the finest buildings belong to the 16th-century **King's College**, which was begun in 1500 and hailed as an outstanding example of Scottish Gothic style.

Marischal College on Broad Street, which was founded in 1593 but rebuilt

Scotland

Aberdeen oil rig support ships

in the 19th century, has the distinction of being the second-largest granite building in the world after El Escorial near Madrid. Nearby is the 14th-century **St Machar's Cathedral** (tel: 01224-485 988; www.stmachar.com; daily Apr–Oct 9am–5pm, Nov–Mar 10am–4pm; free). The **Art Gallery** (tel: 01224-523 700; www.aagm.co.uk; Tue–Sat 10am–5pm, Sun 2–5pm; free), on Schoolhill, contains a fine collection of English, French and Scottish paintings.

Balmoral

The A93 runs some 50 miles (80km) inland from Aberdeen up Royal Deeside to **Balmoral** , where the Queen and the Royal Family spend much of the summer. Balmoral was bought by Prince Albert in 1848, though the estate dates back to the 15th century. Inside the castle, only the ballroom is open to the public, though the grounds can also be visited (tel: 01339-742 534; www.balmoralcastle.com; Apr–July daily 10am–5pm; charge).

The Highlands

The southern edge of the Highland line runs across the country diagonally from a point southwest of Aberdeen near Stonehaven to the Mull of Kintyre, the long spit of land stretching southwards from Argyll on the western edge of the Firth of Clyde. More than half of Scotland lies to the north of this line, most of it mountainous, with just a few fertile glens where crops can be grown and cattle reared. The population is sparse in the northwest – in Sutherland it is fewer than 6 people per sq mile (2.6 people per sq km), compared to the national average of 955 per sq mile (369 per sq km).

Inverness and environs

Inverness  is the vibrant 'Capital of the Highlands'. For long seen as a dull

Inverness, the 'Capital of the Highlands'

nts.org.uk/culloden; daily Apr–Sept 9am–6pm, Oct 9am–5pm, Nov–Dec and Feb Mar 10am–4pm; charge) has many artefacts of the period on display.

To the southeast of Inverness are the rich farmlands of the Laigh of Moray along the River Spey. This is distillery country where many of the famous malt whiskies are made. Follow the signs marked 'Whisky Trail' (www.scotchwhisky.net) from Keith along the A95.

Continuing southwest, the A95 joins the A9 and leads through impressive scenery in the high glens of the Grampians, with the massive summits of the **Cairngorms** towering over the ski resort of **Aviemore** (www.visitaviemore.co.uk).

To Fort William

Heading southwest from Inverness, the A82 skirts the edge of Loch Ness.

241

Scotland

backwater of Presbyterianism, the city has become a major shopping centre with good nightlife, especially at weekends, and is now the fastest-growing city in Britain. With the mouth of Loch Ness only 5 miles (8km) from the town, it is also a good starting point for seeking out one of the world's greatest amphibian celebrity (*see also p.36*).

A few miles east of Inverness, the B9006 runs across **Culloden Moor** where Jacobite forces under Bonnie Prince Charlie were routed in 1746. The defeat of his men by the Hanoverian army represented the end of the struggle for power by the Stuart line. On either side of the road are scattered stones marking the graves of the Highlanders. The **Culloden Moor Visitor Centre** (tel: 0844-493 2159; www.

Castle country

On the way to Balmoral are a number of other fine castles. Just off the A944 is **Castle Fraser** (tel: 0844-493 2164; www.nts.org.uk; Apr–Jun Wed–Sun noon–5pm, Aug daily 11am–5pm, Sept–Oct Wed–Sun noon–5pm; charge), while on the A93 is **Crathes Castle** (tel: 0844-493 2166; www.nts. org.uk; Nov–Mar Sat–Sun 10.30am– 3.45pm, Apr–Oct daily 10.30am– 4.45pm; charge). **Craigievar Castle** (tel: 01339-883 635; www.nts.org.uk; May– June and Sept Fri–Tue 11am–5pm, July–Aug daily 11am–5pm; charge) by the A980, is also impressive.

On the way, it's worth making a stop at the ruins of **Urquhart Castle** (tel: 01456-450 551; www.historic-scotland. gov.uk; daily Apr–Sept 9.30am–6pm, winter until 4.30pm; charge), which was one of the largest in Scotland until 1692 when it was blown up to prevent the Jacobites from using it. Most photos of the Loch Ness monster, known as Nessie, have been taken from this spot.

As the A82 nears Fort William at the head of Loch Linnhe, Britain's highest mountain, **Ben Nevis** looms above at 4,406ft (1,343m). There are numerous routes to the top for both walkers and climbers.

The fortification of **Fort William** ❶❽ itself was constructed in the 17th century to keep out 'savage clans' and sundry other undesirables. Nothing of the fort remains today: it was demolished in the late 19th century to make way for the railway, which led to rapid expansion of the town and its environs. In the town centre, near the tourist information centre, is the **West Highland Museum** (tel: 01397-702 169; www.westhighlandmuseum.org. uk; Jun–Sept Mon–Sat 10am–5pm, July–Aug also Sun 10am–4pm, Oct– May Mon–Sat 10am–4pm; free), which has a number of Jacobite relics including a 'secret portrait' of Bonnie Prince Charlie.

From Fort William, a spectacular train journey runs west to the small port of Mallaig (from where ferries leave for the Isle of Skye). The A830 road follows the same route. This is Bonnie Prince Charlie country, and begins with the stunning view from the viaduct at **Glenfinnan** ❶❾ down

Loch Shiel, and over to the monument on the shore that marks the spot where the Young Pretender himself raised the Stuart standard (visitor centre: tel: 0844-493 2221; www.nts. org.uk; daily Apr–Jun and Sept–Oct 10am–5pm, Jul–Aug 9.30am–5.30pm; charge). Here the clans gathered to begin the Jacobite Rebellion of 1745. It was in this area, too, that the Prince hid with a price of £30,000 on his head after his defeat at Culloden.

Beyond Lochailort there is a view seawards over the bright water and rocky islets of Loch nan Uamh, where the Bonnie Prince landed in 1745 and from where he left 14 months later, despite all the pleadings of the haunting Jacobite songs, never to return. The pebbly beaches

Loch Ness is steeped in tradition and mystery

A train ride on the spectacular Glenfinnan Viaduct

of Loch nan Uamh give way to the silver sands of Morar and Arisaig, shining like snow on the edge of the steel-blue sea.

The northwest

Further up the west coast is the Kyle of Lochalsh, which is linked to the Isle of Skye by a road bridge. Heading north from here is the A890 through Glen Carron and then the A896 via Shieldaig. These roads intersect with the A832 which returns west down Glen Docherty to **Loch Maree**, one of the prettiest lochs in Scotland, and beyond to Loch Ewe and the exotic **Inverewe Garden** (tel: 0844-493 2225; www.nts.org.uk; daily Apr and Sept 10am–5pm, May 10am–

Glencoe

This deep mountain valley stretches more than 7 miles (11km) from Loch Leven to Rannoch Moor through magnificent scenery. The name of Glencoe is also widely associated with a notorious massacre that occurred here in February 1692. By order of the English King William III, more than 200 troops commanded by Robert Campbell of Glenlyon, turned on the MacDonald clan, who had been their hosts for 12 days. Thirty-eight men, women and children were slaughtered as a punishment for the tardiness of their chief in giving allegiance to the English king. The **Glencoe Visitors' Centre** (tel: 0844-493 2222; www.glencoe-nts.org.uk; daily Apr–Oct 9.30am–5.30pm, Nov–Mar 10am–4pm; charge) provides further details of this notorious episode.

5.30pm, June–Aug 10am–6pm, Oct 10am–4pm, Nov–Mar 10am–3pm; donations).

From Inverewe the road heads first north and then winds back to the east, providing many wonderful vistas along the way. The road eventually arrives at the A835, which runs north to **Ullapool** a fishing village on Loch Broom.

Argyll

Stretching south of Fort William is the scenic region of Argyll. Heading down the coast, the first major town is **Oban ⑳**, a faded Victorian resort, but still important as a departure point for ferries to the Hebridean islands. Continuing southwards, the A816 leads to Lochgilphead, and below that, via the A83, the picturesque region of **Knapdale** and the **Crinan Canal**, which connects Loch Fyne with the Atlantic Ocean. Beyond the pretty fishing village of **Tarbert**, the road enters the **Kintyre Peninsula**.

Eventually you come to the ferry port of Tayinloan, from where, during the summer, there are crossings on the hour to the pretty island of **Gigha**. The main attraction here is the **Achamore House Gardens** (tel: 01583-505 400; www. gigha.org.uk; daily 9am to dusk; charge), created by the late Sir James

Houses and shops overlooking Ullapool Harbour

The Oban Distillery gift and tasting shop

eventually rejoin the A83 and follow the road up to **Inveraray** ㉒. To one side of the pretty white town is **Inveraray Castle** (tel: 01499-302 203; www.inveraray-castle.com; Apr–Oct daily 10am–5.45pm; charge) the seat of the dukes of Argyll. In addition to pictures and French furniture, an extensive collection of weaponry reminds visitors that this is headquarters of the fierce Clan Campbell.

From Inveraray, the A83 continues east towards **Loch Lomond**, the largest freshwater lake in Britain, 23 miles (37km) long and 5 miles (8km) across at its widest point. All around is the **Loch Lomond and the Trossachs National Park** ㉓ (tel: 01389-722 600; www.loch lomond-trossachs.org), encompassing 720 sq miles (1,865 sq km) of wonderful scenery.

The islands

Off the west coast of Scotland lie several hundred islands. making up the Inner and Outer Hebrides. The southernmost group comprises Gigha, Islay, Jura and Colonsay. Further north there are the large islands of Mull and Skye and the smaller islands of Iona, Staffa, Tiree, Coll, Muck, Eigg, Rum and Canna. The Outer Hebrides are made up of Lewis, Harris, North Uist, Benbecula, South Uist, Eriskay and Barra. Most of these can be reached by ferry (tel: 0800-066 5000; www.calmac.co.uk).

Off the north coast of Scotland are the Orkney Islands and the Shetlands. They are serviced by ferries departing from Aberdeen and

Horlick, one of the world's great horticulturalists.

Back in Kintyre, the A83 keeps on going all the way to the fishing port of **Campbeltown** ㉑. A local museum, the **Campbeltown Museum** (tel: 01586-559 017; www.museumsgalleriesscotland.org.uk; Mon–Fri 9am–5pm; free) tells the history of the region, and exhibits a fine collection of Scottish paintings. Heading south once more, the road finally runs out at the **Mull of Kintyre**, made famous in a song by one-time local resident, Paul McCartney. The area is now a bird reserve.

Returning north, this time up the east side of the peninsula, you

Scrabster (tel: 0845-6000 449; www.northlinkferries.co.uk).

The Isle of Skye

Perhaps the most impressive of the Hebrides – and certainly the most accessible – is the **Isle of Skye ㉔**. The busy fishing port of Mallaig is one of the ferry departure points for Skye, while the principal crossing is over the bridge at Kyle of Lochalsh, further north.

From the fjord-like sea lochs of the west, across to the sheer Cuillin Mountains in the south, and to the craggy northern tip of the Trotternish Peninsula, Skye epitomises Scotland's wild Celtic appeal. A day's hike or cycle ride around the 50-mile (80km) -long island will still set you squarely in the wilderness.

The **Cuillin Mountains** are a 6-mile (10km) arc of peaks, 15 of which exceed the 3,000ft (900m) needed to make them Munros *(see p.49)*. If the summits seem forbidding, take the walk down Glen Sligachan into the heart of these mountains and through to the other side 8 miles (13km) due south to the beach of Camasunary in Loch Scavaig. In the Sleat area, on the southern tip of Skye, is **Armadale Castle Gardens and Museum of the Isles** (tel: 01471-844 305; www.clandonald.com; daily Apr–Oct 9.30am–5.30pm, gardens year round; charge).

The main attraction of northwestern Skye is **Dunvegan Castle** (tel: 01470-521 206; www.dunvegancastle.com; Apr–mid-Oct daily 10am–5.30pm; charge), which captures the clan spirit of Scotland in its paintings and Macleod relics.

The scenic Isle of Skye

On the west side of the Trotternish Peninsula, **Uig** is an attractive village that encircles a bay from where ferries depart for the outer isles. This northern arm of Skye has been less altered by tourism than any part of the island.

The Orkney Islands

The 70 **Orkney Islands ㉕** were invaded by Norsemen in the 11th century, and did not pass into British hands until late in the 16th century. Ruins from the Norse era are all around.

Everywhere in Orkney there is the feeling of being wide open to the sky, of great cliffs and rocky sea pinnacles. North of Stromness on **Mainland** (the largest island), the coast offers one of the most dramatic cliff walks in Britain, from Black Craig north to the Bay of Skaill. Another excursion for wilderness lovers is the ferry to Moaness Pier on the **Isle of Hoy**.

Kirkwall, 10 miles (16km) east of Stromness, is the largest town in Orkney. It is largely uninspiring except for the **Bishop's Palace**, a 12th-century ruin with a round tower added in the 16th century, and the **Earl's Palace**, one of the finest examples of Renaissance architecture in Scotland (both palaces: tel: 01856-871 918; daily 9.30am–5.30pm, winter until 4.30pm; charge). **St Magnus' Cathedral**, built in 1137, is dedicated to Magnus Erlendsson, martyred first Earl of Orkney.

Places of antiquity grace the countryside under the banner of

Pilgrim destination

One of the most extraordinary islands in the Hebrides is **Iona** (accessible by ferry from Mull). Its major attractions are the Benedictine Iona Abbey (tel: 01681-700 512; www.historic-scotland.gov.uk; daily Apr–Sept 9.30am–5.30pm, winter until 4.30pm; charge) and the relics of the settlement founded here by St Columba in AD563. Celtic Christianity endured here throughout the Dark Ages before spreading out through Scotland and to Europe beyond.

the Unesco World Heritage Heart of Orkney Neolithic Sites. Best known are the wonderfully preserved settlement at **Skara Brae** ㉖ (tel: 01856-841 815; www.historic-scotland.gov.uk; daily Apr–Sept 9.30am–5.30pm, winter until 4.30pm; charge), dating back to *c*.3000BC, and **Maeshowe** (book in advance on tel: 01856-761

The lush coastline at Skara Brae

The Iron Age broch tower on Mousa

606; www.historic-scotland.gov.uk; daily Apr–Sept 9.30am–5pm, winter until 4.30pm; charge), a huge, chambered megalithic tomb from 2700BC with fine, runic graffiti left by 12th-century Norse plunderers. On **Papa Westray**, one of the smaller Orkney islands, is the oldest extant house in Europe.

The Shetland Islands

Britain's most northerly archipelago is the **Shetland Islands** ㉗, just 48 miles (78km) north of the Orkney Islands. **Lerwick** is their only town and there is a small airport on the main island served from most Scottish airports, a frequency maintained because of Shetland's significant oil installations – it has the largest gas and oil terminal in Europe. On the last Tuesday in January, the spectacular fire ceremony of Up-Helly-Aa involves the burning of a replica Viking longship and much revelry.

The tiny island of **Mousa**, off the east coast, is the site of the world's best-preserved Iron Age broch tower, a fortress that has remained intact after more than 1,000 years of battering from Arctic storms. **Unst** is the most northerly of the dozen inhabited islands, and Muness Castle and the ruins of Scalloway Castle, 6 miles (10km) to the west of Lerwick, are also worth visiting (apply to local shops for keys). At the southern tip of the mainland, next door to Sumburgh Airport, is **Jarlshof** (tel: 01950-460 112; www.historic-scotland.gov.uk; Apr–Sept daily 9.30am–5.30pm; charge), a remarkable 'layer-cake' of an archaeological site. Bronze Age dune dwellers, broch builders, Vikings and medieval inhabitants all left their marks.

ACCOMMODATION

A wide range of accommodation is available in Scotland, from country house hotels to traditional bed and breakfasts. Visitors may, however, be surprised to find that even in remote areas prices are often quite high. This is in part due to the fact that the tourist trade is so seasonal, and hoteliers have to make the most of the summer months. Check online before you travel and plan your holiday just outside the peak season to get the best deals.

Edinburgh

Channings
12–16 South Learmonth Gardens
Tel: 0131-315 2226
www.channings.co.uk
A smart series of five adjoining Edwardian houses (including Ernest Shackleton's former home) front on to a quiet cobbled street close to the city centre. **££–£££**

The Scotsman
20 North Bridge, Edinburgh
Tel: 0131-556 5565
www.thescotsmanhotel.co.uk
This highly successful makeover of a newspaper office offers five-star accommodation, as well as a health club, pool and a fine whisky bar. **££££**

The Scottish Borders

Roxburghe Hotel
Kelso
Tel: 01573-450 331
www.roxburghe.net
An 18th-century country house hotel in riverside surroundings offering fishing, clay-pigeon shooting and a championship golf course. **£££**

Westin Turnberry Resort
Turnberry, near Ayr
Tel: 01655-331 000
www.turnberry.co.uk
This luxury country club and spa has two championship golf courses and its own loch. Activities available include horse riding, tennis and off-road driving. **££££**

Glasgow

Malmaison
278 West George Street
Tel: 0141-572 1000
www.malmaison-glasgow.com
A stylish hotel occupying a former church in the centre of town. The brasserie comes particularly recommended. **£££**

One Devonshire Gardens
1 Devonshire Gardens
Tel: 0141-339 2001
www.hotelduvin.com
Head and shoulders better than any other Glasgow hotel, with excellent service, plush rooms and classy bistro restaurant. **£££**

Listings

A sumptuous bathroom at Malmaison

Fife, Tayside, Aberdeen and the Grampian Region

Craigmhor Lodge
27 West Moulin Road, Pitlochry
Tel: 01796-472 123
www.craigmhorlodge.co.uk
Bedrooms in the original Victorian house
are complemented by a further 12 designer
rooms in a smart new courtyard building.
It's an excellent option for families. **£–££**

East Haugh House
Old Perth Road, East Haugh, near Pitlochry
Tel: 01796-473 121
www.easthaugh.co.uk
This family-run hotel offers a warm ambience and excellent food. The public areas
display vintage fishing trophies, and this is
a popular destination for fly-fishermen, as
the hotel even has its own fishing beat on
the Tay. **££**

Gleneagles Hotel
Auchterarder
*Tel: 0800 389 3737 (UK); 01764-662 231
(international)*
www.gleneagles.com
Famous for its golfing and sports facilities,
Gleneagles is a magnificent hotel set on a
country estate. **££££–£££££**

Knock Castle Hotel
Drummond Terrace, Crieff
Tel: 01764-650 088
www.knockcastle.com
Once the home of a shipping magnate, this
Victorian mansion is now a hotel and spa
complex. The rooms are luxurious and the
facilities impressive, but bear in mind that
the hotel operates a no-children policy.
££–£££

Royal Dunkeld Hotel
Atholl Street, Dunkeld
Tel: 01350-727 322
www.royaldunkeld.co.uk
The staff at this 19th-century coaching inn
are unfailingly helpful, the food is hearty and
delicious, and the bar is well stocked. Its reasonable prices are also an attraction. **£–££**

Gleneagles Hotel

The West Coast and the Northwest Highlands

Barcaldine House
Barcaldine, between Oban and Fort William
Tel: 01631-720 219
www.barcaldinehouse.co.uk
This country house retains an old-world feel
with antique furnishings and excellent service. The restaurant showcases the chef's
considerable talents – whether it's the
sumptuous six-course dinner or the bargain-
priced set lunch. **££–£££**

Cairnbaan Hotel
Cairnbaan, near Lochgilphead, Argyll
Tel: 01546-603 668
www.cairnbaan.com
A historic hotel in an idyllic spot on the Crinan
Canal, this country inn is renowned locally for
its welcoming bar and the scrumptious food
served in its restaurant. **£–££**

Holly Tree Hotel
Kentallen Pier, Argyll
Tel: 01631-740 292
www.hollytreehotel.co.uk
The Holly Tree makes an excellent base for
family holidays in Argyll. Facilities include
the award-winning Seafood Restaurant and
a large indoor swimming pool. **££**

Loch Ness Lodge
Brachla, on the A82, Loch Ness-side,
near Inverness
Tel: 01456-459 469

www.loch-ness-lodge.com
This is the finest luxury hotel in the area – ideal for a romantic getaway or a weekend of relaxation. Guests enjoy glorious views over Loch Ness, an award-winning restaurant, and a spa suite. **££££**

The Islands
Duisdale Hotel
Isle of Ornsay, Sleat, Isle of Skye
Tel: 01471-833 202
www.duisdale.com
The Duisdale is the number one hotel choice on Skye, with 18 smart guest rooms looking out over the sea or the extensive gardens. Guests also benefit from day trips on the hotel owner's 42-foot luxury yacht. **£££**

Foveran Hotel
St Ola, Kirkwall
Tel: 01856-872 389

www.foveranhotel.co.uk
This family-run hotel is set in 35 acres (14 hectares) overlooking Scapa Flow. **££**

Grand Hotel
Commercial Street, Lerwick
Tel: 01595-692 826
www.kgqhotels.co.uk
The oldest purpose-built hotel in Shetland is conveniently situated close to the harbour and town centre. **££**

Brach Hotel
Sleat, Isle of Skye
Tel: 01471-820 200
www.skyehotel.co.uk
The rooms are done out in boutique-hotel style, and offer fine views of rugged coastline. The in-house restaurant (which also welcomes non-residents) offers sumptuous cuisine – probably the best on Skye. **££–£££**

RESTAURANTS

Scotland is renowned for its produce from river and sea, farm and moor. Fish is something of a speciality, with salmon, trout, kippers and Abroath Smokies being particular delicacies. Aberdeen Angus beef and Border lamb are second to none, and high-quality game graces many a table in season. Don't forget, though, to try that most Scottish of dishes, haggis, which is probably more enjoyable if you don't know what it's made of…

Restaurant price categories
Prices are for a two-course dinner per person with a glass of house wine.

£ = under £20
££ = £20–30
£££ = £30–50
££££ = over £50

Edinburgh
Oloroso
33 Castle Street
Tel: 0131-226 7614
www.oloroso.co.uk
Innovative dishes are cooked with precision at this fashionable rooftop restaurant.
££–£££

The Witchery
352 Castlehill, Royal Mile
Tel: 0131-225 5613
www.thewitchery.com
The upstairs restaurant is dark and deeply

Oloroso occupies a stunning rooftop setting

Gothic while downstairs is bright with lots of greenery and a small terrace. **££–££££**

The Scottish Borders

Cringletie House Hotel
Edinburgh Road, Peebles
Tel: 01721-725 750
www.cringletie.com
The restaurant of this country house hotel has maintained a high reputation over many years with its French-inspired cuisine. **££–£££**

Glasgow

Mother India
8 Westminster Terrace
Tel: 0141-221 1663
www.motherindiaglasgow.co.uk
This is Glasgow's – and possibly Scotland's – best curry house, known for its legendary home-cooked food. It is licensed but you can also bring your own bottles. **£**

The Ubiquitous Chip
12 Ashton Lane
Tel: 0141-334 5007
www.ubiquitouschip.co.uk

The Ubiquitous Chip

A long-established restaurant in a verdant courtyard off a cobbled street, serving fine traditional and modern Scottish cuisine. **££**

Fife, Tayside, Aberdeen and the Grampian region

Victoria's
45 Atholl Road, Pitlochry
Tel: 01796-472 670
www.victorias-pitlochry.co.uk
Whether for breakfast, lunch, high tea or pre-theatre dinners (the Pitlochry Festival Theatre is close by), the food at Victoria's is comforting and scrumptious, and the service always friendly. Children are welcome too. **£**

The West Coast and the Northwest Highlands

Abstract
20 Ness Bank, Inverness
Tel: 01463-220 220
www.abstractrestaurant.com
Try a tasting menu at the Chef's Table, and whisky from a wide choice in the Piano Bar. **££–£££**

Inverlochy Castle
Torlundy, near Fort William
Tel: 01397-702 177
www.inverlochycastlehotel.com
Expect full ceremony serving modern British cuisine in the three dining rooms. **£££–££££**

The islands

The Creel
Front Road, St Margaret's Hope, Orkney
Tel: 01856-831 311
www.thecreel.co.uk
This friendly fish restaurant is often judged Scotland's best. **££**

The Three Chimneys
Colbost, Dunvegan, Isle of Skye
Tel: 01470-511 258
www.threechimneys.co.uk
This restaurant with rooms and views in a remote crofter's cottage has won awards. **££**

NIGHTLIFE

Pubs are very popular with the locals everywhere in Scotland and are especially crowded around the end of the working day and at weekends. In rural areas, pubs may indeed be the only form of nightlife on offer. In the cities, though, there is the usual variety of clubs and bars, as well as venues for live music, with everything from dance to traditional music on offer.

Pubs

Abbotsford
3–5 Rose Street, Edinburgh
Tel: 0131-225 5276
www.theabbotsford.com
This place is a tribute to the grandeur of Victorian pub design.

Blackfriars
36 Bell Street, Glasgow
Tel: 0141-552 5924
www.blackfriarsglasgow.com
This lively joint is renowned for its good beer and evenings of jazz and comedy.

The Oxford Bar
8 Young Street, Edinburgh
Tel: 0131-539 7119
www.oxfordbar.com
A place replete with literary associations: it's full of Robert Burns' memorabilia and has featured in Ian Rankin's *Inspector Rebus* novels.

The Prince of Wales
7 Street Nicholas Lane, Aberdeen
Tel: 01224-640 597
The Prince of Wales boasts Aberdeen's longest bar counter. Good beer and good food too.

Clubs

Love2Love
9–11 Castle Street, Inverness
Tel: 0844-891 0856
http://love2loveinverness.com/
If you want commercial dance music with no added sophistication, then this is the place to come.

Polo Lounge
84 Wilson Street, Glasgow
Tel: 0141-553 1221
www.socialanimal.co.uk
What is perhaps Glasgow's best-known gay club is thronged every night from Tuesday to Sunday.

Snafu
1 Union Street, Aberdeen
Tel: 01224-596 111
www.clubsnafu.com
From Wednesday to Sunday, there's dancing to house, techno or disco. On other nights, there's comedy and live music (mostly indie).

Wee Red Bar
Edinburgh College of Art,
Lauriston Place, Edinburgh
Tel: 0131-229 1442
www.weeredbar.co.uk
The big night of the week here is on Saturday, when it's 'The Egg' – the city's best indie dance night.

Live Music

Barrowland
244 Gallowgate, East End, Glasgow
Tel: 0141-552 4601
www.glasgow-barrowland.com
Glasgow's premier live music venue fills its capacity of 1,900 on a regular basis for indie, rock and pop acts.

Hootananny
Church Street, Inverness
Tel: 01463-233 651
www.hootananny.co.uk
The best time to turn up to this venue is on a Friday night when local singers and songwriters showcase their talents. Every Saturday afternoon there is also a ceilidh from 2.30pm.

ENTERTAINMENT

While Scotland's major cities offer a wealth of cultural and entertainment options, rural areas of the country are sometimes so sparsely populated that they can't even support a cinema. Nevertheless, community solidarity and ingenuity often seem to have conjured up some of the most eccentric and diminutive theatres, picture houses and concert venues you've seen in your life.

Concert halls

Music Hall
Union Street, Aberdeen
Tel: 01224-641 122
www.boxofficeaberdeen.com
This ornately gilded theatre hosts top orchestras, pop bands, and big-name comedy acts.

The Royal Concert Hall
2 Sauchiehall Street, Glasgow
Tel: 0141-353 8000
www.glasgowconcerthalls.com
This is Glasgow's main venue for orchestral concerts and Celtic music.

Usher Hall
Lothian Road, Edinburgh
Tel: 0131-228 1155
www.usherhall.co.uk
Check the programme here for top-class classical, folk, world and jazz.

Film

Filmhouse
88 Lothian Road, South Edinburgh
Tel: 0131-228 2689
www.filmhousecinema.com
This arthouse cinema presents a diet of new releases and repertory classics.

Glasgow Film Theatre
12 Rose Street, Glasgow
Tel: 0141-332 6535
www.gft.org.uk
Glasgow's arts cinema offers films from around the world, themed seasons and special events.

Wee Picture House
20 Hall Street, Campbeltown, Argyll
Tel: 01586-553 800
www.weepictures.co.uk

Dating back to 1913, this Art Deco building is apparently the oldest purpose-built cinema in Scotland.

Theatre

Aberdeen Arts Centre
King Street, Aberdeen
Tel: 01224-635 208
www.digifresh.co.uk
The theatre here plays host to professional and amateur companies performing all types of material.

Festival Theatre
13–29 Nicholson Street, Edinburgh
Tel: 0131-529 6000
www.fctt.org.uk
Edinburgh's showcase theatre presents major opera, ballet and variety productions.

Mull Little Theatre
Tobermory–Dervaig Road, Druimfin, Isle of Mull
Tel: 01688-302 673
www.multheatre.com
This 43-seat theatre is the smallest professional theatre in Britain, with a season that runs from Easter to September.

Pitlochry Festival Theatre
Port Na Craig, Pitlochry
Tel: 01796-484 626
www.pitlochry.org.uk
From April to October, this theatre presents a programme of plays, concerts and comedy.

Tron Theatre
63 Trongate, Glasgow
Tel: 0141-552 4267
www.tron.co.uk
Stylish venue featuring innovative programmes of contemporary drama and dance.

SPORTS AND ACTIVITIES

Scotland's thousands of miles of rugged coastline, remote beaches, rushing rivers and majestic mountains make it one of the best destinations in Europe for outdoor sports. Despite the weather, the terrain is perfect for fishing, cycling, walking and golf among numerous other sports. *See p.49* for more information about hiking.

Fishing

Scotland's rivers and lochs are renowned for their salmon and trout fishing. The salmon fishing season varies from river to river, starting from January in some places and as late as March in others, and runs until October. The trout season is from mid-March to early October. Local permits are required (details from tourist offices). Sea fishing is found around the entire coast, though it is perhaps best around the Orkney and Shetland Islands. For details of clubs, organisations and fishing locations, visit www.fishing-scotland.net.

Golf

Carnoustie
20 Links Parade, Carnoustie
Tel: 01241-802 270
www.carnoustiegolflinks.co.uk
Carnoustie is home to one of the toughest links courses in the world.

Gleneagles
Auchterarder
Tel: 01764-662 231
www.gleneagles.com/golf
Gleneagles has three 18-hole golf courses, one of which will be the venue for the 40th Ryder Cup Matches in 2014.

Royal Dornoch Golf Club
Tel: 01862-810 219
www.royaldornoch.com
Located 40 miles (64km) to the north of Inverness, this course has more claim than most to being the home of golf, as the game was first played here by monks in 1614.

St Andrews
Tel: 01334-466 666
www.standrews.org.uk
The Old Course at St Andrews is the oldest golf course in the world.

Rugby

Murrayfield
Edinburgh
Tel: 0131-346 5000
www.scottishrugby.org
The highlight of the rugby union calendar is the Six Nations Rugby Championship in early February, when 67,000 fans cram into the Murrayfield stadium for Scotland's home matches.

Skiing

Despite erratic snowfall in recent years, Scotland's five ski centres – Cairngorm, The Lecht, Glenshee, Glencoe and Nevis Range – continue in business, though they have diversified into activities such as mountain biking to balance the books. However, when snow does fall (the main season is between January and April), groomed pistes and challenging off-piste terrain become the playground for skiers, boarders and ski-mountaineers. Consult www.ski-scotland.com for details of resorts and activities.

Blue skies over Gleneagles

Listings

TOURS

From literary tours of Edinburgh's new and old town to wildlife tours on Mull and adventure breaks by bike or on foot in the rugged Highlands, visitors are certainly spoilt for choice. The following are a few of the highlights from the dozens of tours that can be found through local tourist information centres across the country.

Cultural tours

Afternoon Tea Tours
33 Cramond Road North, Edinburgh
Tel: 07873-211 856
www.afternoonteatours.com
This company offers unusual guided tours with themes such as whisky and chocolate, afternoon tea and Scottish aviation history.

Mercat Tours
28 Blair Street, Edinburgh
Tel: 0131-225 5445
www.mercattours.com
Literary and ghost walking tours promise delight and fright.

Bus tours

Haggis Adventures
Tel: 0131-557 9393
www.haggisadventures.com
Especially designed for travellers on a budget, these tours take you to the furthest reaches of the Highlands aboard a yellow 'haggis' bus.

Boat trips

Bella Jane Boat Trips
The Harbourfront, Elgol, Isle of Skye
Tel: 01471-866 244
www.bellajane.co.uk
Between Easter and October, the Bella Jane

Taking to the slopes in Scotland

departs from the pier in the village of Elgol to take you around the rugged coastline of Skye.

Sea Life Surveys
Beadoun, Breidwood, Tobermory, Isle of Mull
Tel: 01688-302 916
www.sealifesurveys.com
You are likely to see whales, dolphins and seals on these Hebridean boat trips.

Tours for the more adventurous

Alba Ballooning
5 Primrose Gardens, Carrington
Tel: 01875-830 709
www.albaballooning.co.uk
Don't forget a woolly hat for these hot-air balloon flights over Edinburgh, the Lothians, Borders and Fife.

Grant Arms Hotel Wildlife Tours
25 The Square, Grantown on Spey
Tel: 0800-043 8585
www.grantarmshotel.com
The Grant Arms operates as a base for a variety of guided wildlife safaris in the Scottish Highlands. In the evenings there are often lectures and films.

Mountain Innovations
Tel: 01479-831 331
www.scotmountain.co.uk
For mountain enthusiasts, these holidays include 'skills' courses on navigation or tackling the mountains in the snow.

Wilderness Scotland
3a St Vincent Street, Edinburgh
Tel: 0131-625 6635
www.wildernessscotland.com
This company organises walking holidays for all levels of ability as well as sea kayaking, mountain biking and skiing breaks.

FESTIVALS AND EVENTS

For a small country, Scotland hosts a staggering number of events. As well as contemporary crowd-pleasers such as the Edinburgh Festival and the Hogmanay (New Year's Eve) parties in the big cities, there are also plenty of celebrations of historical events and national figures – and you may be relieved to know that not all involve kilt-wearing and copious amounts of drinking.

January

Burns Night
Various locations, especially Ayr and Dumfries
www.burnsmuseum.org.uk
Celebrations to honour Robert Burns' birthday on 25 January involve eating haggis and drinking whisky.

March/April

Glasgow Comedy Festival
www.glasgowcomedyfestival.com
Facing a raucous Glaswegian audience is a test of any comedian's mettle. The festival lasts from mid-March to early April.

April/May

Spirit of Speyside Whisky Festival
www.spiritofspeyside.com
In late April and early May the numerous Speyside distilleries lay on special tours, tastings, talks and dinners.

June

RockNess
Loch Ness
www.rockness.co.uk
The shores of Loch Ness play host to a rock festival for a weekend in mid-June.

July

Hebridean Celtic Festival
Isles of Lewis and Harris
www.hebceltfest.com
This is the premier festival for lovers of Scottish folk music. It takes place in mid-July.

August

Edinburgh International Festival
www.eif.co.uk
For three weeks in August the most famous of Britain's arts festivals features concerts, exhibitions, plays and comedy nights. Several festivals take place at the same time.

September

Braemar Gathering
www.braemargathering.org
The Queen often attends this traditional Highland jamboree on the first Saturday in September. Expect pipers, dancers, and burly men tossing the caber.

November

St Andrews Week
www.standrewsfestival.co.uk
This annual festival in the final week of November comprises exhibitions, concerts and fireworks displays.

December

Hogmanay
Edinburgh
www.edinburghshogmanay.org
The most famous Hogmanay (New Year's Eve) party is in Edinburgh around Princes Street and the Royal Mile.

Edinburgh International Festival is the highlight of Scotland's arts calendar

Listings

PRACTICAL ADVICE

Accommodation

Britain offers a wide variety of accommodation for visitors, from luxury hotels in old castles to bed and breakfast (B&B) accommodation in private family homes. By international standards, hotels in Britain are expensive, so if you are on a tight budget you should consider staying in a bed and breakfast or a youth hostel.

It is advisable to book in advance, particularly at Christmas, Easter and in July and August. During the rest of the year there is generally little difficulty in finding somewhere to stay. If travelling in rural Scotland during the low season, you will find that some hotels are closed, especially in January and February. Therefore, it is best to organise accommodation before travelling.

HOTELS

Hotels range from five-star luxury resorts to small family-run concerns. Competition is fierce enough to ensure decent standards wherever you are.

Perhaps the easiest way to book a room is online, through a hotel aggregator website such as www.booking.com or www.hotels.com. Alternatively, you can book directly with a hotel, through a travel agent, or via a tourist office. Most Tourist Information Centres in Britain will book local accommodation (free or for a small fee) for personal callers. All TICs also supply free lists of local hotels and guesthouses. The Britain and London Visitor Centre at 1 Regent Street, London (www.visitbritain.com) provides general information. When booking, check whether the tariff includes breakfast.

A regal room at Amberley Castle in Arundel, Sussex

Hotels are graded according to a number of star ratings schemes. The AA (Automobile Association) operates a simple system, awarding one star for good, but basic accommodation, to five stars for luxury establishments. See www.theaa.co.uk.

Enjoy England (www.enjoyengland.com) runs a nationwide quality assessment scheme, with one to five 'Quality Roses' being awarded in different categories of establishment. Hotels, for example, are in a separate category to bed and breakfasts which come under guest accommodation. Visit Scotland and Visit Wales (national tourism organisations) have a single Quality Assurance Scheme for which star gradings are given by inspectors, again ranging from one to five stars. A Michelin award is the accolade for which the most notable of hoteliers strive.

BUDGET ACCOMMODATION

Travelling in Britain need not be expensive, and there are plenty of options besides hotels for overnight stays. Pubs and inns are a great British institution that have become increasingly popular for accommodation. There are many historic taverns, particularly in rural towns and villages, perhaps situated beside the road, where pilgrims may have rested in the Middle Ages or stagecoaches stopped. Often they retain an old-world character with open fires, low beams, ale on tap and a warm ambience. Standards and food vary from basic to sophisticated. CAMRA (Campaign for Real Ale; tel: 01727-867 201; www.camra.org.uk) publishes a guide, *Beer, Bed & Breakfast*, listing the best inns.

Local bed and breakfasts are convenient and typically good value

Other options include bed and breakfasts and guesthouses, which are generally private homes with a few rooms for rent. Standards vary, but you can expect great hospitality, a hearty breakfast of eggs and bacon with all the trimmings, and helpful advice. Usually identified by a 'B&B' sign outside, they are most abundant on the edges of towns, at the coast and in other prime tourist spots in rural areas. The AA publishes an annual *Bed & Breakfast Guide* to more than 4,000 inspected B&Bs. See also www.theaa.com.

There are well over 200 youth hostels, which range from town houses to beach chalets. Facilities and accommodation are basic, but cheap, often comprising shared dormitories with bunk beds. Some provide full board while others have self-catering kitchens — but hostels are only for those who don't mind mucking-in, communal living and shared bathrooms. You must be a national or international member to stay at a hostel – though anyone (of any age) can join the association. Contact the Youth Hostel Association (tel: 01629-592 700; www.yha.org.uk) or the Scottish Youth Hostels Association (tel: 08701-553 255; www.syha.org.uk).

A taste of the simple life

OTHER ACCOMMODATION

For more unconventional options, the Landmark Trust (tel: 01628-825 925; www.landmarktrust.org.uk) and the National Trust (tel: 0844-800 2070; www.nationaltrustcottages.co.uk) may be able to help. The Landmark Trust is a charity set up to rescue historic buildings. It now has more than 180 properties available for holiday lets, ranging from castles and manor houses to mills, lighthouses and forts. Detailed information can be found in a handbook ordered online or by telephone. The book's price is refunded against bookings. The National Trust and the National Trust for Scotland (tel: 0844-493 2108; www.ntsholidays.com) have over 400 houses and cottages to let.

There are also countless private individuals who rent out self-catering accommodation in Britain. The most popular type is country cottages and seaside apartments. It's a particularly good option for families. A number of agencies run websites where you can peruse photographs of cottages. Try Blakes Country Cottages (www.blakes-cottages.co.uk) or English Country Cottages (www.english-country-cottages.co.uk), for example.

A variation on this theme is staying on a farm. Farm Stay UK (tel: 024-7669 6909; www.farmstay.co.uk) has over 1,200 rural retreats on its books.

In some cities, you may find that universities rent out their student accommodation to visitors during the long summer holidays. This can be an inexpensive option, and some even offer full board. For partcipating universities see www.university-rooms.com.

CAMPING

Despite Britain's reputation for rainy weather (only partially justified!), camping is once again increasing in popularity. Facilities have been improved at campsites, the retro image of camping is appealing to many, and the development of 'glamping' (glamorous camping) is convincing others that it can be a comfortable experience.

There are hundreds of campsites across the country, ranging from camping resorts with excellent facilities (sometimes including swimming pools and children's clubs) to a small field behind a country pub. Websites such as www.ukcampsite.co.uk and www.campinguk.com provide listings. The Forestry Commission also runs a large number of campsites around Britain, some with rustic cabins. See www.forestholidays.co.uk for details.

The fashionable concept of glamping involves staying in yurts, cabins, tipis and bell tents in picturesque locations. Your accommodation usually has standing room, a proper bed, a stove and maybe even a sofa. Sites tend to be very small and have good facilities. See http://goglamping.net for a wide selection of quirky places to stay.

Transport

GETTING TO BRITAIN
By air
A high proportion of the world's major airlines operate flights to Britain so there is plenty of scope for shopping around to get the best deal. Websites such as www.skyscanner.net can assist the process substantially. Departure taxes are included in the price of the flight at the point of purchase.

Britain's two major international airports are:

London Heathrow: LHR; tel: 0844-335 1801; www.heathrowairport.com; 15 miles (24km) to the west of London

London Gatwick: LGW; tel: 0844-335 1802; www.gatwickairport.com; 24 miles (40km) south of London

An increasing number of international flights now arrive at London's other airports, and at regional airports:

London Stansted: STN; tel: 0844-335 1803; www.stanstedairport.com; 30 miles (48km) northeast of London

London Luton: LTN; tel: 01582-405 100; www.london-luton.co.uk; 35 miles (57km) north of London

Birmingham: BHX; tel: 0844-576 6000; www.birminghamairport.co.uk; 6.3 miles (10km) southeast of Birmingham

Manchester: MAN; tel: 08712-710 711; www.manchesterairport.co.uk; 9 miles (14km) southwest of Manchester

Glasgow International: GLA; tel: 0844-481 5555; www.glasgowairport.com; 8 miles (13km) south west of Glasgow

Glasgow Prestwick International: PIK; tel: 0871-223 0700; www.glasgowprestwick.com; 32 miles (51km) south of Glasgow

Cardiff: CWL; tel: 01446-711 111; www.tbicardiffairport.com; 12 miles (19km) west of Cardiff

By rail
Eurostar's regular passenger trains link France and Brussels with Britain. Services run from Paris Gare du Nord (2 hours 15 mins) and Brussels Midi (1 hour 50 minutes) to London's St Pancras International; most trains stop in Ashford, Kent. Booking is not always essential, but recommended; there are offers on tickets bought in advance. For UK bookings, tel: 08705-186 186. From outside the UK, tel: +44 1233-617 575, or visit www.eurostar.com. Fares start from £34.50 for a single.

'Le Shuttle' trains (tel: 08705-353 535; www.eurotunnel.com) travel through the tunnel from Nord-Pas de Calais in France to Folkestone in Kent. There are at least two departures every hour

The Eurostar connects France and Belgium with London

during the day with a reduced service overnight (journey time 35 minutes). Booking is not essential – just turn up and take the next service. Crossings are priced on a single-leg basis and prices vary according to the level of demand (from £44 per car); the further ahead you book, the cheaper the ticket.

By sea
Sea services operate from 12 British ports to more than 20 continental ones. Major ferries have full eating, sleeping and entertainment facilities. The shortest crossing is from Calais in France to Dover in Britain, which takes about 90 minutes by ferry.

Brittany Ferries (tel: 08709-076 103; www.brittany-ferries.co.uk) sail from St Malo, Caen and Cherbourg to Portsmouth; from Cherbourg to Poole; from Roscoff to Plymouth; and from Santander to Plymouth. P&O Ferries (tel: 08716-645 645; www.poferries.com) run from Calais to Dover, from Bilbao to Portsmouth

and from Rotterdam and Zeebruge across the North Sea to Hull. Stena Line (tel: 08705-707 070; www.stenaline.co.uk) sail from Hook of Holland to Harwich. Norfolkline (tel: 0870-870 1020; www.norfolkline.com) operates between Dover and Dunkerque.

GETTING AROUND
Domestic flights
Flying is becoming an ever more popular option for getting around the country. Budget airlines such as easy-Jet (www.easyjet.com) and Ryanair (www.ryanair.com) offer a particularly wide range of flight routes, and often affordable prices as well. Popular routes include London to Newquay, Newcastle, Edinburgh and Glasgow.

Major regional airports include:
Aberdeen ABZ, tel: 0844-481 6666; www.aberdeenairport.com
Bristol BRS, tel: 0871-334 4444; www.bristolairport.co.uk
East Midlands EMA, tel: 0871-919 9000; www.eastmidlandsairport.com
Edinburgh Airport EDI, tel: 0844-481 8989; www.edinburghairport.com
Liverpool John Lennon LPL, tel: 0871-521 8484; www.liverpoolairport.com
Newcastle upon Tyne NCL, tel: 0871-882 1121; www.newcastleairport.com
Newquay NQY, tel: 01637-860 600; www.newquaycornwallairport.com.

Ferries
Ferry services between the mainland and 22 islands off the west coast of Scotland are operated by Caledonian MacBrayne (tel: 0800-066 5000; www.calmac.co.uk). Island Rover tickets

The West Coast Scotland Ferry

allow you to visit as many islands as you wish over eight or 15 days. Ferries to Orkney and Shetland are operated by Northlink (tel: 0845-600 0449; www.northlinkferries.co.uk). Reservations are strongly recommended if you wish to take a car. The ferry to the Isle of Skye from the Kyle of Lochalsh, has been replaced by a toll bridge.

The Talyllyn Railway at Abergynolwyn station

Trains

Railways are run by 27 private regional operating companies. They are not known for punctuality, so allow time for delays. Avoid rush-hour travel in and out of big cities. See www.national rail.co.uk for train times and fares.

There are many money-saving deals, such as cheap-day returns, available. It can be difficult to find out about special offers, so if in doubt, ask again. Generally, tickets bought at least two weeks in advance are vastly cheaper than standard rates, but they sell out fast. Some saver tickets are available only if purchased abroad before arriving.

It is not usually necessary to buy tickets until the day you travel (except to get these special offers), or to make seat reservations, except over the Christmas period when InterCity trains are fully booked well in advance.

For travel in Scotland you can buy a Freedom of Scotland Travelpass giving unlimited travel throughout Scotland and the English Borders on the ScotRail network. The Travelpass also includes some coach travel and scheduled Caledonian MacBrayne ferries to the islands off the west coast. There are two options: four days' travel in an eight-day period, or eight days' travel over 15 consecutive days. Call National Rail Enquiries (tel: 08457-484 950) or see www.firstgroup.com/scotrail.

Intercity coaches

National Express (tel: 08717-818 178; www.nationalexpress.com) operates a large network of long-distance bus services. Fares are usually substantially cheaper than the equivalent journey by train, though you are advised to book your seat in advance. Green Line (tel: 0844-801 7261; www.greenline. co.uk) operates many routes in and around London, including to tourist attractions such as Legoland.

Cycling

There are plenty of opportunities to cycle in Britain (see p.49). In London, a bicycle lending scheme has been established where members of the public can borrow a bike from one of dozens of docking stations all over central London, and then drop it back at any other docking station. There is no need to sign up first: just pay the access fee and usage charge at the docking station with a credit or debit card. See www.tfl. gov.uk for docking stations locations.

There are thousands of bike-hire companies. The following also offer

Transport

Mountain biking in Scotland

cycling holidays and tours:
London: tel: 0207-928 6838;
www.londonbicycle.com
The South: tel: 01590-622 627;
www.countrylanes.co.uk
Wales: tel: 01690-710 766; www.bike
wales.co.uk
Scotland: tel: 07902-242 301;
www.tickettoridehighlands.co.uk.

DRIVING

Driving in Britain is reasonably safe,
though as you might expect from such
a densely populated country, roads are
often busy. In London and many other
major cities, driving is best avoided
in favour of public transport. In rural
areas, however, you will find that a car
is very useful as bus and rail services
are less extensive and less frequent.

Road conditions

Roads are generally well maintained
throughout the country – even in the
more sparsely populated regions of
Scotland. The standard of driving by
local people is also generally good,
though speeding on motorways is
common. Main roads are usually well
serviced with petrol stations, though
less so in more remote areas of Scotland and Wales. Plan ahead if under-
taking long journeys in these areas.

Regulations

Driving is on the left-hand side of
the road and you must observe speed
limits. The top speed limit of 70mph
is applicable on motorways and
dual carriageways. In towns, speed
limits will be indicated on circular
signs edged in red. Beware of speed
cameras, of which there are many,
especially around built-up areas. It is
illegal to use a mobile phone when
driving, and penalties for drink driving are severe. Drivers and their passengers, in both front and back seats,
must wear seat belts where fitted, or
you may be fined. For further information, consult a copy of the *Highway
Code* published by the DSA and
widely available in bookshops, or visit
www.direct.gov.uk.

If you are bringing your own car
into Britain you will need a valid
driving licence or International
Driving Permit, plus insurance cov-
erage and documents proving the
vehicle is licensed and registered in
your country and that you are resident outside the UK.

In central London, drivers must
pay a Congestion Charge. The
boundary of the Congestion Zone –
which extends from Kensington in
the west to the City in the east – is
clearly indicated with signs and road
markings. Cars driving into this
zone between 7am and 6.30pm from
Monday to Friday are filmed and
their drivers are fined if a payment of
£8 has not been made by midnight
the same day (or £10 the following
day). You can pay at many newsagents, by phone or online (tel: 0845-
900 1234; www.cclondon.com).

Motoring associations

The following motoring organisations operate 24-hour breakdown assistance. They have reciprocal arrangements with other national motoring clubs. All calls to these numbers are free.

AA tel: 0800-887 766; www.theaa.com
RAC tel: 0800-828 282; www.rac.co.uk.

Vehicle hire

To hire a car in Britain you must be over 21 years old (over 23 for most companies) and have held a valid full driving licence for more than one year. The cost of hiring a car usually includes third-party insurance, mileage and road tax. Depending on the company, it might also incorporate insurance cover for accidental damage to the car's interior, wheels and tyres. However, it does not include insurance for other drivers without prior arrangement.

Some companies offer special weekend and holiday rates, so shop around. International companies (such as those listed below) are keen to encourage visitors to book in advance before they leave home and may offer holiday packages with discounts of up to 40 percent on advance bookings through travel agents or branches in your own country. Many hire firms provide child seats and luggage racks for a small charge.

Avis tel: 0844-581 0147; www.avis.co.uk
Hertz tel: 08708-448 844; www.hertz.co.uk
Budget tel: 0844-544 3470; www.budget.co.uk
Europcar tel: 08713-849 847; www.europcar.co.uk.

Approximate driving times

Driving times between major cities can vary enormously. You should try to avoid driving at peak times – especially in the early evening on Friday or at the beginnings and ends of bank holidays. All being well, however, estimated drive times are as follows:

London to Cardiff: 3 hours
London to Manchester: 4 hours
London to Edinburgh: 7 hours
Edinburgh to Glasgow: 1 hour.

ACCESSIBILITY

Details of transport access for disabled people can be found on a government website, www.dft.gov.uk/transportforyou/access. Public transport in Britain is gradually becoming more disabled-friendly. New public buses and black taxis are generally wheelchair-friendly, and at railway stations, platform attendants will provide ramps for access to trains. Disabled parking permits allow privileged parking; see the above website for details. Free information and advice is also available from Tourism for All (tel: 0845-124 9971; www.tourismforall.org.uk).

Roads are generally well signposted

Health and safety

MEDICAL CARE

EU nationals are entitled to free medical treatment. Many other countries also have reciprocal arrangements for free treatment. Most other visitors have to pay for medical and dental treatment and should ensure they have adequate health insurance.

In the case of minor accidents, your hotel will know the location of the nearest hospital with a casualty department. Self-catering accommodation should have this information on a notice in the house, together with the telephone number of the local doctor.

If you become seriously ill, you are eligible for free emergency treatment in the Accident and Emergency departments of National Health Service hospitals. However, if you are admitted to hospital as an in-patient, even from the accident and emergency department, or referred to an out-patient clinic, you will be asked to pay unless you fall into the exempted categories mentioned above. For listings of NHS hospitals and clinics, see www.nhs.uk. For a full list of NHS and private hospitals in Britain, see www.drfosterhealth.co.uk.

There are more than 80 National Health Service walk-in centres across the country, usually open seven days a week from early morning to late evening, 365 days a year. A charge may be made to non-EU nationals.

If you need a pharmacy, Boots (www.boots.com) is the largest chain in the country, with branches in most towns. As well as selling over-the-counter medicines, they also make up prescriptions. Opticians can be found on most high streets. Major chains include Specsavers (www.specsavers.co.uk) and Vision Express (www.visionexpress.com).

Tap water is safe to drink throughout the UK.

Major hospitals include:
Charing Cross Hospital, Fulham Palace Road, London (tel: 020-8846 1234)
St Thomas's Hospital, Lambeth Palace Road, London (tel: 020-7188 7188)
Royal Infirmary of Edinburgh, Little France Crescent, Old Dalkeith Road, Edinburgh (tel: 0131-536 1000)
Manchester Royal Infirmary, Oxford Road, Manchester (tel: 0161-276 1234)
John Radcliffe Hospital, Headley

Emergency contacts

In an emergency call 999 for fire, ambulance, police or the coastguard. In the case of a minor accident or illness, go to the nearest hospital's casualty department. For non-urgent calls to the police in London, dial 0300 123 1212; elsewhere, consult online directory www.192.com for the correct number.

Pharmacies are usually easy to find in British towns

Way, Headington, Oxford
(tel: 01865-741 166)
Addenbrookes Hospital, Hills Road,
Cambridge (tel: 01223-245 151)
Bristol Royal Infirmary, Marlborough
Street, Bristol (tel: 0117-923 0000).

CRIME

Serious crime is low, but in big cities
the Dickensian tradition of pick-
pocketing is alive and well. Hold on
tightly to purses, do not put wallets in
back pockets, and do not place hand-
bags on the ground in busy restaurants.
Professional thieves target the Tube in
London, so be watchful of belongings.

In a genuine emergency, dial 999
from any telephone (free of charge).
Report routine thefts to a police station. The threat of terrorism has led to
an increase in police patrols, so don't
hesitate to report suspicious packages.

Be aware that almost all recreational
drugs are illegal in the UK, and possession and use – even of very small
quantities – can incur severe penalties.
Confusingly, personal use of cannabis
was legalised a few years ago, but that
decision has since been reversed.

EMBASSIES AND CONSULATES

Most countries have diplomatic rep-
resentation in London. A selection is
given below, and others can be found
through the Yellow Pages (www.yell.
com). Many countries also have consul-
ates in Edinburgh and Cardiff.
Australia: Australia House, Strand,
London WC2 4LA; tel: 020-7379 4334;
www.australia.org.uk
Canada: 1 Grosvenor Square, London
W1K 4AB; tel: 0207-258 6600; www.

Police officers in central London

dfait-maeci.gc.ca/canadaeuropa
Ireland: 17 Grosvenor Place, London
SW1X 7HR; tel: 0207-235 2171; www.
embassyofireland.co.uk
New Zealand: 80 Haymarket, London
SW1Y 4TQ; tel: 020-7930 8422;
www.nzembassy.com.
South Africa: South Africa House,
London WC2N 5DP; tel: 0207-451
7299; www.southafricahouse.com
United States: 24 Grosvenor Square,
London W1A 1AF; tel: 020-7499 9000;
www.usembassy.org.uk

Gay and lesbian travellers

Gay and lesbian travellers will find that
Britain is generally very welcoming.
Attitudes have changed enormously over
the years, and while there are instances
of prejudice and even violence, they
are, thankfully, less common. If you do
need advice or counselling during your
visit, contact London Lesbian and Gay
Switchboard (tel: 0207-837 7324) or
London Friend (7.30–10pm, tel: 0207-
837 3337; www.londonfriend.org.uk). In
Scotland, speak to LGBT Youth Scotland
(www.lgbtyouth.org.uk) or the Strathclyde
Gay and Lesbian Switchboard (tel: 0141-
847 0447; www.sgls.co.uk).

Health and safety

Money and budgeting

CURRENCY

The pound (£), divided into 100 pence, is the currency for the whole of Britain. Scotland issues its own notes, which are not technically legal tender in England and Wales, though banks and most shops accept them. Exchange rates against the US dollar and the euro can fluctuate significantly. The major banks offer similar rates, so it's worth shopping around only if you have large amounts of money to change. A few shops, services, attractions and hotels accept euro notes, but give change in sterling and will charge a commission.

Some high street travel agents, such as Thomas Cook, operate bureaux de change at rates comparable to banks. There are also many privately run bureaux de change (some of which are open 24 hours a day) where exchange rates can be low but commissions high.

If you are travelling from outside the European Union and you are carrying 10,000 euros or more (or equivalent in another currency), you must complete a cash declaration form at Customs.

CASH AND CARDS

Most banks open between 9.30am and 4.30pm, Monday to Friday, with Saturday morning banking common in shopping areas. The majority of branches have automatic teller machines (ATMs) where international credit or cashpoint cards can be used, in conjunction with a personal number, to withdraw cash.

Banks charge no commission on travellers' cheques presented in sterling. If a bank is affiliated to your own bank at home, it will make no charge for cheques in other currencies either. But there is a charge for changing cash into British currency.

International credit cards are accepted in most shops, hotels and restaurants.

TIPPING

Most hotels and restaurants automatically add a 10–15 percent service charge to your meal bill. It's your right to deduct this amount if you're not happy with the service.

Unless there is a service charge, it's normal to leave a 10–15 percent tip after a meal

Luxury shopping in London

Sometimes when service has been added, the final total on a credit card slip is still left blank, the implication being that a further tip is expected: you do not have to pay this. You don't tip in pubs, cinemas or theatres, but it is customary to give hairdressers, sightseeing guides and cab drivers an extra amount of around 10 percent.

Money and budgeting

Money-saving tips

- Getting an Oyster Card for the Tube in London will prove cheaper than buying ordinary tickets.
- Buy train tickets for off-peak travel.
- Ask for a family/group ticket at museums and popular attractions.
- In restaurants, take advantage of cheaper set-lunch menus.
- Shop around online for cheaper hotel rooms.
- If you're a student, acquire an International Student Identity Card to qualify you for student discounts at museums and on some public transport.

TAX

A standard value-added tax (VAT) of 20 percent is imposed on most goods and services in Britain. Hotel rates and meals in restaurants are taxed at 20 percent; the extra charge should be indicated on your bill. Petrol is subject to both fuel duty and VAT.

Britain imposes a flight departure tax (Air Passenger Duty). The rate depends on the destination and the airline class in which you are travelling, with short-haul economy flights attracting substantially lower duty. The tax is accounted for in the price of your ticket.

BUDGETING FOR YOUR TRIP

Although Britain can still be an expensive place to holiday, the recent devaluation of the pound relative to the euro and the dollar has made it more affordable for many visitors. US travellers will still find petrol expensive, while European visitors may be surprised at the cost of public transport, especially in London.

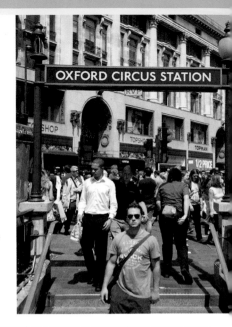

Flights to the UK range in price enormously. Many European visitors may fly with the budget airlines (such as easyJet and Ryanair), which commonly offer return fares from a range of airports across the continent for less than £100 (US$160). Flights from the US start from around £350 (US$570).

For a budget, backpacker-style holiday you will need to set aside £400 (US$650) per person per week. A standard family holiday for four will cost around £2,500 (US$4,100) per week. A luxury, no-expense-spared break can cost over £2,000 (US$3,250) per person per week.

Money and budgeting

Budgeting costs

Top-class/boutique hotel: £150–400 for a double
Standard-class hotel: £90–150 for a double
Bed & breakfast: £50–100 for a double
Motel: £30–70 for a double (or per person)
Youth hostel: £20–40 per person
Campsite: £15–£30 per tent

Domestic flight: £40–200 London to Glasgow
Intercity coach ticket: £25–70 London to Edinburgh
Intercity train ticket: £115–400 London to Edinburgh
Car hire: £15–75 per day
Petrol: £1.40 a litre
10-minute taxi ride: £5–10
Airport shuttle bus: £20
Short bus ride: £1.50

One-day travel pass: £7.30
Breakfast: £5–20
Lunch in a café: £8–25
Coffee/tea in a café: £1.50–4
Main course, budget restaurant: £4–9
Main course, moderate restaurant: £8–13
Main course, expensive restaurant: £15–30
Bottle of wine in a restaurant: £12 upwards
Beer in a pub: £2–4

Museum admission: £3–12
Daytrip to Cambridge: £50–100
Ticket to Legoland: £35
Ticket for a tour bus: £12–30
Cinema ticket: £8–12
Theatre/concert ticket: £10–70
Bottle of whisky: £16–80
Nightclub entry: £3–15

Responsible travel

GETTING THERE
Visitors to Britain from Continental Europe can reduce their carbon footprint by taking the Eurostar train via the Channel Tunnel. See www.eurostar.com for train connections and fares.

Carbonfund (www.carbonfund.org) and TerraPass (www.terrapass.org) provide information on carbon offsetting (ie. offsetting the greenhouse gases emitted during flights). Climate Care (www.climatecare.org) is also useful, providing an online calculator for determining the carbon emissions associated with your trip. The cost of offsetting a return flight from New York to London is around £11.50 per person.

ETHICAL TOURISM
There are a number of organisations that encourage visitors to reduce the negative environmental impact of their visit and even help support local communities. Tourism Concern (www.tourismconcern.org.uk) provides information and ideas about how to travel responsibly, while the website www.ecofriendlytourist.com offers a useful list of eco-friendly hotels across the country. The Slow Food movement (www.slowfood.org.uk) champions fresh local food produced and harvested in sustainable ways.

ECOTOURISM AND VOLUNTEERING HOLIDAYS
For volunteering opportunities, visit the website of the British Trust for Conservation Volunteers (www.btcv.org.uk). It offers a variety of holidays, courses and one-day events where you can help with a range of useful activities, from dry-stone walling to coppicing to monitoring whale movements off the Scottish coast. The National Trust (www.nationaltrust.org.uk/main/w-trust/w-volunteering) and the National Trust for Scotland (www.nts.org.uk/Volunteering) also run a holidays and weekend courses, often based around historic properties or on farms.

Other UK conservation charities which are worth supporting include the Royal Society for the Protection of Birds (tel: 01767-680 551; www.rspb.org.uk). The RSPB manages nature reserves all over the country, and offers volunteering opportunities to help with their maintenance. A much smaller organisation is the International Otter Survival Fund (tel: 01471-822 487; www.otter.org or www.ottershop.co.uk), which offers remarkably good-value holidays in Scotland that allow you a privileged glimpse of this elusive mammal.

THINGS TO AVOID
One of the easiest things you can do to avoid damaging the places you visit is to take your rubbish away with you afterwards. In some cities, dropping litter in the street can earn you an on-the-spot fine, while leaving detritus on beaches or in the countryside is hazardous for wildlife as well as being an eyesore.

Family holidays

PRACTICALITIES

Britain is generally family friendly. While central London can seem somewhat unforgiving, a little planning can make your visit much easier: many parks, attractions and restaurants even in the busiest areas are havens for those with small children. Elsewhere in the country, the pace is more relaxed and congestion less of a problem. Moreover, seaside resorts and attractions in the countryside often depend on making families welcome for their income.

Buying supplies for young children is easy. Infant formula and nappies (diapers) can be purchased in chemists (pharmacies) and supermarkets. An increasing number of public places also offer nappy-changing facilities, and if you are in a large city, you will find that museums are often particularly convenient in this respect.

If you hire a car, you can usually also borrow child seats for a small charge. You will, of course, need to bring pushchairs and other kit with you.

Up to four children aged 11 or under can travel free on London's Underground if accompanied by a ticket-holding adult. Eleven–13-year-olds can get unlimited off-peak travel for £1 per day or 'Kids for a Quid' single fares if travelling with an electronic Oyster card-holding adult, as can 14–15-year-olds providing they have a photo Oyster card. The latter can, however, take up to two weeks to obtain and you need to be an EU national.

Buses are free for all children under 16, but 11–15-year-olds will again need an Oyster photocard. Buses can take up to two unfolded pushchairs (buggies) at one time (they must be parked in a special area halfway down the bus). Any further pushchairs must be folded.

ACCOMMODATION

Most larger hotels will provide a travel cot on request, and many offer a babysitting service. Some – especially the mid-market chain hotels – have kids' clubs, toy chests and children's play areas. Some hotels, however, do not accept children under a certain age, so be sure to check when you book.

Many families prefer the flexibility of self-catering accommodation. Rented cottages, farm stays and camping are popular options. *See Accommodation on p.260 for details.*

FOOD AND DRINK

Most restaurants accept well-behaved children. Only those restaurants that want to encourage families have children's menus and nappy-changing facilities. Dependable chain restaurants with child-friendly policies include

Little ones are bound to have fun in Britain

London has plenty of family-friendly attractions, such as the Natural History Museum

Giraffe (www.giraffe.net) and Carluccio's (www.carluccios.com).

Only pubs with a Children's Certificate can admit children, and even these will usually restrict the hours and areas open to them. Publicans, like restaurateurs, reserve the right to refuse entry. In the countryside, many pubs have gardens where children can play while their parents have a drink.

ATTRACTIONS AND ACTIVITIES

In London, popular attractions for children include London Zoo (*see p.92*), the Science Museum (*see p.90*), the Natural History Museum (*see p.87*), the London Aquarium (*see p.84*) and the London Transport Museum (*see p.73*). There is also St James's Park, where birds congregate around the ponds, and Kensington Gardens, where the Diana, Princess of Wales Memorial Playground should provide some fun.

Britain's coast is dotted with seaside resorts. Brighton and Bournemouth on the south coast are perennially popular, and are easy to get to from London. Cornwall has St Ives and a host of other pretty towns, while Broadstairs and

Whitstable are pleasant places on the north Kent coast. Suffolk and Norfolk have a wide range of resorts, some upmarket (such as Aldeburgh and Southwold), others less so. Wales has long stretches of unspoilt coastline, as well as the old-fashioned destinations of Aberystwyth, Llandudno, Rhyl and Prestatyn. In the north of England, Blackpool is a famous resort, with several attractions – though it has seen better days. Scarborough and Whitby on the east coast of Yorkshire are charming Victorian towns. Pretty beach resorts in Scotland include Stonehaven and Nairn, though the weather is unreliable and the sea fairly chilly.

If you're interested in theme parks, an excellent one for younger children is Peppa Pig World (www.peppapigworld.com), with rides, shops and restaurants. Located in the New Forest in Hampshire, it's easily accessible from the capital, and you can book overnight stays at family-friendly hotels nearby through the park. For slightly older children, Legoland (www.legoland.co.uk) near Windsor comes highly recommended. It offers white-knuckle rides and spectacular Lego models of cities.

SETTING THE SCENE

History – *p.278* **Culture** – *p.286* **Food and drink** – *p.292*

History

Around 7,000 years ago, the last Ice Age ended, and the melting ice flooded the low-lying lands, creating the English Channel and the North Sea, turning Britain into an island. This fact of being 'set apart' from Europe was one of two contradictory factors that would affect every aspect of the country's history. The other was a genius for absorbing every invader and immigrant, creating a mongrel breed whose energies would establish an empire incorporating a quarter of the population of the planet.

EARLY SETTLERS

By about 3000BC tribes of Neolithic people had crossed the water from Europe, probably from the Iberian Peninsula. Farming folk, they also built impressive monuments, such as Stonehenge *(see p.119)*. From about 700BC until the arrival of the Romans came the Celts, most likely from eastern and central Europe, and dominant because, as ironworkers, they had superior weapons.

THE ROMANS

British recorded history begins with the Roman invasion. Julius Caesar first arrived in Britain in 55BC, but, meeting resistance and bad weather, he returned to Gaul. A successful invasion did not take place until AD43, headed by the Emperor Claudius. This time, the island was subdued with relative ease, apart from the country in the far north called

A view of the prehistoric monument, Stonehenge, on a sunny day

Caledonia (Scotland). To repel raids by the warlike Picts ('painted ones'), the Emperor Hadrian had a wall built across the north of England. When the Romans left, nearly 400 years later, to defend Rome against barbarians, they left behind a number of towns and a good road network.

ANGLO-SAXONS, THEN VIKINGS

Invaders from central Europe, Angles, Jutes and Saxons, gradually pushed the native Celts westward into Wales and north into Scotland. In Scotland, the Picts and Scots were eventually united under King Kenneth MacAlpine.

In the mid-9th century the Danes or Norsemen, popularly known as

Vikings, who had been raiding the country for almost a century, decided to settle. Of the local leaders, Alfred of Wessex (871–901) was the only one strong enough to defeat them. In 980, however, Viking invasions resumed. Eventually, Canute, the Danish leader, became king and divided power between the Danes and Saxons; to protect his northern border, he compelled Malcolm II, King of the Scots, to recognise him as overlord.

THE NORMAN CONQUEST

Some semblance of continuity was also achieved by Edward (1042–66), known as the Confessor – a pious man who built Westminster Abbey. However, his heir, Harold II, reigned for less than a year before William of Normandy invaded in October 1066, defeating Harold at the Battle of Hastings and claiming the throne for himself.

The following century incorporated periods of peace interspersed with conflicts over borders and succession. It finally resulted in the founding of the Angevin dynasty (the Plantagenets), by Henry II in 1154.

WARS IN FRANCE AND AT HOME

When Henry died in 1189, his son Richard, who would be known as the Lionheart for his bravery, came to the throne. His death in France was deeply mourned, even though his absences fighting the Crusades had plunged his country into chaos. It was the injustice at home (presided over by Richard's brother and successor John) that produced the Nottingham outlaw, Robin Hood, who supposedly preyed on the rich to give to the poor. Eventually, John submitted to the demands of his barons in the Magna Carta of 1215. His son, Henry III suffered an uprising as well, as the barons summoned a parliament (sometimes referred to as the first House of Commons), representing the chief towns and boroughs.

Under Henry's son, Edward I, Wales was conquered. The Statute of Wales in 1284 placed the country under English law, and Edward styled his newborn son as Prince of Wales, a title held by the heir to the throne ever since. Edward II suffered defeat in Scotland at the hands of Robert the Bruce, which paved the way for a Scottish invasion of Ireland. Edward was eventually deposed, then murdered.

The Cenotaph at Whitehall, one of many war memorials in London

A regal portrait of the infamous King Henry VIII

Edward III spent much of his reign fighting France in the Hundred Years' War (actually 1337–1453), which began when Edward, whose maternal grandfather was Philip IV of France, claimed the French throne. But by 1371 the English had lost most of their French possessions.

After a long peaceful lull, Edward's claim was revived by his great-grandson, Henry V, immortalised by Shakespeare. Henry defeated the French at Agincourt, starved Rouen into submission and made a strategic marriage to a French princess. By the time of his death in 1422 he controlled all of northern France.

On the domestic front, times were hard. The Black Death, which reached England in 1348, killed nearly half the population. However, by leaving land untended and making labour scarce, it gave peasants a better bargaining position. When a Poll Tax was introduced in 1381, they rebelled and took control of London. The Peasants' Revolt was soon suppressed, but landlords became wary about enforcing villeinage, and the feudal system withered away.

Succession conflicts continued over the next century. After Henry VI went mad, and government was put into the hands of a Protector, rivalries between the houses of York (whose emblem was the white rose) and Lancaster (red rose) led to the Wars of the Roses. Violence wasn't confined to the battlefield: one of the most notorious episodes was the murder of the young princes, Edward and Richard, in the Tower of London in 1483. Their uncle, Shakespeare's hunchbacked Richard III, was reputedly responsible. The wars ended with the marriage of Henry VII (1485–1509) to Elizabeth of York, uniting the opposing factions and marking the beginning of the Tudor dynasty.

THE TUDORS

Henry VIII is the most notorious of British kings. He was a gluttonous, licentious ruler who married six times, divorced twice and beheaded two wives. He is famous for bringing about the English Reformation – which made England Protestant rather than Catholic – because the Pope refused to annul his marriage to Catherine of Aragon, who had failed to provide a male heir. Henry also needed the money that could be made from the confiscated monastic property.

When Henry died in 1547, he was succeeded by his only male heir, Edward, a sickly 10-year-old who died six years later. His half-sister 'Bloody Mary' then came to the throne, restoring Catholicism and allowing at least 300 Protestants to be burned as heretics. Her successor, the Protestant Elizabeth I (Henry VIII's daughter by Anne Boleyn), spent nearly 20 years of her reign (1558–1603) resisting Catholic attempts to assassinate her and place Mary Stuart, Queen of Scots, on the throne instead. Eventually, the trial and execution of Mary in 1587 removed the conspirators' focal point, and the defeat of the Spanish Armada the following year secured Elizabeth's position. Elizabeth's rule was also notable for the explorers Sir Walter Raleigh and Sir Francis Drake and the dramatist William Shakespeare.

THE STUARTS

When Elizabeth died without an heir she was, ironically, succeeded by the son of Mary, Queen of Scots. In England, James I (James VI of Scotland) established the Stuart dynasty, and his succession brought a temporary union of the two countries. His reign, though, was bedevilled by further religious controversy. The most famous

An illustration of Oliver Cromwell conferring with lawyers

of the Catholic conspiracies was the Gunpowder Plot of 1605, when Guy Fawkes attempted to blow up the Houses of Parliament. The conspirators were executed, and the episode is commemorated every 5 November, when people burn effigies of Fawkes and set off fireworks.

The Puritan protests were more peaceful, but James had little sympathy with their demands. Some left voluntarily: going first to Holland, a small group that became known as the Pilgrim Fathers set sail in the Mayflower in 1620 and founded New Plymouth in North America, Britain's first toe-hold in the New World.

CROWN VERSUS PARLIAMENT

The other big issue of the Stuart period was the struggle between Crown and Parliament. Under Charles I, relations with Parliament deteriorated, and in 1629 he dissolved Parliament, initiating 11 years of absolute rule. Eventually, however, religious strife and rebellions in Scotland and Ireland forced him to revert to Parliament to raise taxes for armies to deal with the problems. This led to Civil War.

Charles gained the support of the north and west of the country and Wales. Oliver Cromwell, member of Parliament for Cambridge and a Puritan, became leader of the Roundheads – so called because of their short haircuts – and was backed by London, the southern counties and, later, the Scots.

The Royalists were defeated, and Charles was executed in 1649. Cromwell and his followers declared England a Commonwealth and exacted brutal reprisals for the massacres in Ireland. In 1653, Cromwell dissolved Parliament, formed a Protectorate and ruled alone until his death in 1658. Without him republicanism faltered, and, in 1660, monarchy was restored under Charles II (1660–85).

Charles was succeeded by his brother, James II (1685–89), but within a year James had imposed illegal taxation and attempted to restore monarchy and Catholicism, savagely putting down rebellions. In desperation, the two main parliamentary parties, the Whigs and Tories, offered the crown to James's daughter, Mary, and her husband, the Dutch prince William of Orange in 1688.

William and Mary were succeeded by Queen Anne, but, when she died, childless, a reliable Protestant monarch was needed urgently. George of Hanover, great-grandson of James I on his mother's side, was invited to

Britain. Throughout his 13-year reign he never learned to speak English fluently nor particularly liked his subjects.

GEORGIAN BRITAIN AND EMPIRE-BUILDING

The Hanoverian dynasty, under the four Georges, spanned a period of nearly 115 years, and saw the last violent attempts to overthrow a British monarch, in the shape of the two Jacobite Rebellions in support of the 'Pretenders', descendants of James II; the second was led by Bonnie Prince Charlie, who was defeated at the Battle of Culloden.

Meanwhile, Britain was fast becoming the leading world power. The empire had been growing since 1607, when Virginia, the first British colony in America, was established. Britain had since gained control of much of West Africa and the Caribbean. General Wolfe's capture of Quebec ended French power in Canada, and Robert Clive beat both Indians and French for control of India. The Seven Years' War with France concluded in 1763 with a treaty that allowed Britain to keep her overseas possessions. Britain's loss of its American colonies in 1783 was eased by the opening up of the Pacific by Captain Cook, who landed at Botany Bay, Australia in 1770.

Colonial trade, unfortunately, went hand in hand with slavery. European traders bought slaves in West Africa, shipped them to the Americas and sold them to plantation owners, often in exchange for produce that they took back home. It was not until 1807 that the efforts of William Wilberforce made the

The Georgian House is one of Edinburgh's most elegant attractions

Britain was the first industrialised country

then railways and roads were developed to transport goods to market.

THE NAPOLEONIC WARS

Following the French Revolution of 1789–93, Napoleon Bonaparte came to power in France. When he threatened invasion of Belgium and Holland in 1793, European war erupted, with only three years' break until 1815. These wars gave Britain two of its greatest heroes, Admiral Lord Nelson (1758–1805) and the Duke of Wellington (1769–1852), whose victory at Waterloo ended Napoleon's career in 1815.

By contrast, political change in England came not through revolution but gradual reform, as parliamentary acts enfranchised more of the population and regulated working conditions. Britain entered a period of self-confidence and domestic harmony, despite the polarisation of rich and poor evocatively portrayed by Charles Dickens. Queen Victoria's Diamond Jubilee in 1897 celebrated 60 years on the throne for the woman who ruled over the biggest empire in the world.

WORLD WARS

In the early years of the 20th century, the balance of power in Europe was threatened by the growing militarism of Germany, culminating in World War I (1914–18). The next decade was characterised by strikes, political unrest and growing inequality. The effects of the Wall Street Crash of 1929 spread throughout Europe, and by 1931 Britain was entering the Great Depression.

In Germany, the economic

trade illegal and another 27 years before slavery itself was abolished in British colonies.

Back at home, an agricultural revolution brought mechanised farming techniques and the eviction of countless tenant farmers by wealthy landowners. Many of the dispossessed left their homes and looked for work in the towns. In Ireland and the Scottish Highlands there was mass emigration, particularly to America.

The surplus capital accumulated from farming was invested with bankers and merchants, who had prospered from international trade. They in turn provided the finance that made Britain the first industrialised country. The invention of the steam engine, weaving and spinning machinery, and developments in iron production, provided technology to explode industrial output. Canals,

Musicians amusing the shoppers at Columbia Road Flower Market, London

depression helped bring Hitler to power, and by 1939 Britain was drawn into another war. Under the inspirational leadership of Sir Winston Churchill, Britain was saved from invasion, but German bombing wrought destruction on many cities.

When hostilities ended in 1945, the electorate voted overwhelmingly for a Labour government, who, despite the country's near-bankruptcy, managed to lay the basis of the welfare state, providing free medical care, and financial help for the old, sick and unemployed. Another of the effects of the war was to hasten the end of Britain's empire. Starting with India's independence in 1947, the colonies one after another achieved autonomy over the next two decades, although many remained in the Commonwealth, with the new Queen – crowned in 1953 – as their titular head.

BOOM AND BUST

The 1960s saw a rise in living standards and optimism. The introduction of the contraceptive pill prompted a sexual revolution, and the laws relating to abortion, homosexuality and censorship were liberalised.

By contrast, the 1970s were soul-searching years, plagued by strikes, unemployment, and bomb attacks by the IRA. The gloom was only partially offset by Britain's success in finally becoming a member of the Common Market (now the European Union), and the discovery of North Sea oil.

The general election of 1979 brought to power Margaret Thatcher, who set about curbing the trade unions' power, and saw off an Argentine force from the Falkland Islands in 1982. Gradually, unemployment eased, and for many the 1980s signified prosperity.

In 1997, the Labour Party won a landslide election victory under Tony Blair. Early achievements included peace in Northern Ireland and devolution of power to Edinburgh and Cardiff, but Blair's reputation was damaged by his decision to participate in the invasion of Iraq.

In 2008/9, the world financial crisis plunged Britain into recession, and the general election of 2010 brought a change of government. A coalition was formed between the Conservatives and Liberal Democrats, and austerity measures were introduced to tackle the national deficit.

In 2011 the grey mood was relieved by the wedding of Prince William to Catherine Middleton. Optimists hope that two further feel-good events in 2012 – the Olympics and the Queen's Diamond Jubilee – will also boost morale and, through tourism, the economy.

Historical landmarks

5000BC
Britain becomes an island.

700BC
Celts arrive from central Europe.

55BC
Julius Caesar leads the first Roman invasion.

449–550
Arrival of the Jutes, Angles and Saxons.

980–1016
Viking invasions renewed.

1066
William, Duke of Normandy, conquers England.

1277–88
English conquest of Wales.

1348–49
The Black Death plague kills half the population.

1455–85
Wars of the Roses.

1534
Henry VIII abolishes Papal authority in England.

1588
Elizabeth I's navy defeats the Spanish Armada.

1603
James VI of Scotland is also crowned James I of England, uniting the kingdoms.

1642–49
Civil War between Royalists and republican Roundheads.

1666
The Great Fire of London.

1714
George I of Hanover, Germany, is invited to take the throne.

1815
Duke of Wellington defeats Napoleon Bonaparte at Waterloo.

1837
Victoria becomes Queen, aged 18.

1914–18
World War I. More than 1 million Britons die.

1939–45
World War II.

1947
India and Pakistan gain independence.

1953
Queen Elizabeth II is crowned, age 27.

1973
Britain joins the European Community.

1982
Margaret Thatcher oversees victory in the Falkland Islands after Argentina invades.

1997
Tony Blair wins the first general election victory for Labour since 1974.

1998
Northern Ireland peace accord signed.

1999
Scottish and Welsh assemblies begin to exercise a limited degree of devolution.

2010
The General Election results in a Conservative–Liberal Democrat Coalition.

2011
Prince William marries Catherine Middleton.

2012
London hosts the Olympic Games.

Culture

Britain has a cultural heritage born of diversity and assimilation, ranging from the anonymous lines of the Anglo-Saxon poets to the plays of William Shakespeare to the tunes of the Beatles. It is a culture that has been fashioned from the extraordinary history of what were once three distinct nations, England, Scotland and Wales – nations that retain the distinct legacies of their separate pasts. It is a culture that has found expression in all media and genres, from film and music to painting and poetry. In addition to the overview given below, readers may like to refer to *pp.38–45* for information on Britain's literary heritage and *pp.50–55* for Britain's artistic treasures.

THE BRITISH PEOPLE

George Orwell wrote in 1947 that a foreigner would find the salient characteristics of the British people to be 'artistic insensibility, gentleness, respect for legality, suspicion of foreigners, sentimentality about animals, hypocrisy, exaggerated class distinctions, and an obsession with sport'. The Welsh and the Scots would point out that Orwell was thinking primarily of the English, who, to the fury of the Welsh and Scots, persistently equate the terms 'British' and 'English'.

The Brits are famed for their tolerance and sense of humour, yet, as the writer Paul Gallico observed: 'no one can be as calculatedly rude as the British, which amazes Americans, who do not understand studied insult and can only offer abuse as a substitute'. Britain's nearest neighbours can be just as amazed as Americans. André Maurois advised his fellow countrymen: 'in France it is rude to let a conversation drop; in England it is rash to keep it up. No one there will blame you for silence. When you have not opened your mouth for three years, they will think, 'this Frenchman is a nice quiet fellow''.

The truth, as always, is more complicated. If Maurois had been in Liverpool or in Leeds, in Glasgow or in Cardiff, he might not have got a word in, while the Englishman who has 'all the qualities of a poker except

Enjoying the sights and sounds of the day at the Big Tent Festival of Stewardship

its occasional warmth' probably lives in the overcrowded southeast, where standoffishness is a way of protecting precious privacy.

But certain generalisations can be made. Because Britain is an island its people have retained their bachelor outlook despite marrying into the European Union. Because it has not been successfully invaded for almost 1,000 years, Britain remains deeply individualistic. On the one hand, its people perhaps overvalue tradition – a substitute for thought, critics say; on the other hand, they tend not to kill one another in civil conflict and they have absorbed, with relatively little civic pain, large numbers of their former imperial subjects.

To the English, the Welsh seem ebullient, warm-hearted and emotional but also rather garrulous. A certain amount of antipathy exists. Evelyn Waugh, for instance, claimed in his novel *Decline and Fall*: 'We can trace almost all the disasters of English history to the influence of Wales.'

In contrast, the Scots are seen by the English as 'dour', though they'd be hard put to justify the claim in a noisy Glasgow pub. English literature is peppered with anti-Scots aphorisms, such as P.G. Wodehouse's observation that 'it is never difficult to distinguish between a Scotsman with a grievance and a ray of sunshine.' Certainly, the distinct character of the Scots is long established. Unlike the English and Welsh, the Scots were never conquered by the Romans, and they also avoided Norman centralisation after the Conquest in 1066. Their religious experience also set them apart: while

Smartly dressed racegoers evaluate the odds of winning at Ascot

England absorbed the Reformation with a series of cunning compromises, Scotland underwent a revolution, replacing Roman Catholicism with an austere Presbyterianism designed to put the people directly in touch with their God.

POPULATION AND MULTI-CULTURALISM

The population of Britain is estimated at around 60 million people, around 52 million of whom live in England, 3 million in Wales, and 5 million in Scotland. Not only is the population rapidly growing, with a huge increase in immigration – citizens of any EU country can settle in Britain, and recent years have seen an influx of Eastern Europeans – over the last couple of decades, but it is also ageing. According to a report by the Office of National Statistics, the number of people in the UK aged 85 and over was 1.4 million in mid-2009, ie over 2.2 percent of the total population and double the percentage in that age bracket in 1981. Both the country's growth and its

Culture

Award-winning film *The King's Speech* depicts the struggles of King George VI

ageing population present challenges to its creaking transport infrastructure, strained healthcare system and already stretched pension pot.

According to figures for 2009 compiled by the Office for National Statistics (whose figures do not include Scotland), 83.35 percent of the population of England and Wales is White British (unchanged since 2001), with the non-white population increasing from 6.6 million in 2001 to 9.1 million in 2009. The ethnic breakdown is as follows: 1.8 percent of the English/Welsh population is of mixed race, 5.87 percent is Asian or Asian British, 2.81 percent is Black or Black British, 0.82 percent is Chinese, and the rest White Irish and White Other. In London, the population is heavily multicultural, with just 59.5 percent in the White British ethnic category.

FILM

Historically, Britain has played a major role in the development of modern cinema. The British film industry's heyday was the 1940s, when studios led by J. Arthur Rank and Alexander Korda made such classics as Powell and Pressburger's *A Matter of Life and Death* and Laurence Olivier's *Henry V*. Britain has also produced many great directors – Alfred Hitchcock, Carol Reed, David Lean, Mike Leigh and Danny Boyle (whose 2008 film *Slumdog Millionaire* won eight Academy Awards) – and iconic film stars including Charlie Chaplin, David Niven, Peter Sellers and Sean Connery.

In recent decades, however, the British film industry has been largely subsumed into the international (largely American) film industry. While films such as Woody Allen's *Match Point* (2005) were made in London using mainly English actors and technicians, they are not generally regarded as British. Even the James Bond and Harry Potter movies, despite their English backgrounds, have the flavour of international productions. On the other hand, Hugh Grant's caricature Englishness stamps films such as *Four Weddings and a Funeral* (1994) and *Notting Hill* (1999) as British, even though his American co-stars (Andie MacDowell and Julia Roberts) signal a desire for international appeal. Likewise the casting of Keira Knightly, with her clipped vowels, injects the box-office-boosting combination of archetypal English Rose and Hollywood star to a movie. Period films, such as *Atonement* (2007) and *The Duchess* (2008), both starring Knightley, put out the romantic and stereotypical view of the Brits as sexually-repressed, exquisitely-dressed toffs. And the British film industry's most recent success, *The King's Speech* (2010), flies the flag for stereotypical British stiff upper lip. The question of what is a 'British' film is consequently a much-debated question. Whatever the answer, Britain continues to make a significant contribution to the world of cinema from the director's chair to the animator's studio.

THEATRE

In spite of its reputation, the West End of London is not always the place to find the country's dramatic cultural pearls. Here the tradition is as much of the theatre as of performances. This is where velvet-and-gilt Victorian play-houses were designed so that most of the audiences would peer down over the cast, where 'the gods' (the seats high at the back) bring on vertigo and a concern that, had the buildings been conceived today, fire regulations would have ensured they never left the architects' drawing boards.

Nevertheless, the West End is still

The grand interior of the Old Vic, often the venue for classic theatre

a theatrical magnet, because that is where the money is. Catering for audiences by the coach-load, impresarios look to musical spectacles, revivals, and to plays that will please the widest range of tastes. As a result, such middle-of-the-road creative types as composer Andrew Lloyd Webber (now Lord Lloyd Webber) have become both famous and very rich.

Traditionalists claimed that the mania for musicals squeezes out new drama productions. Yet a glance through the theatre listings doesn't entirely bear out this claim. Classics continue to be staged at the National Theatre and the Old Vic, new writing is still put on at the Royal Court, and experimental work and alternative comedy are mounted at the fringe theatres.

Shakespeare is certainly alive and well. The replica of Shakespeare's Globe on London's South Bank has been a triumph of culture over commercialism, with audiences paying to savour the 16th-century ambience by standing for hours in front of the stage or sitting on rock-hard benches. The Royal Shakespeare Company, based in Stratford-upon-Avon, also takes much of its repertoire to London and several regional cities.

In the provinces, most large cities have at least one mainstream theatre, which hosts touring productions, as well as a smattering of fringe theatres. The Cambridge Arts Theatre, the playhouses in Oxford and Nottingham, the Old Vic theatres in Bristol and Stoke, the Leeds Grand, the Sheffield Crucible, Manchester's Royal Exchange, Glasgow Citizens'

Culture

Musicians at Ronnie Scott's, London's legendary jazz bar

and Edinburgh Traverse, to name but a few, all have good reputations, and the Fringe Festival in Edinburgh every August is where myriad actors and comedians clamour to show their earliest promise.

MUSIC

Britain has an active and varied music scene, with plenty to cater to every musical taste. Over the last 50 years, the country has made a major contribution to popular music, and that doesn't look like ceasing any time soon. A visit to Camden in North London is as good a place as any to look for clubs, bars and other venues. Many famous bands played their first gigs at Barfly, for example, and young hopefuls continue to do so today. If, on the other hand, jazz is more your style, there are also many pubs and clubs that host live music – notably in London and Edinburgh. Ronnie Scott's in London's Soho is Britain's best-known jazz venue, showcasing top international artists.

Classical music enthusiasts will find that many British cities have their own professional orchestras and promote seasons of concerts. These include the Royal Liverpool Philharmonic, The Hallé in Manchester, the City of Birmingham Symphony Orchestra and the spectacular ultra-modern St David's Hall in Cardiff. There are numerous professional orchestras in London; perhaps the best at the moment is the London Symphony Orchestra, which usually performs at the Barbican.

In the summer the Scottish National Orchestra (SNO) presents a short Promenade season in Glasgow, while in London the BBC sponsors the Proms festival of around 100 concerts at the Royal Albert Hall. The BBC also funds several of its own orchestras, the BBC Symphony and the BBC Scottish Symphony Orchestra. Also on offer on summer evenings is a programme of open-air concerts at the Kenwood Lakeside Theatre, Kenwood House, Hampstead.

For opera buffs, the Royal Opera and the English National Opera perform regular seasons in London. The Royal Opera House, Covent Garden is home to the Royal Ballet as well as the Royal Opera. Its magnificent theatre presents lavish performances in the original language. Dress is formal and tickets are expensive, unless you are prepared to stand or accept a distant view. English National Opera's home is the London Coliseum on St Martin's Lane. Performances here are often in English, and ticket prices are lower than at Covent Garden.

Elsewhere in the country, Welsh National Opera performs at the Wales Millennium Centre in Cardiff Bay, and Scottish Opera is based at the Theatre Royal in Glasgow. Opera North is based in Leeds at the Grand Theatre but tours in the north of England. The Derbyshire spa town of Buxton hosts a major opera, theatre and music festival for three weeks in July each year.

Perhaps the smartest event in the opera calendar is Glyndebourne. Located off the beaten track in Sussex, it is not the most obvious site for a major international opera festival. But ever since an ex-schoolmaster inherited a mansion there and built an opera house, it has attracted top artists from around the world and become a major event. Performances are in the evening (bring your own Champagne and picnic hampers) from May until August.

BALLET AND DANCE

For ballet, major venues are the Royal Opera House and the London Coliseum, home to the Royal Ballet and English National Ballet respectively. The Royal Ballet also has a home in Birmingham at the Hippodrome Theatre. In Wales, the leading ballet companies perform at the Wales Millennium Centre in Cardiff and the Grand Theatre in Swansea, while the Scottish Ballet is based in Glasgow, but tours the country. The Northern Ballet School, at the Dancehouse Theatre in Manchester, also performs throughout the UK.

For contemporary dance, the main venue is Sadler's Wells, in London's Islington. Its flexible state-of-the-art performance spaces are used for innovative programmes. Other performances of modern dance can be seen at the Peacock Theatre, also in London.

The Royal Opera House in busy tourist hub Covent Garden

Food and drink

Britain's cuisine was once reputed to offer little more than overcooked stodge. Not so now, as well as impressive renditions of just about every other country's cuisine, you can appreciate the finest of Britain's own food heritage.

The last few decades have seen a remarkable transformation in Britain's restaurant scene, bringing it into the international league. The British taste for innovative cooking of the best produce has made the country the envy of foreign nations more traditionally regarded as gastronomically blessed. At one time, however, things were very different, and British food was the butt of many jokes, especially from the French. Former French President Jacques Chirac is quoted as saying that 'you can't trust people who cook as badly as that.' Nowadays, a good pork chop or Scottish lobster would have him eating his words.

NATIONAL CUISINE

The recent blossoming of Britain's restaurant scene is closely related to the re-evaluation of the country's indigenous cuisine. A new generation of energetic head chefs has proved emphatically that British food is much more than meat and two veg, a stodgy pie full of gravy or a buttie stuffed with soggy chips. Now you can feast on Cromer crab, Cornish sprats, Gressingham duck, juicy Herdwick lamb, Galloway beef, and traditional desserts such as bread

Scotland's west coast will delight seafood fans

and butter pudding (deliciously light when well prepared) or Eccles cakes with Lancashire cheese. And this new-found culinary zeal has also filtered down to the local pub, where potted shrimps, shepherd's pie, Lancashire hotpot and bangers and mash are cooked with care and served with pride.

Perhaps the dish with which Britain is most associated is fish and chips. While this is still a popular and inexpensive option for a satisfying meal, the number of fish and chip shops is fast declining. Whereas in the 1930s there were more than 30,000, today there are only 8,600 fish and chip shops in the entire country. The future of those remaining is threatened by dwindling fish stocks and fast-food corporations. This is a shame, since the style of fat

Calendar of seasonal food	
Lamb	May−Sept
Game birds	Sept/Oct−Dec/Jan
Asparagus	May−June
Parsnips	Oct−Feb
Pumpkin	Oct−Dec
Watercress	Apr−May
Gooseberries	June−Aug
Cherries	June−Aug

stubby fried potatoes, quite impossible to replicate in a conventional kitchen, and fish in batter, double fried in beef dripping, is absolutely delicious when done well. In the past, cod was preferred in the south of Britain and haddock in the north. It is skate, however, that is the real test of a fryer's mettle: if it is cooked just right, it is soft and light, but if only 90 percent done, it is a glutinous, bony mess.

Another culinary treat that is particularly popular with the British – and again a fairly inexpensive option for dining out – is curry. A recent foreign minister, Robin Cook, claimed that chicken tikka masala was 'Britain's true national dish'. Indeed, Britain's Indian restaurants now employ more people than her coal, steel and ship-building industries combined.

WHERE TO EAT
High-end restaurants

In recent years, dining out has become fashionable and popular across the country. Whereas in the 1980s, fine dining was considered to be largely the preserve of a metropolitan elite, today it is a far more widespread and democratic activity. Michelin-starred restaurants are scattered around the country, and have raised expectations of what restaurants should be offering. There are currently three that have been awarded the ultimate accolade of three stars: Gordon Ramsay at Royal Hospital Road in Chelsea, London; The Fat Duck at Bray in Berkshire; and The Riverside Inn, also at Bray. There are around 140 other restaurants in Britain that have achieved ratings of one or two stars.

It is easily argued that many high-end restaurants give too much emphasis to design and image and not enough to the food itself. At London restaurants Sketch or China Tang, for example, some feel that if the food is fairly good, it is so as not to distract from the interior decoration. A step further are the likes of The Ivy or Cipriani, where it is the other diners, some of them celebrities, who are the focus of attention.

The Fat Duck restaurant is a prime example of innovative British fare

An array of bitters on offer in a traditional boozer

Many of the restaurants mentioned above require booking weeks, perhaps months, in advance. Beware also, if the restaurant takes your credit card details when you book, you may be charged anyway if you do not then show up.

Pubs

If all this business of booking weeks ahead, hefty bills and embarrassing formality is more than you can take, do not fret; all is not lost. Many of the best eating experiences in Britain are quite inexpensive, relaxed affairs.

A major component of British social history is the public house, which in recent years has been re-evaluated. There is indeed a lot to be said for a pie and a pint, and pub cuisine is a distinctive cuisine in itself (and that does not mean ploughman's lunch with a limp lettuce leaf and a wedge of cheese). Think of steak and kidney pudding, meat loaf, Lancashire hotpot, shepherd's pie, sausage and mash and the traditional Sunday roast. If well executed, these dishes are delicious.

Ethnic restaurants

Another mainstay of Britain's culinary heritage is the huge variety of

Food markets

The first decade of the 21st century has seen considerable growth in the number of high-quality food markets across the country. Many towns host markets where farmers sell their produce directly to the public. Some markets take place once a week (often on a Saturday), others once a month; see www.farmersmarkets.net or www.lfm.org.uk for listings. Perhaps the best of London's food markets for the visitor is Borough Market near London Bridge (Thur 11am–5pm, Fri noon–6pm, Sat 9am–4pm). It offers some of the country's best produce in an historic setting. London's main wholesale markets are Smithfields for meat (Mon–Fri 4–10am), Billingsgate for fish (now in Docklands; offers some guided tours; Tue–Sat 5–8.30am) and Spitalfields for fruit and vegetables (now in Leyton; Mon–Fri midnight–1pm, Sat until 11am). Oxford has the Covered Market, which is renowned for its fine butchers, greengrocers and cheesemongers; it is open daily, and is particularly attractive to visit in the run up to Christmas. In the north of England, Bolton Market (also indoor) is justly famous. Its 300 stalls showcase a wide range of regional specialities. It is open on Tuesday, Thursday, Friday and Saturday, from 9am to 5pm.

ethnic restaurants, especially Indian, Chinese, Japanese, Vietnamese and Thai. In London, visit the Kingsland Road in the East End for Vietnamese, Whitechapel or Tooting (South London) for Indian, and Mayfair for (mostly upmarket) Japanese establishments. Manchester is renowned for its curry mile along Wilmslow Road, and Leicester also has many excellent Indian restaurants. Liverpool's Chinatown is home to the oldest Chinese community in Europe, and is a good place for dining out.

Greasy spoons, pie and mash and fish and chips

Often overlooked is Britain's fast-disappearing old-fashioned working-class grub. Even 15 years ago, wherever you were in a city or major town, there was always a haven close at hand offering a plate of piping hot food at everyday prices. Now, the greasy spoon cafés, fish and chip, and pie and mash shops are being usurped by coffee bars and purveyors of fast food who can pay grasping landlords' higher rents.

'Greasy spoon' cafés serve all-day breakfasts: eggs, bacon, chips and beans, sometimes with manly extras such as black pudding or bubble and squeak. Also, strong tea (in a mug on a saucer) and white bread and butter. Check out www.classiccafes.co.uk for an anthology of the best greasy spoon cafés still open.

Pie and mash shops serve meat pies or eels (jellied or stewed) with liquor (an odd sort of glop based on parsley sauce) and mashed potato. The premises themselves have wonderful tiled interiors, marble-topped tables and wooden benches. You can consult www.pie-and-mash.com for an exhaustive list of shops, though M. Manze's on Tower Bridge Road in London and Whites Pie and Mash in the Essex seaside town of Walton-on-the-Naze are easily recommended.

Food and drink

Borough Market in London is a foodie heaven

Chains

Britain has ever more chain restaurants, more indeed than most other European cities. Some are reasonably good (Carluccio's or the Gourmet Burger Kitchen for example), others are hugely disappointing, with food cooked in the microwave from frozen, and staff as apathetic as you might expect on the minimum wage. Remarkably, it is sometimes the affluent areas (Hampstead in London or Knutsford near Manchester, for example) that are the most intensive breeding ground for chains and have little else to offer besides.

DRINKS
Beer

Traditionally, beer was to Britain what wine was to France. It comes in various forms, from lager (now the most popular form in Britain) to ale (brewed using only top-fermenting yeasts; sweeter and fuller bodied) to stout (creamy, almost coffee-like beer made from roasted malts or roast barley), of which the most famous brand is probably Guinness. Pubs generally serve beer either 'draught' or from the cask. In the case of the former, a keg is pressurised with carbon-dioxide gas, which drives the beer to the dispensing tap. For the latter, beer is pulled from the cask via a beer line with a hand pump at the bar. This method is generally used for what is often termed 'real ale': unfiltered and unpasteurised beer, which, unlike industrially produced lagers, requires careful storage at the correct temperature.

Wine

The popularity of wine-drinking in Britain has increased dramatically in the last 20 years. In the unenlightened days, many pubs served only Liebfraumilch and perhaps Lambrusco, but nowadays you can expect a more grown-up selection, and New World wines are at least as widely offered by

Beer festival advert in southwest Scotland

Just one of the many varieties of whisky served in British pubs

pubs as European wines. The growing popularity of wine in Britain has even encouraged some to start producing English varieties. Vineyards in the south of England now produce around 4 million bottles annually. Sparkling white wine is a particular forte, with recommended producers including Camel Valley, Ridgeview and Nyetimber. If you are interested in visiting a vineyard, try Chapel Down Winery (tel: 01580-763 033; www.englishwinesgroup. com) near Tenterden in Kent, where guided tours are offered daily from June to September. In East Anglia, the Wyken Vineyards (tel: 01359-250 287; ww.wykenvineyards.co.uk) are situated on the edge of a country estate near Bury St Edmunds.

Cider

A longer-established English tipple is cider, produced in south-west England since before the Romans arrived. Made from the fermented juice of apples, it is also known as 'scrumpy' (windfalls are 'scrumps'). The pear equivalent is called 'perry'. Unfortunately, many pubs only offer mass-produced cider made from apple concentrate. In order to sample the real thing, you may wish to visit a cider festival. The website www.cider festivals.co.uk provides details of the main ones, which are mostly in the southwest of England, in places such as Bath and Bristol.

Whisky

Another speciality is whisky *(see also pp.234–5)*, produced in Scotland and Ireland. This is available as 'single malt' (malt whisky from a single distillery), as well as 'blended' – cheaper whiskies are normally made from a mixture of malt and grain whiskies from many distilleries. Smarter pubs in England and Wales will offer a small selection of both, while in Scotland many hostelries pride themselves on offering a large range of single malts.

Last orders

Most pubs ring a bell for 'last orders' at 11pm and then expect you to drink up and depart by 11.30pm. However, in 2003 new legislation was introduced allowing pub landlords to apply for extended opening hours, up to 24 hours a day, 7 days a week. In practice, only a small minority of pubs has made such an application, though this has not stopped renewed concern about Britain's supposed 'binge-drinking' culture.

Food and drink

Index

299

Index

301

Index

Accommodation index

Index

Credits for Berlitz Handbook Great Britain

Written by: Michael Macaroon
Series Editor: Tom Stainer
Map Production: Stephen Ramsay and Apa Cartography Department
Production: Linton Donaldson, Rebeka Ellam
Picture Manager: Steven Lawrence
Picture and design editor: Tom Smyth
Photography: akg images 127B, 283; Alamy 9CL, 168, 251; Alnwick Castle 213; Amberley Castle 260; Back Page Images/Rex 117; Finn Beales/Hay Festival 39; Blenheim Palace 153; Britain on View 191T; Burgh Island 44; Burghley House 164; Celtic Manor 185; Chatsworth House Trust 7B; Cliveden 104, 114; John Constable 145; Corbis 27; David Cruickshanks/APA 2R, 8BR, 14, 49, 59, 231, 232, 234, 235T&B, 238, 239, 240, 241, 242, 243, 244, 245, 252, 264, 266, 267, 276/277, 282, 286, 292, 296, 297; Steve Cutner/APA 6BL, 108, 110, 111; Lydia Evans/APA 2L, 4B, 13, 37, 38, 47, 50, 60/61, 119T&B, 121, 122, 125, 128, 129, 130, 155, 158, 159, 258/259; Fairmont Hotels & Resorts 7TL, 94; Fotolia 161, 163; Glyn Genin/APA 9BL; Getty Images 7CR, 28, 29, 36, 54, 57, 77T&B; Glasgow Science Centre 237; Gleneagles Hotels Ltd 250, 255; The Goring Hotel 93; Liu Haifa 257; Tony Halliday/APA 109T, 156, 157; Robert Harding World Imagery 106, 126, 127T; Historic Royal Palaces 91; Hotel du Vin 167; Hotel Portmeirion 186; iStockphoto.com 5TR&BR, 6TR, 33, 34, 139, 141B, 160, 173B, 175, 176, 193, 194, 195T&B, 210, 212, 220, 246, 247, 248, 261, 278, 280, 281; Legoland Windsor 8BL, 103T; London 2012 76; London News Pictures/Rex Features 15; Ian Lowe/NewImage 196; Douglas Macgilvray/APA 6TL, 9BR, 25, 55, 223T&B, 225, 227, 229, 230, 233; Malmaison 214, 249; Le Manoir aux Quat'Saisons 166; Midsummer House 148; Derry Moore/The Royal Collection 22; Morston Hall 147; Frank Noon/APA 42, 151B; James Osmond/The Travel Library/Rex Features 8T; The Old Vic 289; A. Plamer-Watts/Fat Duck 115, 293; Photolibrary 19, 30, 41, 56, 58, 89, 95, 103B, 133, 135, 141T, 142, 171, 173T, 177, 181, 256, 287; Mike Powles/FLPA 140; RHS/Jon Enoch 31, 101; Sadler's Wells 98; Ronnie Scott's 97, 290; William Shaw/APA 6BR, 7TR, 9TR, 10/11, 12, 43, 45, 46, 48, 165, 178, 179, 182, 183, 184, 189, 197, 199, 200, 201, 202, 203, 204, 205, 206, 208, 209, 211, 216, 219, 216, 219, 262, 265; Ston Easton 131; Superstock 4TL; Ming Tang-Evans/APA 3L, 4TR, 5TL, CL&BL, 6CR, 16, 18, 23, 24, 32, 40, 51, 52, 53, 65T&B, 69, 70, 71, 72, 73, 74, 75, 78, 79, 80, 81, 82, 83, 84, 85, 87, 88, 90, 92, 99, 100, 263, 268, 269, 271, 272, 275, 279, 284, 291, 295; Tate Liverpool 191B; Travel Pictures 180; walespressphoto 9TL; Corrie Wingate/APA 3R, 17, 20/21, 26, 35, 107, 109B, 113, 123, 124, 137T&B, 143, 144, 146, 151T, 270, 274, 294

Cover: front: photolibrary.com; back left and right: Corbis; back centre: photolibrary.com

Printed by: CTPS-China

© 2012 APA Publications (UK) Limited
First Edition 2012

Contacting Us

At Berlitz we strive to keep our guides as accurate and up to date as possible, but if you find anything that has changed, or if you have any suggestions on ways to improve this guide, then we would be delighted to hear from you. Write to Berlitz Publishing, PO Box 7910, London SE1 1WE, UK or email: berlitz@apaguide.co.uk

Worldwide: APA Publications GmbH & Co. Verlag KG (Singapore branch), 7030 Ang Mo Kio Ave 5, 08-65 Northstar @ AMK, Singapore 569880; tel: (65) 570 1051; email: apasin@singnet.com.sg

UK and Ireland: Dorling Kindersley Ltd, a Penguin Group company 80 Strand, London, WC2R 0RL, UK; email: customerservice@dk.com

United States: Ingram Publisher Services, 1 Ingram Boulevard, PO Box 3006, La Vergne, TN 37086-1986; email: customer.service@ingrampublisherservices.com

Australia: Universal Publishers, 1 Waterloo Road, Macquarie Park, NSW 2113; tel: (61) 2-9857 3700; email: sales@universalpublishers.com.au

www.berlitzpublishing.com